West of Emerson

West of Emerson

The Design of Manifest Destiny

Kris Fresonke

UNIVERSITY OF CALIFORNIA PRESS

Berkeley   Los Angeles   London

Chapter 6 of this book previously appeared in somewhat different form as "Thoreau and the Design of Dissent" in *Religion and the Arts* 2–2 (1998): 221–41. Figures 1–6, from the *Journal of Voyages and Travels of a Corps of Discovery . . .* , by Patrick Gass, are reprinted here courtesy of the Bancroft Library, University of California, Berkeley; figures 7–12, from William H. Emory, *Report on the United States and Mexican Boundary Survey,* vol. 1, are reprinted here courtesy of the American Philosophical Society.

University of California Press
Berkeley and Los Angeles, California

University of California Press, Ltd.
London, England

Library of Congress Cataloging-in-Publication Data

Fresonke, Kris, 1966–.
 West of Emerson : the design of manifest destiny / Kris Fresonke.
  p.   cm.
 Includes bibliographical references (p.) and index.
 ISBN 0-520-22509-0 (alk. paper).—ISBN 0-520-23185-6 (pbk. : alk. paper)
 1. Emerson, Ralph Waldo, 1803–1882—Knowledge—West (U.S.)
 2. Thoreau, Henry David, 1817–1862—Knowledge—West (U.S.)
 3. Frontier and pioneer life—West (U.S.)—Historiography.
 4. United States—Territorial expansion—Historiography.
 5. West (U.S.)—Historiography. I. Title.

PS1642.W48 F74   2003
810.9′358—dc21   2001058522

Manufactured in the United States of America
12 11 10 09 08 07 06 05 04 03
10 9 8 7 6 5 4 3 2 1

The paper used in this publication is both acid-free and totally chlorine-free (TCF). It meets the minimum requirements of ANSI/ NISO Z39.48–1992 (R 1997) *(Permanence of Paper).* ⊗

And they said unto Joshua, Truly the Lord hath delivered into our hands all the land; for even all the inhabitants of the country do faint because of us.

CONTENTS

ILLUSTRATIONS

ACKNOWLEDGMENTS

In 1982, a member of my family, in a mood of mirth and big spending, paid a psychic to tell me about my past lives. The best of these (all otherwise tending toward Cleopatra and Napoleon, for the psychic knew her market) was a nineteenth-century life in which I, the daughter of homesteaders somewhere on the southern Plains, was the only survivor of a Comanche raid. Traumatized and orphaned, I went native for a while, the psychic declared. I ended up working in a brothel somewhere in San Francisco, but (she was firm on this point) I wore my hair in braids, Indian style, until I died.

Yes, gentle reader: in my former life, I was Natalie Wood in John Ford's *The Searchers.*

Thus I trace the origin of my suspicions toward Western destiny to about 1982. On the other hand, since that date, it has taken many better minds than my own to help me tell the "past lives" story that follows, of geographical and theological fate in nineteenth-century America.

I would like to acknowledge the following people for their help. As I once heard an Air France employee say, explaining a delayed flight out of Charles de Gaulle airport, "Thank you for your *comprehension.*"

Michael Colacurcio deserves much more than my thanks for introducing me not only to Emerson but to the concept of an ideal reader: he is one, and he kindly read this manuscript in its raggedest forms in just that spirit. Blake Allmendinger put the *Journals* of Lewis and Clark into my hands in 1993, and for this good deed and others, he is forever my rodeo queen. Bill Handley will, like a friend, see the forest for the trees, no matter the logjam in my ideas; I am indebted to him for the sympathetic and intelligent ways he helped to refine this book. To Linda Norton, my gracious and encouraging editor at the University of California Press, for her enthusiasm about this book in its loutish early drafts, I wish a trip to the church of Santo Spirito.

To the outstanding Randy Heyman at the University of California Press, kudos and thanks. To Victoria Silver, I can only offer the thanks, as vast as all the wide-open spaces, of a fellow Westerner who appreciates the predicament of irony. For my colleague and friend M. H. Dunlop, a deluge of diamonds, red velvet, and blue china for helping me to get out of Dodge. UCLA, where I wrote my dissertation, was home to a set of graduate students while I was a doctoral student in English who made intellectual life a true happiness; I include in that list Luke Bresky, Lorraine Valestuk, Maurice Lee, Jayne Devens, Rebecca Humenuk, Martin Kevorkian, Will Moddelmog, Ilana Nash, and Willene Van Blair. I am also in the debt of Jayne Lewis, Barbara Packer, Christopher Grose, and Eric Sundquist at UCLA, and José Amaya and Constance Post at Iowa State University, for encouragement and help. Kevin Van Anglen gave, and still gives, time and thoughtful scrutiny to my work, for which he has my continuing thanks.

The American Philosophical Society gave me, in 1996, a precious month in their archive, with a Mellon Fellowship, where I did the majority of the research for the chapters on Lewis and Clark, William Emory, Stephen Long, and Zebulon Pike. Edward C. Carter II was gracious and helpful to me all month, and I was lucky to have the excellent aid of librarians Beth Carroll-Horrocks, Rita Dockery, and Roy E. Goodman. I also thank the American Philosophical Society for permission to reprint the illustrations to William Emory's *Report*.

Thanks, finally, for the permission of Boston College to reprint my article "Thoreau and the Design of Dissent," now revised as chapter 6 of this book. It originally appeared in *Religion and the Arts* 2–2 (1998): 221–41.

To my parents, and to my brother and sister, the thanks of the youngest child.

To Richard Major, my manifest destination—*Questa è lingua di cui si vanta Amore.*

Introduction

Possess this Country, free from all annoye
THOMAS TILLAM, "Upon the First Sight
of New England" (1638)

Design! It is all design.
RALPH WALDO EMERSON, *On the Relation
of Man to the Globe* (1834)

My first sight of New England was from a rented Toyota along that grim wilderness of highways that migrate out of New York City into Connecticut. We were off to Vermont, or something. At nineteen, I was just noticing Easternness, which to my Seattle mind was *truly* Eastern, as in the Orient—imperial, courtly, corrupt, mandarin, something in Puccini. (Of course, the Orient is due west of Seattle.) I'd failed so far to notice that the East Coast was American cultural headquarters: if you don't live there, as John Updike says, you're somehow *kidding*.

Travel narrows the mind, and as we drove north through Connecticut and Massachusetts to some vile weekend chalet in Vermont to grill the steaks a boyfriend had mail-ordered from Colorado from an ad in the *New Yorker*, I was not doing high-prophetic intellectual work about American regions. I was not memorizing New England for recitation later, when it would be intellectually useful to imagine barbecuing in Emerson's backyard, or Hawthorne's. (Anyway, Nabokov calls this fraudulence of memory "future recollection . . . you know, trying to see things as you will remember having seen them."[1] It happens to Humbert Humbert while he meditates murdering Lolita's mother.) It hardly impressed me. I was trying to memorize the words to a Gilbert and Sullivan chorus for a show. Major John Wesley Powell, who took rafts down the Colorado River three times in the 1870s and mapped the Grand Canyon, used to read *Hiawatha* and *The Lady of the Lake* aloud to his men. For my part, I was a little maid from school, practicing out loud a Victorian comic opera about the East (kimonos, kohl eye pencil, paper fans) while speeding in a Japanese car to Western beefsteaks on a sodden Vermont barbecue. We passed a Massachusetts town where ancestors of mine are buried, but didn't stop. It is a complex fate to be an American.

Americans can also, however, set standards of genius in this problem of how to see new lands. Ralph Waldo Emerson observed, on his first trip abroad, that St. Peter's in Rome and St. Paul's in London were only ghosts to Americans, who had seen pictures of them too often, and who were over-qualified in European ancestor worship. Two American ladies I saw in a medieval Tuscan town one afternoon were shaking their heads at the view: "Oh, it looks just like *Europe.*" Because Americans are haunted by such ghosts all the time, we're the best at rational explanations, followed by howling doubt, followed again by the rational, followed again by the howl.

The purpose of this book—its rational explanation—is twofold: to describe the theological lineage of manifest destiny, or the quasi-sacred explanation for the way America looked to Americans in the nineteenth century, and then to see key texts of our nature canon, *Nature* and *Walden,* in this new line of descent. My evidence is a set of exploration narratives and the nature writing of Emerson and Thoreau. I have not written an exhaustive history of exploration writing, nor a thorough reexamination of Transcendentalism. Instead I have attempted to place some canonical New England texts in a different historical context: namely, in the expansion and exploration of the Far West in Jacksonian America. My target is the usual story of Emerson and Thoreau, our official Romantics, setting up shop in Concord, Massachusetts, and determining the course of the national literature; the context for these literary giants is not in the civilized East, nor the far East (that is, Europe), but in the wide open West of the Louisiana Purchase. Instead of theorizing familiarly that *Nature* and *Walden* represent the high point of New England Romantic thought, this book tracks down texts by explorers of the Far West who contributed to these "classics," and uncovers, for instance, the parodic Western politics included in Emerson's most famous essay, and the westward-looking forms of resistance in Thoreau's writings. Westerns, I argue, helped create some of our "Easterns."

One of the central problems of our national literature is a local version of Emerson's ghosts: not that no one had ever seen America before, but that we have never *stopped* seeing it. There is insanity built in to our reports from the frontier, the kind arising from familiarity. Familiarity is a part of looking at the new, and it is the ability to have seen it already. Exploration is an intellectually conservative act, reinforcing what the explorer knows already. One way of describing this ability in nineteenth-century America is the argument from design, or the theological idea of seeing the Creator in the manifest order of the creation.

A SURVIVAL FROM the Age of Reason, the design argument is actually classical (or at least medieval) in coinage.[2] In simplest terms, the argument goes like this: from the manifest design of the world, we can infer the presence of a designer. The idea or impression that nature is so orderly that it must have been consciously crafted is almost too fundamental to the Western mind to have a name, though "natural theology" is the phrase we use most often. Greek philosophy developed this idea as a technical proof of the existence of a creator God. Aristotle gave it a particular shape in his *Metaphysics* as the "teleological argument": things don't just exist, they all have a function, an end, a coherent goal—and an infinite God must have set all these goals. Thomas Aquinas took up the teleological argument from Aristotle as one of his famous *Quinque Viæ* of proving monotheism, and it has remained a staple of Christian apologetics.

This last of Aquinas's proofs in the *Quinque Viæ* was for him the least important, and was offered mainly on the authority of Aristotle. Aquinas's four other proofs struck the seventeenth century as fusty, monkish metaphysics; but in a mood not only empirical but also exhausted by the European wars of religion, that century approved of the fifth one. Religious feeling, for the seventeenth century, rested more on the exclusive foundation of observed order in the physical universe, and less on the mysteries of faith. Among the first to formulate such a sense of order was George Herbert's elder brother Edward, Lord Herbert of Cherbury, who published the forerunning work of Deism titled, imposingly, *De Veritate prout distinguitur a revelatione, a verisimili, a possibili, et a falso* (1624), drawing religion away from revelation and basing it on the argument from design. He was among the first to begin a trend that spread across Europe. Later in the century it reached its apogee with John Toland's *Christianity Not Mysterious* (1696), in which Christian faith is indistinguishable from the untutored piety of a man admiring the craftsmanship of the stars.[3]

So from the middle of the seventeenth century, the teleological argument began to eclipse all other proofs of God in the form of the "argument from design." This version of the theory argues not from Aristotle's teleological nature of things, but from the observation that there is more order in the world than can be accounted for by anything but intelligent design. This line of thought makes fewer metaphysical assumptions than Aristotle or Aquinas, and it claims less belief, for in fact it indicates the existence of an architect who shaped the visible world, but did not necessarily create it, is not necessarily infinite, and is not necessarily good. But this minimal proof suited the minimal God of that age: even when advanced by orthodox Christians, it sounds frugally Deist—as in this hymn by Joseph Addison, inspired in the 1720s by the Nineteenth Psalm, in which God is merely an exalted adjective form:

> The spacious firmament on high,
> With all the blue ethereal sky,

> And spangled heavens, a shining frame,
> Their great Original proclaim.

In 1711, William Derham's influential Boyle lectures drew attention to the physical or empirical nature of the contemporary argument from design by calling it the "physico-theological" argument, a term later picked up by Immanuel Kant. And as late as 1803 William Paley, in *Natural Theology,* famously defended and popularized the argument from design, using narrowly mechanistic language (God as "watch-maker"), and his form of the argument lingered, especially in America.[4]

This was the philosophical environment in which Romanticism claimed to detect, by intuition, rather more about God in nature than the fact of coherent and universal craftsmanship; and it was the environment in which Darwinism could be felt like a shattering bolt, because "physico-theology" rested so much upon the nonadaptation of species. It was also the setting, as it happens, for Emerson and Thoreau to turn their eyes to the American West, where they found that arguments from design had become a national pastime of the Jacksonian Democrats.

In this book, I refer to the argument from design, which I sometimes shorten to "design," to mean the tendency of thought that reads aesthetic qualities and divine volition in the orderly appearance of the world. I include in the term more strictly philosophical conjectures, deducing classic monotheism from the appearance of the world, as well as the ambient sense (which in the nineteenth century often has an Idealist tinge, by no means orthodoxly Christian) that cosmic order is so compelling it somehow points beyond itself.

Design is a conservative theory, no matter the Romantic or Idealist ecstasies it may eventually inspire. It combines sober empirical observation with a temperate faithful conclusion; nature was now able to furnish the principal evidences of religion. (Design in the eighteenth century was a subset of the field of natural theology; in other words, nature's religious theory.) By the early nineteenth century, design was nearly devoid of a following: no one could be persuaded that its admirable logical strictness made up for its problems of dubious content. David Hume had coolly pointed out how many versions of the argument left something to be desired, resting as they did on faulty notions of cause and effect; and it was claimed gleefully by Voltaire that one design-addled theologian had insisted that God invented tides in order to make it easier for ships to sail into ports.[5]

But the design manifestos were still appearing in America by the 1830s, and in sermons throughout the century. It was a basic element of Christian education. William Paley, whose 1804 *Natural Theology* introduced American readers to the formal description of design, could regularly be found on the Harvard curriculum and was furthermore "reprinted endlessly . . . and

assiduously conned by the self-educated" in the nineteenth century.[6] Design survived to become a crucial line of reasoning to nineteenth-century
nature writers, such as Emerson and Thoreau, who saw in it the ideal alloy
of the scientific and the spiritual temperaments.

Furthermore, design began to appeal to politicians. America is an argument from design: America looks American, and its appearance lets us infer God's designs for its settlement by Americans. One of John O'Sullivan's
editorials in the *Democratic Review* taught the apprehension of democracy in
landscapes, even to the extent of quieting Whig "convulsions": "Adopting
Nature as the best guide, we cannot disregard the lesson which she teaches
when she accomplishes her most mighty results of the good and beautiful
by the silent and slow operation of great principles, without the convulsions
of too rapid action."[7]

For his part, Andrew Jackson noted in his *Farewell Address* that destiny had
a way of coming to pass: "We encountered . . . trials with our new Constitution. . . . But we have passed triumphantly through all these difficulties. . . .
The States which had so long been retarded in their improvement by the Indian tribes residing in the midst of them are at length relieved from the evil."

Can any of us distinguish that passage from one of Henry David Thoreau's,
in "Walking"? "I think that the farmer displaces the Indian even because he
redeems the meadow, and so makes himself stronger and in some respects
more natural."[8] And Jackson concluded, ringingly, that "Providence has
showered on this favored land blessings without number and has chosen
you as the guardians of freedom to preserve it for the benefit of the human
race."[9]

Design was apt for the expanding American continent at a time when
ideologies for exalting the American destiny were rapidly being consolidated by Jacksonian Democrats—who realized, after 1828 (Jackson's first
presidential victory), that it belonged to them. The argument for the
world's design, by the 1820s, was becoming particularized as the argument
of America's manifest destiny.

Design is the key to the attempts to make nature, particularly in the Far
West, look American. Americans, who always believe more easily in God than
in America, like to perform sacraments of landscape, transubstantiating the
West into a national-theological proof, a region that proves we exist. Myra
Jehlen, describing Amerigo Vespucci—who not only saw design in the New
World, but saw it named after himself—calls this process "the archetypal
conjunction of personal identity and national identification." Wayne Franklin identifies it in exploration writing as "the border between language and
event." Even F. O. Matthiessen found an incipient blueprint to land and its
destiny in our literature, observing "the triumph of a new age . . . foreshad-
owed in the gold rush."[10]

I argue that, through this crucial notion of design, nature writing also has a politics. Walt Whitman endorsed, in 1847 in the *Brooklyn Daily Eagle,* the total subjugation of nature to Jacksonian designs: "The great winds [of democracy] that purify the air and without which nature would flag into ruin —are they to be condemned because a tree is prostrated here and there in their course?"[11] Skirmishes in American politics became increasingly organized around what design you placed on the continent.

ONE EXAMPLE OF a Transcendentalist's fight with the Jacksonian heresy, discussed at greater length in chapter 6, is Thoreau's essay "Walking."

Thoreau read widely and often in the literature of exploration and rattled off long lists of explorers' names in his works *Cape Cod* and *The Maine Woods.* He read Lewis and Clark. He read Zebulon Pike. He adored Columbus. "Walking" displays a knowledge of not only the exploration canon, but also its major debate, left over from the eighteenth century: that is, the claim by naturalist Georges Buffon that American species were inferior and inclined toward extinction. To this gallic hauteur, Thoreau replied in "Walking," sounding like a Jacksonian: "I must walk toward Oregon, and not toward Europe."[12]

But Thoreau was never to embrace fully the Jacksonian politics suggested by his love for the Far West, despite the apparent depth of that passion. As chapter 6 details, Thoreau went to some trouble to learn the identity of the players in *l'affaire Buffon,* such as Thomas Jefferson and his fellow scientists. In "Walking" Thoreau reminds us of "the Society for the Diffusion of Useful Knowledge," frequently understood as the 1830s British society by that name; but he also alludes specifically to the American Philosophical Society in Philadelphia, with its mission defined as "the Promotion of Useful Knowledge."[13] The APS, of course, famously had sponsored the Lewis and Clark expedition. Thoreau upbraids what is, for him, a national defense league for going about its work too aristocratically. In "Walking" he urges, oddly, the formation of a Society for the Diffusion of Useful Ignorance, surely a satirical description—and also a warm endorsement—of the Jacksonians.

The legacy of Jefferson for Thoreau, in opening the West for exploration, had mixed virtues at best: its merits were in its American rejoinder (what Stephen Greenblatt now calls "the native riposte") to European charges of mediocrity, and its defects were in its excess of erudition and refinement, or its lack of native wit. Thoreau's "useful ignorance" would correct this overnicety, despite its ties to the Democrats.

"Walking," overall, offers contradictory judgments on democracy, and the exploration of the West is where these contradictions fall out. For all of Thoreau's scorn for elite institutions, he appreciated Jefferson's efforts to stifle European invective against America. And yet for all of his democratic embrace of "useful ignorance," he calls in "Walking" quite specifically for only a "select class" of walkers. The question of national amour propre is framed by Thoreau as an issue of how to use the Far West. When the West answers doubts about national promise—doubts that the Jacksonians were also busily discharging, in their way—Thoreau embraces it: "Westward," he crows, "I go free." When it furnishes the crude substance of egalitarianism, such as a vast space undifferentiated by any "select classes," Thoreau demurs. Whitman, for his part, jeered at Thoreau and "the fashion of a certain set to despise 'politics' and . . . the unmanageableness of the masses; they look at the fierce struggle and at the battle of principles and candidates, and their weak nerves retreat dismayed from the neighborhood of such scenes of convulsion. But to our view the spectacle is always a grand one."[14]

Such were the seductions of manifest destiny.

MANIFEST DESTINY IS one of the most wearied phrases left us from the nineteenth century. Peter Gay, exasperated with the scholarly industry on Rousseau, once famously declared that he thought the concept of the noble savage had run its course intellectually and that nothing more need be said about it, *ever*. Manifest destiny may suffer from the same intellectual supersaturation; it's a feature of American politics that seems not so much invented new in the nineteenth century as paradoxically welcomed as an old favorite into our political tradition. It is as if will could immemorialize what time had not. Manifest destiny has no primary statement as such, only John O'Sullivan's editorial in his *Democratic Review* in 1845. It's a surprise to find the term in print for the first time at such a late date; the idea held currency long before it was sloganized.

Historians, of course, have themselves wearied manifest destiny as a useful tool of analyzing Jacksonian politics and culture until, perhaps inevitably, some have declared that it never existed in the first place.[15] My use of the term here is with an understanding of its limits: I accept Marvin Meyers's proposal simply to consider the eclecticism of the Jacksonian *persuasion*.[16] For an example of Jacksonian eclecticism, we might consider the case of Abner Kneeland, a radical who, after a career as a preacher, rejected Christianity to administer Boston's First Society of Free Enquirers. He made his most outrageous declaration in 1833, in his magazine *The Investigator*, and got himself arrested for blasphemy: amid standard fulminations against organized religion, he compared prayers answered by God to pork barrels doled out by Andrew Jackson. The implied reverse comparison, of Jackson as a God, delighted New England. Kneeland was defended by W. E. Channing in a petition for the remission of his sentence, a document signed by Emerson, Theodore Parker, George Ripley, William Lloyd Garrison, and Bronson Alcott. Kneeland was praised by Orestes Brownson, the first Transcendentalist to join Jackson's party, in tones that are a bit waggish: Kneeland, he wrote, had "shown himself a democrat."[17]

My emphasis on manifest destiny in this book is mainly to consider the expansionist endeavors by Democrats in the 1840s (such as the Mexican War), justified in bald political terms as America's mission and fate, and occasioning a cultural tone of veneration toward that mission. Unluckily for us all, Andrew Jackson never wrote a book on the subject.[18] But I take it that this veneration was audible, if no longer to us, to New England—since New England is the focus in this book of the changing myths of the American West—where major writers had no choice but to talk back to it. Those books we have.

The concept of manifest destiny is not strictly an American invention. It originates under other names in the general process of European conquest in the New World, and manifest destiny retains obvious resonances from those centuries of *translatio imperii*. When Las Casas concludes that the Aztecs are "better than other nations" because they compare favorably to early Christian martyrs in their victimization by the Spanish, or when Valladolid declares that "wars may be undertaken by a very civilized nation [such as Spain] against uncivilized people who . . . devour human flesh," we can hear the murmur of semidivine aspiration even in the contest to rationalize the novel difficulties of conquest.[19] Like the landscapes it was to conquer ideologically, manifest destiny was born old, to offer authority to a young nation. It is no wonder, really, that manifest destiny plagiarized a concept with the vintage and European ancestry of design: there was pedigree in it, and intellectual gravitas.

In the nineteenth century, expansion of the Western frontier and explorers' texts about it absorbed the respectability of a particular theological argument—one long shouldered, as it happens, in the religious plot of American origins. That plot is summarized succinctly by Sacvan Bercovitch as the transit from godly "errand to manifest destiny to dream."[20] In other words, the seventeenth-century Puritan conception of divine planning, which raised a New Jerusalem in Massachusetts, did not abate even as a secular national government then centered in Philadelphia made Constitutional in 1789 the old Puritan territory. And those impulses to imagine God's hand creating and cultivating America—the Puritan origins of the American self, as Bercovitch has termed it elsewhere—had transmuted into a boisterous party rhetoric by the mid-nineteenth century. Jacksonians were simply reading God's map: Americans "came to indigenous peoples," points out one historian, "as missionaries, not conquistadores." Mexico, exhorted a congressman in 1847, needed us to "civilize, Christianize, and moralize" it.[21] In the Jacksonian sense of mission we can scarcely miss the noise of destiny, and it surfaces mainly in religious language.

My point is that during Western expansion in 1840s America, a Christian plot is still too much with us. Theological vainglory in America is familiar from at least the moment when John Winthrop cut the ribbon on the city on a hill, or perhaps from the instant that Columbus fell to his knees at first sight of the West Indies to beseech hopefully that God, not Satan, had put it there.

Annette Kolodny has challenged critics to dispense with the merely "imputed continuities" from the Puritans when it comes to American intellectual history, but I confess myself unable to do so when the evidence tells me that the errand is still being run.[22] The plot of manifest destiny, bequeathed to us from the religious community that launches so much of our canonical literature, expands in the nineteenth century along with the territories it has to absorb. It nearly collapses under its own weight. Exploration narratives convey as much: explorers such as Meriwether Lewis and William Clark wrote about *terra nova* with a comparative anxiety about which theoretical approach might work best. They simply cannot force American nature into one ideology, and they try out them all. In the *Journals* even the Puritan plot is drowned out by that of the Enlightenment sublime, and the Romantic ruin, or the dreaded possibility of no sovereign theory whatsoever. Frank Bergon has intelligently called this superabundance "epic"—another sovereign theory, of course, and one that indicates to me we still have no comprehensive theory for the *Journals*. Jehlen has assigned to Meriwether Lewis the heady Romantic spirit, a useful explication of some of the *Journals,* and less applicable, perhaps, to narrative questions drawn primarily from Lewis's impulses toward design.[23]

It is in such a setting that the interchangeable use of *nature* and *landscape* appears, a shorthand in evidence throughout exploration narratives, for whose authors the empirical or quasi-scientific connotations of "nature" spill over without remark into the cultural and aesthetic undertone of "landscape." For explorers, the exploration of nature was generally a case of deciding how to describe landscape. I have, myself, retained this equation here, not to perpetuate a conceptual error, but to convey what such language tells us about exploration narratives and their view of the two terms.

By way of introducing a few of this book's chapters in a preliminary fashion, I would like to review some of the aesthetic options of exploration and their political attachments. The uncertainty of Lewis and Clark lasted only about a generation, and included the explorer Zebulon Pike, whose self-interested drive to create a transcendent American nature in his picturesque exploration narrative must now be seen for its failed effort to keep political ideology from creeping in. The harder he tried to achieve innocence, the greater the ideological liability. Pike wrote in an old-fashioned genre, the picturesque, which offered readers charming "sketches" of nature. His choice was mainly to protect himself from accusations of being Aaron Burr's traitorous hireling, but it was an aesthetic selection that would prove lasting in later accounts.

Thus picturesque exploration accounts after Pike, such as Stephen Long's and William Emory's, offer not the anxious Puritan sense of "errand," in which patterns of divine intention appear in the awful and punishing language of Protestant discipline. Rather, they are triumphalist, unreconstructed descriptions of God's plan for (say) an American war with Mexico, not in the rage of the Calvinist Jehovah, but in the calm of the post-Enlightenment clock-maker God. The picturesque is a lasting literary mode in exploration, and one that dulls the mind, in its repetitions, toward what nature might contain. Its popularity accounts, in part, for the Transcendentalist desire to revivify American nature.

But it was in no sense a randomly selected literary genre for Pike and the others. One of its chief British theorists, William Gilpin, had specified in his 1794 manifesto *On Picturesque Travel* that "we suppose the [picturesque] country to have been unexplored."[24] Lands imagined to be virgin, therefore, were simply awaiting their picturesque destiny. It is otherwise difficult to account, in nineteenth-century exploration narratives, for the fashionableness of the picturesque—a literary mode that aims not high, but middle —unless we grasp how it flattered American destiny. A. J. Downing, the American picturesque landscape designer, declared that the picturesque, more than the beautiful or even the sublime, demonstrates and aggrandizes power.[25] What better mode for conveying the progress of a nation besotted with its own perverse symmetries? How else to narrate a landscape that welcomed its absorption into an empire than to describe in picturesque aesthetics its immemorial longing to do so? Such designs are sham judgments on the Far West, and contain all the wonder and calamity of Jacksonian propaganda.

Finally, the two-point view among Jacksonians—that there was order in American nature, and that God put it there for Americans to profit by—becomes combined and foreshortened in the simple assertion that we could expand perpetually and blamelessly westward, Americanizing nature. The divine presence becomes implied in the errand itself, no matter who is now the errand boy. The language of order, whether aesthetic or theological, whether picturesque or design, conveys the pressures, accumulated since Plymouth colony or perhaps Columbus, of cosmic intent. In Jacksonian America, such heaped-up confidence in having God's ear attended mainly the national *devoir* of expansion and offered far less explicit concern for the Creator Himself. When Henry Adams's Democrat brother John ran for governor in 1868, Adams lamented simply, solemnly, that John had chosen "the wrong side."[26] And when John O'Sullivan published an early issue of the *Democratic Review,* he exulted that nature was the godhead of American politics. The principle of political freedom, he wrote, "is borrowed from the example of the perfect self-government of the physical universe, being written in letters of light on every page of the great bible of Nature."[27]

The idea of the United States' imperial fate used the same mental muscles as the notion—usually admitted in the eighteenth century—that the world was fated to be useful to humanity because our imperium, likewise, was intended by God. Other nations might have let slip the same cosmic self-esteem, such as Russia or England or China. But this American conviction specifically inherited the ancient New England Puritan sense of mission, which colored its rhetoric at least, and made it of immediate concern to the New England intelligentsia then enduring Jackson and his successors in the White House—wistful-skeptical heirs of Puritans as they were, and scandalized by Jackson's godless misuse of such divine favoritism as they felt. Nineteenth-century manifest destiny descends, oddly, from this vigorous and grave Puritan errand, and an intervening eighteenth-century sense of cosmic optimism.

IT IS FITTING to point out, before I turn to each of the chapters in this book, that the familiarity and conservatism of explorers toward American nature is intellectual fraud, a fact that is evident in our literature also: once we run to the end of what we know, we have to improvise. (The old argument about the "origins" of American literature—native genius or transatlantic influence?—falls under this cognitive habit too: either we improvise or we borrow.) But talk about "somehow *kidding*"! Most of the equipment of exploration was the bogus aesthetic plans for what explorers would see. Thomas Jefferson famously advised Lewis and Clark to be on the lookout for hills made of salt, woolly mammoths, and a range of gentle, shining mountains that would tidily mirror the Appalachians. The funhouse distorting mirror of Jefferson's symmetrical mind is Humbert Humbert's, practicing "future recollection." In Humbert Humbert's Old World childhood, he gloated over the Appalachians as the high point of Romantic westerliness: "a gigantic Switzerland or even Tibet, all mountain, glorious diamond peak upon peak, giant conifers, *le montagnard emigré* in his bear skin glory, and . . . Red Indians under the catalpas"—in fact, he imagined them as the Rockies. Heading west in depraved middle age, Humbert and Lolita find the Eastern mountains "boiled down to a measly suburban lawn and a smoking garbage incinerator. . . . Farewell, Appalachia!"[28]

And under Jefferson's aegis, Lewis and Clark underwent the obverse experience, even, of having landscape look unfamiliar, *on the second viewing:* the trip back from the Pacific to St. Louis was the one that began to worry them. There were fewer tributes to European architecture to be seen in the western geology; fewer symmetries as formulated in Thomas More and Georges Buffon; fewer signs that the Northwest Passage, itself a fraud, would advance them westward to Japan. They just wanted to get home.

After I went west again, to Los Angeles—farewell, Appalachia!—I never stopped thinking of the West as the familiar region where Easterners go mad. But the thing is, Easterners found the West, well, *everywhere*. The regions, always permeable, begin to switch places. Meriwether Lewis, a manic depressive who killed himself, gazed at eroded cliffs and saw the Gothick, and his tormented dreams back home were filled with western geology. Zebulon Pike, probably in conspiracy to break the United States in two, weathered mutiny and starvation in order to prove that the Rocky Mountains were picturesque. William Emory looked at the borderland between America and Mexico and found the self-evident truth that the borderline was not placed, or even replaced, but revealed. Henry Thoreau turned right outside his Walden Pond cabin instead of left and not only liked the view better (it faced west), but said it was where the woodchucks roamed, and twelve thousand woodchucks can't be wrong. Ralph Waldo Emerson, that fox among hedgehogs, or perhaps woodchucks, venerated Columbus and his discovery—or found him, in the words of his friend Almira Barlow, "a little beyond."[29]

Meanwhile, even though the West is everywhere, the literary canon in America has fraudulently settled into regions. One of the correctives of this book is to point out that our regions are promiscuous, cross-breeding, interdependent, and obsessed with one another. When I began writing the chapter on Lewis and Clark, a specialist I know in Western literature said to me that he was fed up with being called a "regionalist." He pointed out that it was at the very least an error of scale to call the fifty miles around Walden Pond "America" when everything west of the Mississippi River was only a region. The same argument has been made by classicists about Athens and Greece when describing the regional spread of literature to that other Wild West, Rome.

In nature's nation, literature is Western. This book reviews the presence of westering in various works of nineteenth-century American literature, from its first great national exploration, the Lewis and Clark expedition, to the Civil War, when slavery finally compromised all the possibilities of continental expansion, and of continued geographical symmetry. My purpose has not been to insist that the Lewis and Clark *Journals* are, say, the same as *Walden* or *Nature,* but rather that they write the same plot.

The difficulty in a universal and destinarian exploration plot, of course, is that its intellectually conservative qualities of reasserting the glories of the nation rather than pursuing strange and novel regions that might not (yet) be American tend to nettle a community like New England. Exploration and conquest were appealing in New England because they seemed at least intellectually intrepid, and they stirred the imaginations of Emerson and Thoreau, who were inspired by Western exploration narratives. (Chapters 4, 5, and 6 describe their extended readings in the genre.) But the trap was laid for New Englanders who could not avoid Jacksonian rhetoric any more than they could avoid Jackson himself. "The West," Albert J. von Frank reminds us, "was too American, too representative of essential national values, to be allowed to go its crazy way unguided by the shaping hand of eastern

institutions." And New Englanders, he continues, soberly "prepared themselves to supply the required aid."[30]

But the too-American destiny in exploration narratives appeals both to
high-minded Transcendentalists as well as opportunistic political hacks; they
begin to sound like each other. Thus William Henry Channing protested the
Mexican War not out of any dispute with the destinarian terms of national
development, but because the war "divert[ed] our whole people from the
fulfillment of the destiny to which Providence plainly summons us."[31]

LET ME NOW review the chapters in this book. Eventually, explorers such as
Lewis and Clark (the subject of chapter 1) and Zebulon Pike (chapter 2)
pointed out that the effects of nature on the human mind during an expedition are not a joyous instance of contact with the divine; instead, it is a failure of the will, because most of the time there is no explanation for what
you see. Nature is having its way with you, not the other way around. Jacksonian politics were organized never to permit such failures; "unmixed error," intoned George Bancroft, "can have no existence in the public mind."[32]
Even Aaron Burr might have found this position intellectually empty.

Zebulon Pike, who departed for the southern Rocky Mountains while
Lewis and Clark were still in the field, continued to display the hunger for
symmetry and order promised by the crooked old statesmen who commis-
sioned the maps and surveys of the new continent. Design, especially when
seen through the picturesque, is the key metaphor in his account. Pike's
statesmanlike notions of order in nature were colored by his probable involvement in the Burr Conspiracy. Aaron Burr's plans to set up a rival empire in the western territories of America dispatched Pike to reconnoiter
the Southwest region bordering Spanish territory. In his account of his exploration, written while treason charges were being leveled against Burr after the Conspiracy was exposed, Pike seeks to exonerate himself. His gentlemanly persona in the account, a version of Washington Irving's Federalist
picturesque style, simply cannot be that of a guilty man; nature itself, in picturesque shades that only Pike could appreciate, showed his innocence. The
insistence that what looked like treason was actually patriotism was made
possible by the conservative rhetoric of exploration: even if something looks
new and menacing, you can be assured it is familiar and safe. Pike could not
be guilty, because he was too picturesque (and gentlemanly) a conqueror.
The picturesque finally ends up an intellectual cul de sac, conventionalized
into mere checklists of aesthetic feeling, as later picturesque writers tell us.

The accounts of Stephen Long and William Emory (discussed in chapter 3) extend and solidify these attempts at political evasion combined with
geographical erratum. Long, who explored but failed to find the source of
the Red River, is famous for another great error of design: the designation
of the rich grasslands west of the Missouri as "the Great American Desert."

Emory's account, written at the same time as *Walden,* is a survey for the U.S. government in the territory won in the Mexican War, searching for a suitable route for the western railway. His narrative is an uneasy companion text to *Walden,* as I show in chapter 3, because Emory is unreconstructed in his enthusiasm for taking over the Southwest and making it prosper. The 1850s saw statements by a number of New Englanders on Mexico's loss, including Theodore Parker, who shrugged that simply "by being better than Mexico, wiser, humaner, more free and manly," the United States won the Mexican War.[33] By this time, the rhetoric of design had become interchangeable with the rhetoric of destiny; Emory's own politics were straightforwardly pro–Anglo Saxon and pro-expansionist. He was also a picturesque writer, like Pike, who saw in unsettled landscapes only the potential for cultivation and the design of American conquest. Emory's is a narrative that looks at the West to find out what its purpose is. He finds, along the new border with Mexico, that the West is proof that America exists, and that it is victorious. It is no wonder that later explorers, such as Long and Emory, offer a triumphalist version of unknown lands, and their narratives are as untroubled as early drafts of the exploration story are haunted.

The landscape problem, by the 1830s, was that when explorers could not account for everything they saw, they bluffed, and with mixed successes. But Emerson and Thoreau attempted—rather urgently—a solution to this problem in response to landscape (see chapters 4, 5, and 6). For Emerson, design had too much intellectual potential to be discarded. And America, for Emerson, was where design was fulfilled. The lessons of exploration (Emerson frequently considered the moral law that the Columbian discovery might teach us) were to remind us that our vision of America was somehow inadequate to its actual topography.

In this light, Thoreau's project, reviewed in chapter 6, responds by narrating some of the rare moments of topographical exultation, whether by walking to Wachusett, trying to live deliberately, or eating a woodchuck raw. Thoreau's insistence upon a frontiersman figure who symbolically "settles" Walden Pond uneasily takes over a classic trope of the Jacksonian Democrats, their Rugged Individual. Thoreau's "exploration narrative" is an attempt to reclaim this genre, its wonder and its inner life, for those who share his antipathy to slavery and his classic resistance to Jacksonian democracy. His attacks in "Slavery in Massachusetts," too, are likewise shared between immediate political protest and general intellectual dissent, so that Thoreau condemns not only the horror of endorsing slavery, but also the horror of what endorsing slavery looks like from the inside of the endorsing mind. That mind resorts again and again to political slogans, not to mention aesthetic clichés about nature. For Thoreau, intellectual shortcuts are just moral foreshortening; and they're signals of our depravity.

The shared effort between Emerson and Thoreau, essentially to save the design argument from itself, was a corrective to this depravity, and a corrective, they hoped, to the political retrograding in the Far West. To do so, they still wrote about *design* in a way that makes it sound, at turns, more like *destiny*.

The nature writer in the nineteenth century wrote again and again and again about the West, investing it at turns with genius and corrective, and also menace and terror. Regardless of what landscapes writers described, they were expert at having seen it already: it was brave, new, Arcadian, Edenic, sublime, beautiful, picturesque, pastoral, Gothic, ecological, a *jardin anglais*, usually non-Mexican, free or slave, lousy with resources, virgin, unoccupied, and, most of all, *ours, by design*. The design argument transformed mere scenery into national landscapes.

Its rhetoric was providential and cheerful: anyone could see that God made nature for Americans. But the dilemma—untheorized, but built, it seems to me, into nineteenth-century politics—was in opposing the expansionist politics in manifest destiny while remaining committed to the nation. It was difficult to resist the design argument, its intellectual tradition, its providential rhetoric, and its confidence in American progress, and then in the process not to become saddled with manifest destiny. All successes in solving this dilemma were qualified. Each time Emerson stooped to correct the Jacksonian prose style and its central idea of manifest destiny, he was admitting its force.

New England writers, particularly Emerson and Thoreau, could easily recognize political opportunism in Jacksonian rhetoric; but refuting it was another matter. Thoreau is one of the few New Englanders to have had a discernible (irascible, responsible) politics, and his were anti-Jacksonian, but he also worshipped the effort at western expansion. He wanted a nation of Walden Ponds, just as Jefferson, equally at odds with his own political impetus, wanted a nation of yeoman Monticellos. Emerson's politics were less straightforward than Thoreau's, and they tackled their subjects with abstraction. ("The tedium of an assigned theme," one critic detects as the tone of Emerson's political writing.) [34] He also found the West mesmerizing, and as much the repository of American progress as Jackson said it was. But Emerson was so shrewd about Jacksonian rhetoric that he could even parody it in *Nature,* as chapter 5 shows.

Even before the specifically political protests in Transcendentalist nature writing, though, the writers of exploration narratives found themselves ensnared by rhetorical promises about American nature. All exploration narratives begin buoyantly, and most of them lapse into confusion and despair when the landscape fails to live up to its promised symmetry and order. If there is less evidence of resistant politics in these narratives, it is probably because the confusion is so real: how could national missions westward fail to live up to national promises? How could America disappoint?

The decades before 1860 share the coincidence of enormous literary production and continental expansion westward, something of which even F. O. Matthiessen makes relatively little in *American Renaissance*. It would be appropriate now to reconsider, at least, how to write a syllabus in a nineteenth-century American literature course in light of the westward-facing tendency I have pointed out in works of apparently entrenched New England regionalism, and in light of the Eastern personality of Western exploration narratives. Our prime meridian seems uprooted: perhaps literary Transcendentalism is a species of Western exploration narrative; perhaps the most suitable companion text to Lewis and Clark is *Leaves of Grass*. Or *Huckleberry Finn*. Or that narrative that (like Pike's) must tread so carefully through political accusations, by Frederick Douglass.

THE OTHER QUESTION I have raised involves dissenting American politics in the nineteenth century and what options it had in an age of conquest: whether to warm to Jackson's common touch, or despise his vulgarized mass politics; whether to free slaves by force, or hope for slavery's peaceful decline; whether to seize California, or defend Mexico; whether to see design (and its philosophical seriousness), or destiny (and its land grabs); or whether, in Matthiessen's formulation about Herman Melville, to side with Pierre, or Ahab. Dissenting New England, it seems to me (I have specifically not termed it "liberal," for reasons I detail in chapter 4), would eventually have to make up its mind to be annihilated, again in the Melvillean sense of the problem: the choices were always going to be imperfect. Moreover, the limits of dissent, even in a democracy, were reached by the spring of 1861, when war began and a winter of Compromises ended, when all the nation's politics came to one explosive point, and when even the West itself seemed to come to a stop.

But neither Jacksonians nor their enemies could have predicted what place westward expansion would take in tautening, and then breaking off, relations between slaveholding and free regions. The deferral of the slavery question, first in time (put off at independence for future negotiation) and then in space (permitted in a limited number of western states), eventually altered the destiny manifesting itself in the West. In empire's republic, politics looked west. The Civil War proved, as no temporary sectional squabble or vulgar presidential politics did, that endless expansion into redemptive Western nature was bound to go bad, and so reveal itself not as redemption, but as what Thoreau called murder to the state.

In the frenzy of causal logic during the Age of Jackson, design was an obvious choice; it was not a perfect solution. Of course destinarianism, confusing antecedents with causes, might even insist that Lewis and Clark (or Jefferson, or perhaps Bonaparte) caused the Civil War, because exploring the Louisiana Purchase added so much to the territory to fight over. A providential plot may well be the defining characteristic of nineteenth-century American literature, and the West provided an infinite number of such plots.

During the crisis of 1860, the *New York Times* editorialized from the obvious fact of America's geographical ecstasy—"there is no nation in the world . . . so thoroughly pervaded with the spirit of conquest—so filled will dreams of enlarged dominions"—and appealed to *this* manifest destiny as the reason the North must not give in to secession. What exploration narratives were really saying, hints the paper of record, was that the war must be fought for fear of losing "all prospect of ever extending our growth and national development. . . . We should [wrongly] be limiting ourselves to that narrow band of the continent."

"We frequently talk," declared the Charleston *Mercury* at the same time,

> of the future glories of our republican destiny on the continent—of the spread of our civilization and free institutions over Mexico and the Tropics. Already we have absorbed two of her States, Texas and California. Is it expected that our onward march is to stop here? Is it not more probable and more philosophic to suppose that, as in the past, so in the future, the Anglo-Saxon race will . . . occupy and absorb the whole of that splendid but ill-peopled country, and to remove . . . the worthless mongrel races that now . . . curse the land?[35]

If design is the philosophic blessing of the land with intent, Mexicans must be a mistake, an infection of undestinedness, unpromising preliminaries in the Promised Land. Picturesqueness, discovered by Pike in what was still northern Mexico, delimited by Emory to this side of Polk's border in the Southwest, was now a concrete fact of *all* pre-American lands: the country was imperially splendid and groaned for the free institutions of the slave power. And this design, insists the paper of South Carolina, was too manifest to be handed back to the besieging North.

Slavery was probably the final perverse symmetry of American landscape theory, one that destined some states to be free and others not. You were meant to know just by looking which was which, just as you were meant programmatically to be moved by American nature. We can glimpse in the Civil War the logical extreme of the design impulse: aggressive paranoia. The 1860s represent the collapse of a broad geographical will into sections finally declared hopelessly unlike each other, destined to separate. There was no sovereign theory left; fighting began in two differently designed Kansases. Easterners allegedly wrote the Western plot, in conquest and exploration narratives, and then in Western eyes were all their sins remembered. The West recapitulated, vengefully, that conquest plot back into the national epic, extending the territorial prerogatives of North and South and then forcing, as in a retrograde march, those two contenders to defend their claims. Design out West was the author of destruction back East.

Sectional disquisitions, after 1865, were as extravagant as the opening propositions had been; when the siege was over and the surrender signed at Appomattox, the Priams and Hecubas of the defeated South sometimes even recognized themselves in the world's first destinarian war. How could they not read their own experience back into the ultimate eastwardness and pastness of Troy? Even Edgar Allan Poe, like Paris, abducted Helen for his war captive and his muse: "the weary, way-worn wanderer bore [her] / To his own native shore."[36]

The North had the antique Sheridans and Grants, Yankee Ajaxes and Odysseuses, who had burned "the topless towers of Ilium." They recognized the everlasting Greek type, and it was their type: Emerson gnomically detected "immortality . . . in [the ancient Greeks'] very rags."[37] Thoreau, tucked away in his tame woods, never ordering his woodchucks from Colorado, also thought himself a Greek. (He always referred to Greek classics familiarly, "as though he himself had just written them.")[38]

Before Sherman had burned his last topless tower, someone else was preparing to read the pattern of the *Iliad* back into the soil of Turkey. Heinrich Schliemann, a middle-aged German, had recently taken up archaeology and thought it would be interesting to look for Homer's Troy. He found it, too, or thought he had—burned towers and walls, and even "Priam's gold," on a barren hill above the Straits of the Dardanelles.

Gold was not a new experience for Schliemann. He owed, and we owe, his excavation of Troy (the archaeologization and bringing-up-to-date, the Westernization of Homer's design) to Western gold. He had been a forty-niner. Schliemann had made the capital for ancient Ilium from modern prospecting, from newly conquered California.

1

Natural Causes

The Journals *of Lewis and Clark*

The problem which the Lewis and Clark expedition was sent to solve originated with the discovery of America. Columbus, the discoverer, was primarily intent on finding, not a new world, but a new way to an old one, and the accidental discovery of America constituted, in reality, the great tragedy of his career.
M. M. QUAIFE, *The Journals of Captain Meriwether Lewis and Sergeant John Ordway, Kept on the Expedition of Western Exploration, 1803–1806* (1916)

May I get out again with my life, you shall possess the brave country alone for me.
JOHN BUNYAN, *Pilgrim's Progress* (1678)

Piracy was the first problem of the published story of Lewis and Clark. Sergeant Patrick Gass was the official carpenter of the Corps of Discovery, and during his travels he kept, as a few of his fellow explorers also did, a private journal. Lewis and Clark were shrewd enough to buy up the journal of Sergeant John Ordway for $150, but in 1807 a Pittsburgh publisher, David Mc-Keehan, slyly bought the rights to Gass's account and rushed it into print. Lewis, who had stalled for months in preparing the official journal for publication—much to the vexation of Thomas Jefferson, who wanted a close-fisted Congress to know exactly what they'd bought from Napoleon—found himself busy not with the *Journals* but with letters to the editor. McKeehan, he complained, was going to distract the public with "unauthorized and spurious publications"; the expedition merited the words of the commanders, not of the supporting actors. The public, Lewis himself objected, "may be taught to depreciate the worth of the work which I am myself preparing for publication. . . . Much time, labor, and expense are absolutely necessary" before it would be ready.[1]

Lewis lost. That year Gass's unauthorized account appeared at the price of one dollar. It went through four editions. In 1810 it was even translated into French, and in 1811 into German.[2]

This book begins with the story of the Lewis and Clark *Journals* and some of its discontents (such as Patrick Gass) because, in my view, Lewis and Clark's text offers a significant case of failure. Its burden was the demand for comprehensive description of several million square miles of new territory, or the directive to find a design for Louisiana; its undoing was a direct result of that commission. The explorers and writers who followed Lewis and Clark, from Zebulon Pike to Henry David Thoreau, noticed more than we, so far, about such an inevitable drubbing in the face of *terra incognita*. To make clear the obstinacy of Jacksonian rhetoric in the nineteenth century, this chapter will describe a pre-Jacksonian moment, when exploration had in it more genres than even the fluent Meriwether Lewis could pronounce. The successive narratives to Lewis and Clark—and their Jacksonian clamorings—will, I suspect, show in high relief.

What did the West look like just before Lewis and Clark's *Journals* appeared, and what was its destiny? The Gass journal is an important document, because it is the only nineteenth-century account of the expedition to include illustrations.[3] Unsigned and probably created by Gass, they are described in McKeehan's advertising as "charming woodcuts," and indeed, the pictures are crude, appealing depictions of Western adventures.[4] (See figures 1 through 6.) They offer a naive pictorial version of the contradictions in exploration narratives: the attempt to discover, alongside the effort to have seen things already, or the mixed narrative of wonder and retrospection.

Gass presents exploration, in other words, with the deck stacked. Unlike the Lewis and Clark *Journals,* of which they are the fugitive precursor, Gass's pictures and diary find a simple but lasting moral in westering, one that the *Journals* finally will not abide. Where Gass makes plain the expedition's amusements, so that even minor trials are rehearsals of major pleasantries, the *Journals* will lose their nerve; Lewis and Clark in their own text will insist on reporting their boredom, their hunger, and their exhaustion. My argument is not that Lewis and Clark were realists (they were not). Rather, it is that, within the genre of exploration narratives, such concessions to melancholy and hardship become primary with the *Journals,* and not much before them. We should be more surprised than we are to read about such calamities. Historian William H. Goetzmann has specified helpfully that calamity can occur during discovery, but not during exploration: discovery is for surprises and mishaps, and exploration is for the careful display and exercise, calamity free, of one's cultural training and expertise.

Lewis and Clark's literary reputations, which have steadily risen as we approach their bicentennial and reread them, have in many instances been based on mistaking them, so to speak, for Patrick Gass. Quite apart from the sentimentality dedicated to their heroics (the usual offering of history buffs),[5] a consistent critical line has been to find in the *Journals* the commonplaces of empire narratives. That is easily done with Gass and his parable of conquest, as I will describe. Lewis and Clark have attracted similar observations: Goetzmann finds them "foreshadowing" manifest destiny; Clyde A. Milner declares the expedition "the long prelude" to a century of

Western expansion. But even to go ahead and credit Lewis, specifically, with the conscience of an up-to-date Romantic, as Goetzmann and Myra Jehlen have done, is only to read the voyage out.[6] So far we have imagined Lewis and Clark as insufficiently self-aware and overly devout, in literary and political terms, toward the delusion of empire. Indeed, even later explorers read them this way, as chapter 3 describes. Such a devotion is evident in their *Journals*, in fact, only until about mid-1805, or halfway through.

For some reason Western American literature keeps having to fight this characterization: it is largely cherished for its rusticity and its artifact status, and for its relevance as the documents of empire.[7] Exploration narratives are only beginning to sound literary to us. We seem to be shambling toward Annette Kolodny's appeal: "the challenge," she writes of our judgments of noncanonical American literatures, "is not to decide *beforehand* what constitutes literariness."[8]

It is part of the purpose of the current chapter to reorient a prevailing view of Lewis and Clark, and to find them not a latterly example of sinister conquerors or agents of empire—itself a naive set of accusations—but rather to take seriously, for one thing, the bleak mood of the entire return journey. Mere victims, in one account, of the Romantic sublime, Lewis and Clark are also thinking their way well past it, so that they commence an American habit of mind for the nineteenth century. That habit, as this study will track down, is in the careful and sometimes poignant discrimination among designs, or among master plans for the expanding continent. Western landscapes, by about 1800, were supposed to be well consolidated into Western thought: you could have your choice of the sublime, the Arcadian, the picturesque, or the virgin (among many others); you had no anxiety that the landscapes on your journey, like the specimens in a natural history museum, would or could lack for descriptive captions.

Lewis and Clark tell us how this contrivance fails. They make no new claims to having found their way to political utopia, or to the best American design, any more than they can point out exactly where the Northwest Passage is; but they do try to find both, and their confessed failure is what distinguishes the *Journals* from other white North American exploration narratives. Failures of design do not sound the same in other explorers' accounts; they seldom see print. John Ledyard, another of Jefferson's exploring protégés, who in 1788 was arrested by the Russians on his way east across Eurasia to the Pacific and to Oregon, had much more to own up to for his foolhardiness and errors, and yet his account has hardly the depth of Lewis and Clark's.[9] Captain James Cook, who despite his triumph of global circumnavigation is another famous case of failure (his death in Hawaii was immediately termed an "apotheosis," and lately a "transfiguration"), is likewise less memorable for his journal prose than his deeds.[10] And Stephen Long and Zebulon Pike (as I discuss later), who failed to find the source of the

Red River on separate expeditions, somehow find in their nonsuccesses the evidence of national triumph. If Lewis and Clark's *Journals* do foreshadow the advent of manifest destiny, they are among the least qualified, despite their heroics, to do so.

But to return to Patrick Gass. With Lewis and Clark's *Journals* frustratingly unpublished until 1814, the Gass journal, its pictures, and the associated squabbles over literary piracy offer an unintentional but vivid portrait of this source text, and one that can prepare us for how to read it freshly. The first plate in Gass, entitled *A Canoe striking on a Tree* (see figure 1), was selected as the frontispiece to the journal, although it represents a pair of explorers at, perhaps, a fairly low moment—their canoe sinking, and their hands raised in alarm. Kenneth Haltman, an art historian who has written the only study of these illustrations to date, points out that the woodcut borrows its iconography from a popular eighteenth-century print of *Pilgrim's Progress*, namely *Christian and Pliable in the Slough of Despond* (1781).[11] Christian and Pliable, like Gass's two explorers (one assumes they're Lewis and Clark: the troupe, some forty people, was always known eponymously as "the Lewis and Clark expedition"), sink into a pond with raised hands, because, as John Bunyan tells it, "they, being heedless, did both fall suddenly into the bog." The subtitle of *Christian and Pliable* is the short colloquy from Bunyan on moral disorientation: "Then said Pliable ah! neighbour Christian, where are you now? Truly said Christian I do not know."

Haltman sees in this initial illustration the evidence of Lewis and Clark's journey as a quest narrative, signaled by the placelessness and danger that the troupe must overcome. He also finds that, as the illustrations go on, we witness "allegorical succession," from failure to triumph. And indeed, as the journal progresses, so do the illustrations in their sense of victory over the wilderness. Here is a list of the other five (see figures 2 through 6):

Captains Lewis & Clark holding a Council with the Indians
Captain Clark & his men building a line of Huts
Captain Clark and his men shooting Bears
An American having struck a Bear but not killed him, escapes into a Tree
Captain Lewis shooting an Indian

While it is possible to trace a straightforward conquest story in these woodcut titles—from Indian council to Indian slaughter, for one thing, and the establishment of defensive architecture in the land of bears—it is also the case that the moral tone, following the Bunyanesque opening, gets a bit loose.[12] Here, for instance, is the way Bunyan had continued that scene in the Slough of Despond:

> Pliable began to be offended, and angrily said to his fellow, Is this the happiness you have told me all this while of? If we have such ill speed at our first setting out, what may we expect betwixt this and our journey's end? May I get out

Figure 1. *A Canoe striking on a Tree*, from the *Journal of Voyages and Travels of a Corps of Discovery . . .* , by Patrick Gass.

again with my life, you shall possess the brave country alone for me. And, with that, he gave a desperate struggle or two, and got out of the mire on that side of the slough which was next to his own house: so away he went, and Christian saw him no more. Wherefore Christian was left to tumble in the Slough of Despond alone.[13]

With Bunyan's allegory in mind, the Gass illustrations don't exactly simplify the terms for understanding Lewis and Clark. For one thing, who's who? Should Lewis, popularly understood as the moody, "deep" explorer, correspond to Christian, whose long and complex journey leads to salvation? Or does Clark, with his reputation for sincerity and simplicity, more closely resemble the morally absorbed Christian? Which of the explorers is, in other words, too Pliable?

The solution is that Gass and McKeehan did not anticipate the moral confusion that this woodcut's allegorical echoes might set in motion. Few exploration journalists did, though their narratives are generally packed with allegory and literary allusion. The genre of exploration narratives works this way: the mythic allusions and the classical references pile up so quickly that the author is, in Bunyan's terms, bogged down; he's no longer observing the new, but busy predicting it, or even busier making the new into the old.

Captains Lewis & Clark holding a Council with the Indians

Figure 2. *Captains Lewis & Clark holding a Council with the Indians*, from Gass's *Journal of Voyages and Travels.*

Captain Clark & his men building a line of Huts.

Figure 3. *Captain Clark & his men building a line of Huts*, from Gass's *Journal of Voyages and Travels.*

Captain Clark and his men shooting Bears.

Figure 4. *Captain Clark and his men shooting Bears,* from Gass's *Journal of Voyages and Travels.*

An American having struck a Bear but not killed him, escapes into a Tree.

Figure 5. *An American having struck a Bear but not killed him, escapes into a Tree,* from Gass's *Journal of Voyages and Travels.*

Page.245.

Captain Lewis shooting an Indian.

Figure 6. *Captain Lewis shooting an Indian,* from Gass's *Journal of Voyages and Travels.*

McKeehan's response to Lewis's complaints about the infringement on his original *Journals,* then, is also instructive: he can describe, even if he may not have cared about, the inner life of the exploration narrative. Lewis had protested that none of the spurious accounts presented accurate renderings of Louisiana's "celestial observations, mineralogy, botany, or zoology." McKeehan replies that Lewis cannot suppress reports of the expedition simply in the interest of scientific accuracy—for Lewis will bore his readers with "too long and learned dissertations," while Gass, "who does not speak scientifically," is at least "homespun."[14] McKeehan unwittingly presents Lewis as a philosophe, or perhaps simply a quantitative drudge; in any case it is hard to miss the encyclopedic bent of Lewis's mind, even presented in McKeehan's hostile account: a mind that finds truth in the sheer accumulation of knowledge, and that cannot take seriously any lesser effort to describe the natural world. The authoritative account of the expedition, published in his own way and for readers who did not "depreciate" it, provides for Lewis a certainty of knowledge with an audience who consent to that certainty. It is hard to imagine the Enlightenment mind more vividly.

On the other hand, flailing at Lewis for calling only his own account authoritative (the pirate pointing out piracy), McKeehan also illuminates a different side of Lewis's mind. McKeehan contends that no one has the right to claim unique interest in the recent expedition, because the facts about Louisiana were probably plagiarized from Alexander Mackenzie, who had trekked across the Canadian Rockies to the Pacific for Great Britain in 1789 and 1793. It is true that Lewis and Clark carried Mackenzie's account with them during the expedition; indeed, many explorers after Lewis and Clark carried the Biddle edition of Lewis and Clark with them.

For all we know, Gass was right to depict the moral outcome of the exploration as he did, in the terms of didactic Protestant literature, especially given the providential feel of future exploration narratives, from bog to empire. McKeehan's second objection, though—presented crossly, amid complaints that Lewis walked to the Pacific and back only for the money—seems to me to get to the heart of the matter. *Of course* the Lewis and Clark journey was plagiarized; *of course* the route had essentially been traveled before; *of course* there was little novelty left in the Far West in 1806. Everyone knows the plot, McKeehan seems to be saying: you have no monopoly on it. Lewis, preoccupied with publication squabbles and the governorship of Missouri, did not comment on McKeehan's accusation, nor did he return to work on his own manuscript. After his death in 1809, Clark had to hire Nicholas Biddle to make the journals publishable.

The essential contradiction of an exploration narrative, and of formal exploration projects generally, lies in its mandate simply to explore, which sits alongside a detailed list of exactly what to look for. McKeehan, jeering at Lewis's notion of "the genuine work" and attacking Lewis for his editorial "expunging fingers," could claim that differing accounts of the expedition made no difference to the public—that, indeed, readers of Gass or of Lewis and Clark would find little meaningful, subjective variance in the way the story came out. The West was going to be American; the details were irrelevant. And to claim that an exploration narrative contained irreducible, singular literary interest was simply a stratagem by Lewis to prevent McKeehan's making a profit.

Perhaps it is hard to imagine the Romantic mind more vividly than this (its devotion to a subjective, individual report of the world) unless we can bring to bear the multiple intellectual attitudes of the *Journals.* They are a text not simply as thrilling as an Enlightenment catalogue nor as dull as a first-person Romantic lyric, but truly "a little beyond." Emerson's friend meant Transcendentalism, and I don't; I mean that enterprise in the *Journals* to make language fit a new landscape, rather than the other way around. And the *Journals,* with every literary option available, finally want them all. (This desire, of course, is strikingly Emersonian.)

As this chapter will suggest, Lewis and Clark's *Journals* have precisely the uniqueness—perhaps it is "literary"—that Lewis insisted on in 1807. The McKeehan dispute shows Lewis's sense that the American West had shifted in meaning, or design, from disposable imperial press release to something like an aid to reflection. But not even Romanticism accounts for the gloom of the return trip. I always know I am reading the literature of the American West when I observe "genre trouble" like this; should we need a new definition of a Western, as many critics have said we do,[15] there may be a beginning of one in this generic maelstrom.

Furthermore, that shift in the senses of design, like the insistence on calamity, is more vivid than it ought to be in a mild corporate document like the Lewis and Clark *Journals*. As my discussion of the round-trip journey suggests, the explorers' mental universe, before new Western landscapes, reacts strongly: it stirs, it shudders, and it finds little peace. The response is even more obvious during the voyage back, when those landscapes lose even the charm of novelty.

It is the purpose of exploration to impose order on unmapped territory, and in narrating this process, the exploration journal records those ordering principles that have taken imaginative hold for the explorer. In the case of Lewis and Clark, called America's "writingest" explorers by Donald Jackson, the trials of order are vivid, for being first, and also for failing. In this chapter, I discuss these trials of order and their near-successes. It is my claim that Lewis and Clark merit a foundational status for writing about that failure, and for discovering the limits of being the "writingest." By finding in exploration both the deep structures of art and literature and the chaos of real events, they bring the exploration narrative into American literary practice. This is not an "influence" model of literature, for the *Journals* were only available in Biddle's shortened (and hugely rewritten) edition in 1814, and not at full length until the early twentieth century. The struggles in the *Journals* to find merit in antique national designs, while noting painstakingly just how deficient those designs were, place Lewis and Clark first in a nineteenth-century process, described in the Introduction, of saving design from itself.

AN EARLY STAB at the *Journals* termed them an "Enlightenment epic,"[16] suggesting reasonably that Lewis and Clark wrote more than just a period piece, and that they were indebted to one sensibility (the eighteenth century's) while showing signs of another. Duality happens to be a key metaphor for critics who divide up the cognitive work of the *Journals:* Lewis is aesthetic, ethereal, and aristocratic, while Clark is practical, direct, and speaks for the common man.[17] (He certainly spells like him.) My argument is not unlike this one, but I find the *Journals* so actively engaged in trying out a variety of master plans that, finally, the Enlightenment is just another on the list.

Some critics who chart the course of the Enlightenment in America reach a dark conclusion, what Peter Gay called "the shadow," John P. Diggins "pathos," and Robert A. Ferguson "uncertainty"[18]—namely that in high-stakes intellectual and political events, such as the American Revolution, the prospect of success, resulting in political stability and a more perfect union, is about equal to the risk of failure, or political chaos. For all its associations with human perfectibility in politics and heavy-handed taxonomic realism in science, the Enlightenment had its share of unease. There was mob violence, undeterred, and tyranny, unfettered, and mysteries, unilluminated. It had as much to dread from internal chaos as it did to commend in outward order. The dark side of the Enlightenment *was* the Enlightenment in America; insufficiently skeptical (and provincially anti-intellectual), Americans simply never took part in it.

There is also the counterpoint, that America is where the Enlightenment was fulfilled. Henry Steele Commager's account is perhaps the most familiar, a story of an intellectual movement's apotheosis in the founding of a nation: an empire of reason. Commager, like Henry May, narrates an agreeable history in which paradigms (social, political, scientific, artistic) multiply and prosper, and rationalism governs them all. Significantly, *this* American Enlightenment is the age of atheist Thomas Paine and the English treatise *Christianity Not Mysterious* (1696); religious life is gauntly Deist, and primarily organized around its own carefully measured last rites. ("As freezing persons recollect the snow," Emily Dickinson said.)

The call for a desecularized Enlightenment history has been audible for some time;[19] indeed, the attempt to describe the theological origins of manifest destiny (as in this book) is dependent upon such an effort. The merit of an American Enlightenment imagined—in my view, more subtly—as a dialectic between reason and faith, rather than reason's mere temporary indulgence of faith, is that, by the 1830s in New England, the two categories were almost as contentious, again, as in the Middle Ages.[20] Such a reemergence is more impressive if we consider earlier decades not so much a religious recess as an incubation of the debates.

There is more anxiety in the confident treatises of the eighteenth century than intellectual historians have previously stressed. Ferguson, for instance, now finds the (secular) transit of American Enlightenment not through *Common Sense, The Federalist* and the Declaration of Independence, but in two works sometimes demoted in the ranking of foundational literary texts: Francis Scott Key's "Star-Spangled Banner" (1814) and George Washington's *Farewell Address* (1783). The key to these two texts is their "consuming anxiety," conveyed in the song's urgent, repeated question, "O! say does that star-spangled banner yet wave?" In such a case, argues Ferguson, one isn't sure whether the elaborate verbiage quite outweighs the fact that it's a question, not a declamation. Enlightenment anxiety, it seems, inheres in its star-spangled conviction of progress.

And among religious thinkers and leaders in particular, the reasoned assurances of the design argument, as well as the gusto of the attacks on historical Christianity, were balanced (for instance) by the fervor of revivalist piety lingering from the Great Awakening. For Alan Heimert these two positions, reason and piety, are the central strains of American religious thought in the period (and he acknowledges, justly, that they're hardly unique to America);[21] it was the century, writes Michael J. Colacurcio, of "Paley against Hume, Bishop Butler against the Deists, Yale University against Thomas Paine."[22] The long withdrawing roar of religious faith on the part of Deists, it seems, was kept in check by the heirs of Jonathan Edwards. The design of the universe was very much an unsettled question, no matter what Alexander Pope's couplet on the smooth functioning of nature might suggest:

> Nature and Nature's Law lay hid in Night;
> God said, *Let Newton Be!* and all was Light.

Long odds, generally, are built into the mechanism of the Enlightenment (a favorite metaphor of the age): the very optimism toward natural order and natural law that offers, say, Thomas Jefferson the taxonomic method and the contract theory of government can also, in the same moment, give way to pessimism and confusion and despair. Familiar as unhappy endings are in the list of the world's intellectual systems—what poststructuralist among us can't describe structuralism this way? what Puritan couldn't describe the Halfway Covenant this way?—the eighteenth century struggled, in the view of historians, more mightily with its contradictions, and wrote more vividly of its complexity. These are the chief qualities, as it happens, of the latter half of Lewis and Clark's *Journals*.

Exploration journals during the American Enlightenment, of course, did not invent the general narrative shape that Lewis and Clark would use. The diary of Columbus, and the narratives of Spaniards such as Cortés, would kick off the morphology of New World discovery along with a mania for record keeping that, for its indelibility and longevity, seems partly to have influenced Jefferson's own views on the matter. William Bartram, who wandered in Georgia and Florida in the 1770s, has had his lists of Latin nomenclature for flora and fauna scrutinized sufficiently, so that we may now, with Jehlen, declare him botanically devotional, or in other words, politically abstracted.[23] And, as she points out, highly abstractable: his *Travels* (1791) were the model for a romance by Chateaubriand.

The exploration narrative, by the late eighteenth century, had a shape that Europeans had been fine-tuning for some three centuries. Its characteristics were chiefly these three: one, it contained encyclopedic descriptions of flora, fauna, and indigenous peoples, which made those things "real" (and not fanciful); two, one's own civilization was projected imperially forward into (that is, described as prospering in the near future of) unoccupied, untamed nature; and three, it had a chronicling style that did not so much receive data as select or create it, and tended to see a cosmic (or sometimes European political) plot, or design, in every scene and story. (A fourth feature might be the explicit aestheticization of landscapes according to strict rules of sublimity or beauty, though such a habit, emerging relatively late, falls under the third item on this list.)

As it happens, European novels picked up on the shape of the exploration narrative, such as Chateaubriand's debt to Bartram for the story of *Atala;* and it may be more convincing, rather than review heavily theorized examples of explorers' texts such as Bartram's or John Smith's, to see exploration in its reflected light, as this book will do in succeeding chapters on the Transcendentalists.[24] Daniel Defoe's *Robinson Crusoe* (1719), once the classic story for Ian Watt of *homo economicus,* is now the postcolonial critic's evidence of imperial "symbolic production . . . linked to proto-capitalist methods of distribution," or, more succinctly, the fraud of facts in natural history. Crusoe, speaking in first person and nominally writing his own story, is "an author who is also an explorer."[25] Aphra Behn's *Oroonoko* (1688), mentioned only twice by Watt in the history of the novel, is now cherished for Oroonoko's likeness, during his study of natural history in Surinam, to "a gentleman virtuoso of the Royal Society"—one of the main audiences for exploration narratives.[26] The long-theorized issue of novelists and their claims to be telling the truth (the avowals of authenticity in the front matter of novels, the phrase "true history" in the title) has expanded to take into account the influence of the literature of New World exploration. And not simply for content: Edward Said, for instance, has altered the way one may read about income from West Indian plantations in Jane Austen, so that she is not simply name-dropping to have Sir Thomas Bertram farm in Antigua, but rather she is engaged in a narrative technique.[27] Her novels aren't colonial, but *colonialized.*

In other words, the history of the novel has been revamped to include the influence both of empire and of exploration literature, a theory now as accredited as Watt's well-known claims about the novel and the rise of the middle class. That influence, in my view, may be understood not only as the deep emphasis on realism and facticity, but also on the overdetermination of plot, or on a tenacious sense of design. Patrick Gass can stand in for many writers about the New World, such as William Bradford in his history of Plymouth colony (1651), or Jedediah Morse in his textbook on American geology (1789), or "Scotus Americanus" in his description of North Carolina (1773), or John Smith, Thomas Jefferson, William Byrd, or Hugh Jones in their natural histories of Virginia. They share the rage for order. It is well beyond the scope of this study to chart the development of plot in the novel; but rather than reproach novelists for luring exploration narratives into the shifty realm of fiction, we might better notice the ways that it was perhaps exploration narratives that taught novelists the sense of an ending. Exploration narratives, as I will suggest, pass on the possibilities of national design to Emerson and Thoreau.

To return to two general conditions in the late eighteenth century (the tendency of reason to give way to sensation, revelation, or doubt, especially religious; and the design-faculty of the exploration narrative, which distinguishes a national or cosmic plot where other observers might see only "data," or nothing at all): they are also the conditions of Lewis and Clark's *Journals*. In this context, it is extraordinary to continue to find them credited with ostentatiously democratic politics, or imagined as carrying out the imperial errand with unreflective resolve. Confused with their precedents in the exploration narrative genre (as well as with their competitors, such as Gass), Lewis and Clark are bafflingly imagined as one part Cincinnatus and the other part Napoleon. The most outrageous portrait was in the documentary by Ken Burns, in which the pair is credited with practicing democracy in the wilderness simply because the company once took a vote about which route to take. (Meanwhile, the expedition, a military enterprise, had been marked all along by whippings and other disciplinary measures.)

In fact the politics that we can infer from the *Journals*, scant as they are, are inconsistent and uneasy. Like most foundational American literature, the *Journals* seek to allay, for one thing, that basic anxiety that "a vast and still mysterious continent will somehow swallow the promise of representative government."[28]

Instead of doing here what the rest of this book does, namely, read nature texts for an emerging discourse of manifest destiny, it is appropriate to see in Lewis and Clark the originary worries of explorers for whom manifest destiny was still just another of many designs, rather than the final one. As such, their worries about republican virtues are implicit and unliterary: they are visible mostly in other forms of anxiety; in aesthetic and scientific questions about how nature looks; and in composition crises such as how to continue to express delight in landscapes that had become boring to the point of outrage or mania, or in Native Americans who had resisted imperial absorption. American politics may have been consensual to the point of invisibility, or they may have been contentious to the point of unrelenting affliction. In the *Journals*, these issues are absorbed into a fairly opportunistic medley of no particular ideology. Lewis and Clark are by turns hierarchical, autocratic, egalitarian, and indifferent toward politics; moreover, they differ from each other in styles of command. Indeed, their mix of approaches is in keeping with their responses to landscape, and fickle politics may be partly a cause of the changes in tone: if the first months of travel are merry and spirited, it is probably because of the recent sanction of their president-patron. And if the return trip is gloomy, it is because the approval of empire could not be more remote or impractical.

In the next section, I look at the *Journals* according to the mixed terms I have established in this review of their historical and literary contexts. I also hope to revive some of the drama of the *Journals* that originally interested me in them. Just as it is easy to forget that the expedition was a success in carrying out eight thousand miles of arduous overland travel, it is also easy to forget that the intellectual and imaginative projects of the expedition—the Northwest Passage, for one; the total scientific mastery of *terra incognita,* for another—were failures. Meriwether Lewis died of self-inflicted wounds in 1809. It is a stretch, of course, to imagine that Lewis committed suicide because of the collapse of Enlightenment science in the face of too much nineteenth-century Doubt; but on the other hand, it is also less satisfactory to imagine it was simply the harassing questions from Washington, D.C., over the expedition's expense reports that drove him to shoot himself in the head and chest with a pistol and then slash his wrists and then, over many hours, thirsty and calling for water, to bleed to death under a tree as a terrified innkeeper and two servants looked on.[29]

ON FEBRUARY 14, 1806, it was William Clark's turn to make the daily entry in the field journal. During a winter encamped at Fort Clatsop on the Columbia River, the company was preoccupied with trade negotiations among Pacific Coast Indians, trying to buy canoes and horses for the return trip without losing their shirts. Clark, usually a writer of less spontaneity and speculation than Lewis, on this day turned away from immediate concerns and declared: "We now discover that we have found the most practicable and navigable passage across the continent of North America."[30]

This passage that Clark bleakly describes, nothing like the legendary Passage westward back to Europe, had tested the company for nearly two years of backcountry travel, and Clark was not persuaded that it had any commercial potential. His sentence, as emotional as the laconic Clark ever becomes in the *Journals,* offers us a glimpse of the expedition just before it begins the journey back to St. Louis. Following the disappointment of waiting, in vain, for a ship to take them home, and after the rigors and privations of the long winter of 1805, Lewis and Clark must also, on this return, encounter *terra nova* again. But with one difference: they have seen it before. For Lewis and Clark, the return trip is, following Stephen Greenblatt's comparison of first encounters to "the systole of the heart,"[31] a *diastolic* experience. The explorers have not only been tested by their excursion into unknown land; they will be plagued all over again, on their return, by the extraordinary reassessment of what they know, and how they know it.

But exploration journals are most buoyant when they are, as we can say now, most deluded. In the case of Lewis and Clark, the pair began their journey with assurance and poise, urged on by President Jefferson's confidence in their sure course through the Northwest Passage. But the expedition arrived at the Pacific Ocean on November 7, 1805, without finding the continuous water route. After a winter at Fort Clatsop, during which Clark made his bleak claim about navigability, they retraced the same, tragically landlocked route. The return trip was a grim and hungry one. The initial send-off from Jefferson had diminished in its force; the president had even, inexplicably, failed to send a ship to the Pacific Coast in order to bring Lewis and Clark home.[32] The explorers had recorded sublime landscapes on the voyage out. On second viewing, these visions were dull and irksome.

And as they learned upon their return, Lewis and Clark were presumed dead. National neglect replaced Jefferson's sweeping and princely farewell of 1803. Lewis and Clark were dispatched to explore the westernmost boundary of the United States, and in disappearing for so long from the view of both sponsor and nation, they dropped over the horizon of American rhetorical dominion: no one wrote to them, no one wrote about them, and they themselves began to question their enterprise and the purpose of their field journal. It is no wonder the *Journals* change after November 1805, when Lewis and Clark begin to plan the retreat: the nostalgia for civilization is more poignant, and the experience of the unknown is less susceptible to paraphrase. Language is no longer the loyal and able instrument it was in the first months; instead it is bafflingly inadequate for transmitting their experiences. It would have been gratifying to Lewis and Clark to discover the Northwest Passage for commercial reasons, but also because they were, conceptually, fully prepared to find it. The absence of the Passage leads, again and again, to an absence of any written passage that might validate their preconceptions: it leads to a failure of the word.

With such a tragic view of the *Journals* in mind, it is easy, as I mentioned, to forget that the expedition was a success. If Jefferson learned from Lewis and Clark that the vast western half of America looked nothing like the state of Virginia, he could still consider that *incognita* a temporary matter. But Lewis and Clark could not.

Jefferson, as sponsor, offered a ringingly eighteenth-century rationale for exploration: as he recommends in his *Notes on the State of Virginia* (1787), continents can be brought to order with an inventory of their contents. Greenblatt, describing the similar habit of Herodotus in his *Histories,* calls such inventories "a calculation-effect"—calculations that "measure and hence master an alien object."[33] The abundance of verbal detail in *Notes on Virginia* effectively "explores" and masters Jefferson's home state. (It was Jefferson, after all, who devised the settlement plans for new lands west of the Mississippi—the orderly grid still visible from an airplane flying over the American West.)

Jefferson's view of the exploration of Louisiana was also, in his words, "literary," an adjective that denoted in 1803 the many disciplines that would benefit from Lewis and Clark's findings. While Jefferson's term *literary* is general, it is also exact: it presumes that language will effectively mediate, describe, and commemorate events. Moreover, the different genres of writing that must coexist in a single text—journal, travelogue, scientific observation, military record, political theory, and so on—are all unified by their single goal of describing the new land, and by their single "literary" bearing.

Larzer Ziff's study of Jefferson is helpful here, for it confirms Jefferson's utterly nontragic reliance on language as the means of apprehending the expanding American continent.[34] Particularly in his encounters with American Indians, Jefferson consistently emphasized the power of language to redeem Indian history, since Indian culture left no literary traces. Jefferson maintained, for example, in *Notes on Virginia* that the noble origins of American Indians would eventually be documented and preserved by extended philological analysis—in effect, by integrating Indian language into the print culture (and anthropological hierarchy) of Europe.

Jefferson's view of the Lewis and Clark expedition was similarly centered on the power of language; he left notes, like those on Virginia, that suggest as much. The instructions that sponsors offer to explorers before their expeditions, since the time of Columbus, have traditionally emphasized—and attempted to solve—the problem of translation, specifically from indigenous into colonial languages.[35] The promise of "understanding," with the implication of successful conquest, originates in the belief of the sponsoring nation that not only could a Babel of languages be rendered successfully into one universal language, but that landscape itself—analogous to the stubbornly taciturn Indian—is also susceptible to translation. It is no wonder, therefore, that Jefferson's instructions to Lewis and Clark conspicuously feature the correct methods for keeping the field journal.

For Jefferson, documentation is the central feature of discovery. First, he remarks in his instructions that he expects Lewis to send "occasional communications, adapted to circumstances as they arise," and furthermore that Lewis and Clark's passage through *terra incognita,* formerly French territory, is guaranteed by French-issued travel documents. Lewis and Clark were also issued letters of recommendation from Jefferson himself. These documentary details suggest that the exploration enterprise, for Jefferson, brought the word to the wilderness. But then you brought it back: the balance of the instructions, some five pages more, advise Lewis on the format of logbook entries and scientific observations. Jefferson's devotion to preserving the written word is practical, but he acknowledges also that the information Lewis and Clark will gain is tantalizingly precious and subject to misfortune. Careful record keeping will prevent a tragic loss:

> Your observations are to be taken with great pains & accuracy, to be entered distinctly, & intelligibly for others as well as yourself. . . . several copies of these, as well as your other notes, should be made at leisure times & put into the care of the most trustworthy of your attendants, to guard by multiplying them, against the accidental losses to which they will be exposed. [A] further written guard would be that one of these copies be written on the paper of the birch, as less liable to injury from damp than common paper.[36]

Jefferson's anxiety is understandable because, as he cautions later, "in the loss of yourselves, we should lose the information you will have acquired."[37] (Elizabeth Bishop reprises this advice in her poem on loss, "One Art": *"Write it!"* yells the poem's grieving speaker to herself.) Jefferson places full confidence in the field journal as the immediate expression of the exploration experience. The dangers are an illegible script and an unlucky exposure. There is no thought of a different kind of "accidental loss," or of Lewis and Clark's "loss of themselves"—the failures of their ability to decipher their experience, and of the journal to absorb their rage for order.

The American Western itself, of which the *Journals* are one of the initial drafts, may cause the linguistic ambitions of its authors to fail. "The Western," notes one critic, "flattens language and removes the mystery";[38] the physical heroics of the Western protagonist effectively silence the range of languages that an empty land can hold. (It does not contain multitudes. That is how the West is one.) Jefferson's optimistic sense of positivist conquest fails in advance, because the Western inevitably "reverts to [linguistic] stasis" in its quest for definitive *symbolic* action and cannot maintain a merely writerly view of the unknown that is even healthfully curious, let alone authoritative.

There is no reason for exploration journals to register this loss as conspicuously as they do. In expeditions of commercial motivation (and one of Jefferson's chief goals was to control transcontinental passage in advance of the British in Canada), we might expect the journal to be as emotionally stirring as, say, the annual report of a corporation. But in the case of Lewis and Clark, the sense of crisis is quite insistent.

The evidence tells me so. The early months of the *Journals* are uncomplicated: the Missouri River, while tending not to flow in a straight line, is at least calm during the spring of 1804 as Lewis and Clark voyage toward the Rocky Mountains. The sense of purpose of these early months is reflected in their calm and appreciative language. The landscape is pleasing: Clark notes "the most butifull prospect of the River up & Down the countrey Opsd. prosented it Self which I ever beheld" (6:14). Game food is abundant, and Lewis notes that the flocks of birds are "so gentle that they did not quit the place untill we had arrived within a fiew feet of them" (6:24). The Missouri, in explicit pastoral terms,

> passes through a rich fertile and one of the most beautifully picturesque countries that I ever beheld . . . innumerable herds of living anamals are seen, it's borders garnished with one continued garden of roses, while it's lofty and open forrests are the habitation of miriads of feathered tribes who salute the ear of the passing traveler with their wild and simple, yet sweet and cheerfull melody (6:132).

Clark remarks on July 30, 1804, in terms that summarize the journey's auspicious beginning, that "every thing in prime order men in high Spirits. a fair still evening Great no. Musquitors this evening" (2:430). Clark's comment is typical for its emphasis on "prime order" and for mentioning the mosquitoes, which were the explorers' only affliction along the Missouri.

Encounters with Indian tribes are similarly orderly, ritualized almost immediately into what Seelye terms "imperial theatrics,"[39] a ceremony of gift exchanges, political speeches (translated by guides), loyalty oaths to the Great White Father in Washington, and finally participation in Indian meals or dances. Lewis and Clark use each diplomatic session to practice anthropology, describing the appearance and cultural habits of each tribe. Their mania for order predisposes them, as it did Robinson Crusoe, to favor "tidy savages," such as the Mandans.

The intertribal negotiations Lewis and Clark attempted, partially on the Mandans' behalf, are also extraordinary for their determination to rearrange the intricate preexisting relationships among tribes. Lewis and Clark's efforts were unquestionably sincere (indeed, the two are often commended for their ethnographic sensitivities), but their diplomatic results would prove transient. The Sioux, for example, were a considerable nuisance to the navigation of the Missouri, repeatedly raiding travelers and demanding trade goods in exchange for safe passage. (Clark duly describes the Sioux as "Durtey, Kind, pore and extravigent" [3:161].) In September 1804, Lewis and Clark learned that the Sioux meant to attack and had circled their camp. After four days of tense waiting, the Sioux were persuaded that the explorers would not capitulate, and the warriors retreated. In the Journals, Lewis and Clark regard the matter as closed: they are confident this military stand will have a lasting diplomatic effect. Clark recounts a meeting with Mandan chiefs a few weeks later in language that becomes typical of such encounters: "we ... give them some account of the Magnitude & power of our Countrey which pleased them and astonished them verry much" (3:160–61). Clark also notes that "the [Sioux] poison the minds [of the Mandans] and keep them in perpetial dread," but that, having generously subdued the Sioux without firing a shot, the explorers depart confident that they made "a firm peace" (3:163). As with most events during the voyage out, the treaties Lewis and Clark arranged among the Mandan, Ricaree, Sioux, and Menataree tribes were optimistic pageants of readily met expectations. The explorers, as representatives of the United States, regarded the treaties as stable national agreements and were gratified to bring not only the news of the Great White Father but also the theory of contractual government to the wilderness.

Like most American explorers, Lewis and Clark were conscious of their status as government representatives. The sense of national purpose that launched their enterprise, however, deteriorates, so that the second half of the Journals records the destabilization of every term of the national landscape set forth in the first half. When the geographical destination has been reached and does not live up to its mythic promise, then, in Perry Miller's phrase, the errand has failed. Critical discussion of exploration narratives has largely focused on the first half of an exploration journey, during which the directives of the sponsor are steadily sustained and enhanced by the explorer.[40] Thus we have accounted, so far, for only half the journey. The return trip is of course necessary for the explorer's news to reach his audience; otherwise exploration becomes a rather elaborate and private means of suicide. The return is also a reencounter with *terra nova*, which alters dramatically the meaning of the land, since it is, quite simply, no longer new. Instead of exploring, it discloses, on the return trip, its own geographic closure. The *Journals* of Lewis and Clark acknowledge this process only with enormous resistance. It is partly in the accounts of intertribal negotiations that this shift in temperament becomes evident after 1805.

RETURNING TO THE Missouri plains in 1806, Lewis and Clark discover that their treaty network, achieved in a miraculous few months, has not lasted the winter. Clark describes a reunion with the chief of the Minatarees:

> When he saw us last we told him that we had made peace with all the nations below, Since that time the Seioux had killed 8 of their people and Stole a number of their horses. he Said that he had opened his ears and followed our Councils, he had made peace with the Cheyennes and rocky Mountains indians. . . . if the Seioux were at peace with them and could be depended on he as also other Chiefs of the villages would be glad to go and See their great father, but as they were afraid of the Seioux they should not go down &c (8:304).

Clark continues his attempts to reaffirm the treaties of the last year—in discussion with Ricara chiefs, for example, where he "was very sorrey to here that they were not on friendly terms with their neighbours the Mandans and the Menetarras, and had not listened to what we had said to them but Suffered their young men to join the Seioux" (8:315–16). Although the Ricaras are "anxious to be at peace," they are still confirmedly at war with the Sioux, and "should kill them whenever they came into their country." Indeed, Lewis and Clark are surrounded by raiding parties and violence: "our back was scercely turned before a war party from the two [Minetare] villages followed on and attacked and killed the Snake Indians whome we had seen" (8:304). These circumstances—along with the anxiety of diminished supplies, and the fact that Lewis has just been shot accidentally by one of his own men on a hunting party—are the context for Lewis's exasperated remark about his stopped watch, which seems the last straw during a bad month: "as if the fates were against me," laments Lewis, "my chronometer from some unknown cause stoped today" (8:127). The collapse of the treaties is one of the signals to Lewis and Clark that their imprint on the new land has not been indelible, and that their discoveries—entirely new to them and their national audience—are not especially meaningful to the current inhabitants of the West. More significantly, Lewis and Clark begin to acquire a tragic sensibility and realize that their exploration is less the enactment of American sovereignty than it is an errand into the wilderness.

Even before attempting the return route, the company lived in straitened circumstances in the winter of 1805–6 among the Pacific Coast tribes at Fort Clatsop. Because the Pacific Coast Indians were experienced and cosmopolitan traders, Lewis and Clark could only with difficulty continue to exchange their dwindling supply of trade goods—handkerchiefs, medals, knives, and so on—for food. Prices were higher, trade practices sharper, and outright theft common. Lewis recounts the negotiations of Sergeant Drouillard (which Lewis spells phonetically) of their party toward the end of their stay:

> Drewyer returned late this evening from Cathlamahs with . . . a canoe which
> he had purchased from those people. for this canoe he gave my uniform laced
> coat and nearly half a carrot of tobacco. it seems that nothing except this coat
> would induce them to dispose of a canoe. . . . I think the U'States are indebted
> to me another Uniform coat for that of which I have disposed on this occa-
> sion. . . . we want yet another canoe, and as the Clatsops will not sell us one at
> a price which we can afford to give we will take one from them in lue of the
> six Elk which they stol from us in the winter (6:426).

Lewis has lost his military uniform—perhaps his military status, too—in an unfair trade, and has begun to run a tab for the ordeal of the journey. The company has adopted the practices of the tribes they live among and now regards theft as a legitimate trade option.

But even as the explorers took their commercial cues from their neighbors, they were isolated inside Fort Clatsop. The company met during the day with chiefs who wished to visit, but they locked its gates at sunset. Insularity is so adamantly asserted in the *Journals* that Lewis and Clark seem vexed as much by the possibilities of theft as by the corruptions of contact. Lewis ruminates on February 20, 1806, that "the treachery of the aborigenes of America and the too great confusion of our countrymen in their sincerity and friendship, has caused the distruction of many hundreds of us" (6:331). He reflects uncannily on the relative ease of the voyage out (and the comparatively lapsed conditions of the present moment) when he continues: "so long have our men been accustomed to a friendly intercourse with the natives, that we find it difficult to impress on their minds the necessity of always being on their guard . . . this confidence on our part, we know to be the effect of a series of uninterrupted friendly intercourse, but the well known treachery of the natives by no means entitle them to such confidence" (6:331). Lewis concludes, sounding like a watchful Puritan on the incursion of Satan, that "our preservation depends on never losing sight of this trait in their character, and being always prepared to meet it in whatever shape it may present itself."

The plenitude of the first months is gone, and with it the innocence and promise of their mission. The return trip is characterized chiefly by troubles. The explorers and their company—some thirty-five people in all—were frequently on the verge of starvation. Clark notes over and over during the journey back the scarcity of game and supplies—especially in the Bitterroot Mountains of Idaho, where they traveled along, coincidentally, "hungary creek." "Our fare," writes Lewis in a typical 1806 entry, "is the flesh of lean elk boiled with pure water, and a little salt." Their trade goods once again change in value, as they had on the Pacific Coast. Where formerly the Indians had accepted medals and handkerchiefs and ribbons, now, Clark notes, they "seem anxious always to riceve articles of utility, such as knives, axes, Kittles, blankets and mockerson awls" (6:385). Thus, instead of relying upon the symbolic currency of their national sponsor, Jefferson—in whose image the trade medals were struck—Lewis and Clark must now traffic in useful goods that yield up no symbolic value at all. The decline in the American president as a valuable commodity indicates the change in Lewis and Clark's mission generally, from a broadly construed national enterprise to a local struggle for survival.

The landscape descriptions in the latter half of the *Journals* follow this pattern of decline as well. Certainly the hurry to return home before the winter temperatures froze the Missouri River accounts for the distractedness of the explorers, but generally Lewis and Clark, upon seeing again what they had celebrated the first time, find their natural surroundings less splendid and more troublesome. Lewis had in May 1805 rhapsodized about a canyon of the Missouri, comparing its parapets and cliffs to "eligant ranges of lofty freestone buildings; some collumns standing and almost entire with their pedestals and capitals; . . . some lying prostrate and broken[,] others in the form of vast pyramids. . . . As we passed on it seemed as if those seens of visionary inchantment would never have an end" (4:225–26). Lewis, indulging his meditative side, found this scene of ruins "most romantic in appearance." Indeed, Lewis's tastes are derived, as he mentions, from Salvator Rosa—a ruins painter—and the sublime.

On the return, however, there is more economy to their descriptions. If fewer words are wasted, it is because the rhetoric of the voyage out—whether that rhetoric was inspired by Jefferson, or Wordsworth—has proved untenable. The explorers observe that waterfalls on the Missouri they had admired "had abated much of their grandeur since we have first arrived at them in June 1805" (8:112). If their original impressions were exaggerated, and if that response was prompted in part by more comfortable traveling conditions, it is also true that the explorers' sense of mission inspired an exaggerated sense of beauty—the appreciation that comes from proprietorship. Lewis and Clark would commonly remark of a delightful scene that it was also noteworthy "from a commercial point of view" (8:132). Their willingness to expend linguistic space in the *Journals* on a landscape corresponds most often to the continued sense of presidential endorsement. When that backing seems more remote, then the landscape becomes tedious, as on June 27, 1806: "we arrived at a Situation very similar to that of our situation of last night" (8:58).

Overall, a diminishing national sanction has this effect on the *Journals:* the landscape garners less space for descriptive paeans and is replaced by complaints of injury, hunger, and worry. Lewis, the more divulgent writer of the two, is especially so during the trauma of being shot. Peter Cruzatte, a hapless member of the company, shoots him by mistake. Still bleeding, Lewis grills Cruzatte about his blunder and records the exchange in detail:

> Cruzatte seemed much allarmed and declared if he had shot me it was not his intention. . . . I asked him whether he did not hear me when I called to him so frequently which he absolutely denied. I do not believe that the fellow did it intentionally but after finding that he had shot me was anxious to conceal his knowledge that he had done so. the ball was lodged in my breeches which I knew to be the ball of the short rifles such as that he had, and there being no person out with me but him and no indians that we could discover I have no doubt in my own mind of his having shot me (8:155–56).

The event may well indicate the interpersonal tensions of the company whose members had by now spent over two years together in arduous military duty. Lewis's description exhibits his extraordinary self-command in this crisis, but clearly the environment is getting the best of them: Cruzatte cannot see his commanding officer for the trees. Lewis practices a form of "calculation effect" here, with his analytical review of the facts. No further mention of this event occurs in the *Journals,* except for Clark's notes that Lewis's wounds are healing apace. But the shooting suggests the level at which the company came to function, which was no longer heroic and inspired by an exalted mytho-geographic hope. Instead they were simply trying to return home, across an irritatingly impassable expanse of boring terrain, and the continued frustrations and delays outweighed the fact that they were the first white Americans to reach the Pacific.

A promise has been reneged upon, as in the unreasonable trade Lewis made for his military coat. The national myth that exploration narratives are meant to enhance, especially as nineteenth-century settlement realized the fiction of manifest destiny, is effectively erased as Lewis and Clark become preoccupied and disillusioned. Retrograde motion in Lewis and Clark's *Journals* is the cause of this disillusion. The return introduces recursiveness, both in the terrain covered and in the scenes described, which endangers the essential and compelling feature of the exploration narrative—

that of continually describing the new. And the Lewis and Clark expedition shudders collectively at retreats. On one occasion on the voyage out, the company escapes a forced retreat with characteristic good luck. The men seek the passage from the Missouri to the Columbia and have to choose between the two sides of a forked river. Lewis comments that their choice is crucial, because if they selected wrongly and were "obliged to return . . . [it] would not only lose us the whole of this season but would probably so dishearten the party that it might defeat the expedition altogether" (8: 125). (Their choice proves the correct one.) Later, three months before reaching St. Louis, the party finds that snow has made the Rockies impassable and decides, rather than starving their horses with several days' fruitless travel, to backtrack and hire another Indian guide. The effect of the retreat is extremely demoralizing, according to Clark:

> We began our retrograde march at 1 P.M. haveing remaind. about three hours on this Snowey mountain. we returned by the rout we had advanced to hungary creek. . . . here we had more grass for our horses. . . . the party were a good deel dejected, though not so much as I had apprehended they would have been. this is the first time since we have been on this tour that we have ever been compelled to retreat or make a retragrade march (8:32).

Clark's entries in the *Journals* tend to concentrate on the immediate terrain and the day's movements and seldom speculate on the journey as a whole. His comments are therefore extraordinary for their long view and the meditative tone prompted by the company's serious disappointment.

The final pages of the *Journals* display Lewis and Clark's relief at resuming urban surroundings. Following their welcome in St. Louis, Clark continues the journal for three days and records the fact that they immediately "rose early and commenced wrighting our letters," the documents to Jefferson and others that both explorers knew would be instantly published in newspapers. The final entry of the *Journals* sees the two continuing this activity—"a fine morning. we commenced wrighting &c."—and suggests that Lewis and Clark had become so habituated to keeping a journal that they would even record the fact that they were now writing about the contents of the journal.

This circularity is hard to miss: the end of the *Journals* writes the beginning. Lewis and Clark have wrestled throughout with the descriptive inadequacies of their sponsor's rhetoric. The *Journals* have changed from the linear account of events to a round-trip story. Lewis and Clark, it seems, possess the sense of an ending.

This ending is, of course, grimly aware of the transformation and loss from the beginning. The *Journals* are characterized, finally, by a skepticism toward their own efficacy. They do not sustain their initial levels of patriotic enthusiasm, scientific abstraction, or commercial ambition. Contact with the new is initially responsible for this lapse, challenging the explorer's rhetoric to encompass utter novelty in its lexicon. Then, however, a *re*-encounter with the discovered land introduces another burden on that already strained rhetoric, and as the *Journals* indicate, language eventually offers fewer assurances or consolations. An exploration journal is invigorated by the first challenge—naming new rivers and mountains is as pleasing as successfully navigating the wilderness—but cannot stand up to the second. Indeed, the definition of exploration as discovering the new should be qualified: instead, it is encountering the predicted. The importance of the return trip is in its admission of the distance between the order imposed on the landscape and the landscape itself: the gap widens and widens.

Leo Marx has described one basic inconsistency of the nineteenth century in America as the impulse to honor the pastoral by means of its obliteration through technology: we commemorate the garden through the intrusion of the machine.[41] Exploration has a similar internal tension. Explorers are dispatched to discover the new, and yet their attitude toward it is incorporative and proprietary: they want it to look like the old. Exploration maps are made in advance: they do not "report a place, but . . . impose an *idea* of a place on a new continent." They are what Myra Jehlen terms "narratives of recognition."[42]

Exploration, one critic has argued, is a means of saturating the landscape with our own metaphors.[43] These metaphors are our most habitual means of defining ourselves—by establishing a rhetorical relationship with the landscape, and more generally by mastering phenomena through language. In a fully saturated landscape, there is no further need to explore; and in the process of settling the land (its features and its meanings), exploration meanwhile discovers, in the company of metaphor, a region of obsolescence.

Zebulon Pike, Federalist Gloom, and Western Lands

Whatever other objects may be comprehended by the mind, they are always consider'd with a view to ourselves; otherwise they wou'd never be able either to excite these passions, or produce the smallest encrease or diminution of them.
DAVID HUME, *Treatise of Human Understanding* (1740)

Who is it that says that America is not picturesque? I forget.
FANNY TROLLOPE, *Domestic Manners of the Americans* (1832)

The effect of Lewis and Clark on the nineteenth century was not only boundless geographical fiat: their *Journals* found a devotee in none other than Edgar Allan Poe, who read the Nicholas Biddle edition of the *Journals* in the 1830s and made use of it in his adventure story *The Narrative of Arthur Gordon Pym*.[1] The *Journals* were a text that explorers and travelers, and even the hacks who didn't get out of the dining car, carried with them. John Charles Frémont in the Rockies and Stephen Long in the Plains, dime novelists in California, Walt Whitman tramping through Wisconsin, Thomas Campbell while composing his long ode, *Gertrude of Wyoming*—all read it. And even an explorer who had no opportunity to see it, Zebulon Pike, grasped immediately that he was Lewis and Clark's heir apparent.

Dispatched in 1805 to reconnoiter the American southwest, Pike was the next explorer of the lands west of the Mississippi River, and the next player in the melodrama of American expansion. It is fitting that his expedition should have been organized by Aaron Burr as a clandestine attempt by the former vice president to invade Spanish America and set himself up as president for life. Pike was a beneficiary of Lewis and Clark's territorial prerogatives as well as their (initial, Jeffersonian) sense of national designs. The Burr Conspiracy has a doomed grandiosity to it that even the rationalist Jefferson might have approved—a man, after all, who had a taste for the headaches that the deep sublimity of nature gave him, and who would have had to admire the sublime flamboyance of Burr's schemes.

But even before the little-known Burr Conspiracy made its way into Pike's narrative, Pike wrote his way into the literary record by taking an intrepid literary form, the exploration narrative, and turning it into the polite, picturesque travel account. Such a domestication was perhaps what Lewis and Clark needed all along, but they were too genre-happy to give the picturesque their exclusive attention. Given the anxious and certainly repeatable responses by Lewis and Clark to *terra nova*, Pike himself might have intensified loss, rehearsed privation, and made exploration narrative, in fact, an elaborate suicide note, as it was for Meriwether Lewis. But instead, Pike tried out a different version of American design, in which the rage for order dissolves into a cultivated blindness to disorder. His narrative contains so much high artifice and gentility that we find ourselves thinking of the sentimental *Man of Feeling*, or of the redoubtable *Columbiad*. (By comparison, Lewis and Clark's *Journals* always makes me think of *Notes from the Underground*.) Given the options in the literature of the early republic, Pike's choice was not inevitable. He took the exploration narrative into new, but also identifiably old, territory—not with the catalogs of wonders in European discovery, nor the dread-narrative of Lewis and Clark, but into something of a stylistic cul-de-sac: the picturesque style of the persevering, though outmoded, Federalist writer. It was a style that Washington Irving made his signature: his early works even appeared under the pseudonym "Jonathan Oldstyle, Gent."

Pike's decision was in part motivated by the political mess he found himself in, as his boss, Burr, was indicted for treason in 1806. It is also traceable to the literary fashion of the picturesque, a beneficiary of eighteenth-century values of political moderation. Very little happens in Pike's exploration narrative beyond a polite review of gentlemanly feeling, so that in his *Journals* he is guilty only of putting the heart before the coarse. His interest was in a narrative mode that all but removed politics from the American landscape. He perceived, and his readers were invited to perceive, in these rich provinces the tokens of a refined and timeless moral code: a code not ratified by party orthodoxies nor tied to specific moments of history, but one that assured the masters of wide lands of the perpetual extension (and not the perversion) of the orderly republic. It was an answer to key questions posed by nature that had so vexed Lewis and Clark: Why does American nature look so calculated and then so unplanned? How can its features be brought under steady aesthetic control?

In this chapter, I first review the Federalist literary culture of which Pike was a product, and the picturesque aesthetic to which he, like Washington Irving, was devoted. In the political climate of the early republic, after the "Revolution of 1800," as it was called—which can be described as post-rationalist, post-Constitutionalist, and nascent-Jacksonian—Pike and Irving both found in the picturesque some consolation for their growing sense of obsolescence as gentlemen and as political moderates. I then address Pike's involvement in the colorful Burr Conspiracy and the ways in which his narrative seeks his exculpation in narrowly picturesque terms.

IN MY EFFORT to describe the transformation of strictly theological design into manifest destiny in the early nineteenth century, the picturesque is significant as a middle term. Explorers are educated and subtle writers, but they are not members of the New England coterie of Emerson and Thoreau. The picturesque fad is therefore of interest for its position outside those specific intellectual circles (except, at times, in Thoreau's case), despite its extraordinary versatility and ubiquity as an ordering principle and as a nationalist mode. The implicit inquiry, then, is to discover the intellectual limits of the picturesque—limits that apparently were all too obvious to thinkers like Emerson and Thoreau by the 1830s (both remained, in the fine phrase of John Conron, "New Englandly cool" about the picturesque) [2] but not yet for, say, Washington Irving. The picturesque would leave off at the point where design was taken up by Emerson, and this aesthetic code therefore would contribute to a history of American design, especially in descriptions of nature. Its decline has to do with its limited successes in conquering, or even engaging with, the central institutions and concerns of the age of Jackson.

Although Federalism is not the sole political analog to the picturesque (it was resorted to by most parties during the nineteenth century), the two bear comparison for their eventual moods of collapse and diminution. Federalism was a serious political party before 1800, and indeed achieved a happy monopoly during George Washington's second term. After 1800, and especially during the War of 1812, although Federalist candidates were still fielded in elections, the party's political force weakened and it became, instead, a philosophy, a style, a tone, and a personality type. There were many Americans, such as Pike and Irving, who *felt* Federalist, but there was less and less active Federalism left for them to cling to. (The Whig party, commencing only in 1833, is often mistakenly perceived as the retooled Federalist party. In fact it arose from divisions among Jeffersonian Republicans.) [3] The result among Federalists was a refined sense of their own irrelevance. This response was the case with Pike, and also with the better-documented figure, Washington Irving, the salon man of letters and a contemporary whose case suggests to us what Pike, the explorer and intriguer, was up to.

The Federalist personality surfaces in Pike's literary choices, if we may take Irving as our model. Irving's politics were moderate, as admirers would say, or almost excruciatingly circumspect. This circumspection is the case especially when Irving contemplated the westward, Democratic, and imperial course of the republic after 1800. It did not occur to the author of *Astoria,* for instance, ever to comment skeptically that John Jacob Astor was in a fight for fur sales with empire as much as profit in mind. With the fascination of the leisured class for the new commercial set, Irving found Astor energetic and visionary. (Such enchantment pops up again when Emerson, against better judgment, considers what he likes about Andrew Jackson.) It was Astor himself who suggested that Irving write the history of the fur business out West, a patronage arrangement that critics have long seen to account for Irving's celebratory version of events on the Columbia River. It was certainly auspicious for Astor that the writer in his pay just *happened* to find the beaver trade a fit subject for praise literature. Recently, Irving's ties to Astor have been assessed more closely, revealing that in this most commercial of transactions each man used the other for reasons that had nothing to do with profit, and which offer an old-fashioned, top-down circulation of resources: Astor's enterprise in pelts was polished with lush prose, and Irving, the placeman, reveled in being court artist to America's Trimalchio.[4]

Irving's view of money and trade drifted over the course of his career, so that by the writing of *Astoria* he had left off complaints about the vulgarity of commerce and was willing to make it over into a national apotheosis with Astor as its prophet. Whatever his reasons for changing his view of trade— out of expediency toward scant opportunities for professional writing, or genuine enthusiasm about the fur business—Irving's patrician politics also took a turn that we might predict: the spirit of the age had its effect. In his early career he had had innocuous ideas about labor and money and elections, views that would make him welcome in Knickerbocker drawing rooms. Half a century later, the social bedrock of Edith Wharton's *Age of Innocence* would lament the current scurrility of the writing class in comparison to Irving: "Mrs. Archer was always at pains to tell her children how much more agreeable and cultivated society had been when it included such figures as Washington Irving. . . . The most celebrated authors of that generation had been 'gentlemen.'"[5] (It is a similar tribute to gentlemanly values that from 1802 to 1817, Harvard University awarded honorary degrees only to Federalists.)[6]

But by the 1830s, when he returned from Europe, Irving began to countenance, though not soften to, the movement of westward expansion in America, and the party that most vocally called for it. Vernon Parrington has reviewed this transformation in Irving from "smallclothes and tie-wigs" to a vague Sansculottism, or from urbane Federalist playboy to party hack. Irving went from Federalist paranoia about the "imported nightmares" of clamorous democratic mobs to praise of those same mobs of imports.[7] The transformation was not absolute, but after a certain date, Irving warmed appreciably to Democrats.

The evidence is mainly Irving's relationship, after 1832, with Vice President Martin Van Buren, who, after assuming the presidency himself in 1837, would eventually reward him with a choice diplomatic post in Spain. Irving wasn't noticeably Jacksonian through all this sponsorship, any more than he was much of a businessman after writing about Astor. And in 1838, he grumbled in a famous letter to a friend about Locofoco extremism. (The Locofocos were a radical group of New York Democrats organized in 1835 who opposed the regular party.) He insisted, in his lingering Augustan manner, that "ours is a government of compromise."[8] His complaints may sound Whiggish, but they are different in kind from those lodged by an arch-Whig journalist who wrote under the pseudonym "Richelieu" for Horace Greeley's *New York Tribune.* "Richelieu" denounced "Loco-Foco mismanagement" of the Mexican War and called for "Whig blood and Whig courage" to prevail. (Emerson later satirized this phrase by drolly recommending "whig preaching, whig poetry, whig philosophy [and] whig marriages.")[9] The *Tribune*'s approach in 1846 reflected the bellicose tone of a serious party objecting to an expansionist war; Irving's in 1838 was the mournful entreaty of an obsolete Federalist, and the automatic remark of a man who had always belonged to a powerful class: the government, he specified possessively, is *ours*.

That he should call the government "ours" during the reign of Little Van is a mark of Irving's obsolescence; but so is his other catchword, compromise. A continuing loyalty to eighteenth-century ideals was, as I argue later, part of the trap that Jacksonian Democracy laid for New England *bien-paisance.* Superannuated by the Age of Jackson, Transcendentalists still bore a lingering devotion to what by the 1840s were antique systems of providential thinking, such as the argument from design, which rendered them a harmless opposition. The sense of being outmoded eventually stirred in many Transcendentalists an ill-advised enthusiasm for what seemed the closest surviving relation to providence, namely manifest destiny, the great Jacksonian heresy.

So with "compromise" for Irving, at least at first. He meant it as a riposte to the uncompromising, vulgar, common-man politics of his age; he meant it also as the word of the Founders, who steadied the republic by compromise and consensus. But his old-fashioned rhetorical choice took him quite out of the running. No Tammany Hall Democrat would take seriously the compromises suggested by a Jonathan Oldstyle, Gent., because only a Jonathan Oldstyle, Gent., would suggest them. The politics of compromise was so out of date that it effectively debilitated Irving's politics as it gentled them. Irving, in the end, disenfranchised himself, which perhaps was his purpose. Federalism became for him not a politics, but a way out of politics.

Compromise, once cutting-edge, had meant for the earlier generation the vivid and challenging job of keeping the government going, or what one literary historian calls "the creativity of agreement."[10] Federalism had viewed governing as intellectual work, like drafting the Constitution. Its values were imagined to be generally inclusive, even if its practitioners were patrician; its goals were to contain differences and create unity not by imposing ideological consistency, but by containing, tolerating, and dissembling differences—slavery most of all. It maintained legitimacy at times by deception (such as ignoring slavery) and verbal insistence ("We the people"). Compromise was the ruling term for such expedients: compromise justified them because they averted political collapse.

Federalism by the 1830s was not a party, but a mood of nostalgia for it-self. Alexis de Tocqueville himself, in *Democracy in America,* had famously lamented the party's demise. The Whigs and Democrats were now the com-batants on the field, and regret for the nation's "founding" values was acute. One historian singles out Fisher Ames of Massachusetts as the personifica-tion of the party's "curiously enervating melancholy," for his anti-Jacobin ravings and his tragic sense of history: "I fear," he wrote in 1807, "that Fed-eralism will not only die, but all remembrance of it be lost."[11] In other words, after 1807, success for the Federalists could be defined as being re-membered to have failed. The party had built, in its own view, the national institutions that smoothly managed the economy and the national defenses and the day-to-day workings of the law courts. By the time Jefferson took of-fice in 1801, that dominion was over; it was for the relics of the party, like Ames, to carry on and to oppose, among other policies, that Jeffersonian en-deavor that would so influence the course of Jacksonian America: the Loui-siana Purchase. It is thus singular for Pike to deploy what is in large part a Fed-eralist mood, in a Jacksonian genre, for a Republican project—that is, the melancholy picturesque for the exploration narrative about western lands.

Jacksonian Democrats, by the late 1820s, reasoned from an essentially Jacobin position of imagined homogeneity, or a unified front, rather than the Founders' paternal compromises toward diverse political persuasions and moods. Their foe at first was simply the Bank of the United States, but then they took on the Bank's related mischiefs: privilege and plutocracy, and centers of power such as the treasury. Naturally such a cartoon version of the Age of Jackson magnifies its political unity and ignores party infight-ing over tariffs, nativism, and slavery through the 1840s (not to mention the impressive Whig electoral feat of 1844, when Henry Clay made a serious try for the presidency). But Jackson was a success precisely because he capital-ized on a constituency no one else had been able, or willing, to marshal: the homogenized common man, who had played little part in the largely aris-tocratic reserve of Revolutionary politics. Even Jefferson's fondness for the yeoman farmer, and his model of decentralized government (which the Jack-sonians adopted), was by the 1830s comparatively the politics of a parvenu, whose fancy velvet knee-breeches Irving himself mocked in *Salmagundi.*[12] This gentility was part of the inheritance of the Whigs from Jefferson, and in the view of one observer in 1870, it extinguished the party: "too much re-spectability," he complained, "and not enough people."[13]

In many ways, if the Louisiana Purchase and the expedition to explore it were not the last gestures of the American eighteenth century, they were the first gestures of the nineteenth. Whig designs on the continent contended in the 1830s with Democratic: thoroughgoing distaste for expansionism in Henry Clay fought its rough champions in Jackson and Van Buren. But meanwhile, Jefferson had specified in his *Notes on the State of Virginia* (1783) the rational progress of democratic institutions across uninhabited lands, with Virginia as a model: government was as lucid as a map. The Jacksonian approach to exploration was far less lofty—both Jackson and Van Buren were chiefly occupied with the business of expansion, the regulation of prices and borders, and the "rudeness in the social condition" on the frontier—even as exploration narratives began to indulge in more exalted literary values.[14] Decades before Whig scions Henry Clay or Daniel Webster defended themselves as "the party of order," Pike clung to a recognizably Federalist propriety. Pike's preference was for inflated rhetoric, which made little of *terra nova* and much of the fineness of the explorer's "social condition" within it.

Irving's case, as I have suggested, indicates the ways in which literature of the early republic was created in response to a mixed audience, one that, like Wharton's Mrs. Archer, held deeply nostalgic ideas about the gentility of the writer, and one that observed with alarm the old order yielding before the new. Over a long and varied professional life, Irving wrote again and again in the picturesque style, and as I discuss, such an aesthetic choice would come to signify both a stand against political change, and an admission of its certainty.

"LANDSCAPE," DECLARES TOM Stoppard in his play *Arcadia,* describing the picturesque gardens laid out by "Capability" Brown and others of his school, "was invented by gardeners imitating foreign painters who were evoking classical authors. The whole thing was brought home in the luggage from the grand tour."[15]

The picturesque, which simply means looking like a picture, is also "a notoriously difficult category to define."[16] It is both a literary and visual aesthetic: a set of philosophical assumptions about nature that underlie writing, painting, and particularly landscape gardening. Indeed, writing and scenery were closely tied as a mutual effort at picturesque "seeing." The picturesque traveler had a method for translating landscapes, one that was both rigidly aesthetic and (as it was thought) generally applicable to all cases. The picturesque posited that natural scenery was worth notice and description because it reminded the viewer of art. The picturesque tourist was "engaged in an experiment in controlled aesthetic responses to a range of new and often intimidating visual experiences"; he was eager to point out resemblances between nature and paintings.[17] And perhaps overeager: one American writer satirized the numerous British picturesque travelers who

> sketch the scenes they pass when half-asleep.
> Some best describe indeed what pass'd by night,
> 'Tis done by all, who travel but to write.[18]

Samuel Coleridge also chimed in to mock the fashionable habit of picturesque travel:

Tour, Journey, Voyage, Lounge, Ride, Walk,
Skim, Sketch, Excursion, Travel-talk-
For move you must! 'Tis now the rage,
The law and fashion of the Age.[19]

Such laws of fashion in the picturesque suggest that nature was susceptible to, if not utterly dependent upon, the mastery of its human observers:
scenery could not exist without the human eye to take it in. This suggestion
of mastery lends to the picturesque its ready adoption in narratives of nationalism. Indeed, it is one of the paradoxes of the picturesque that its apparently nationless, ready-made aesthetics actually contained a powerful
machinery of specific national heat. Pike's *Journals* are especially attuned to
this tendency. James Kirke Paulding, another American picturesque travel
writer, published his 1822 *Sketch of Old England, by a New-England Man* specifically to correct widespread misinformation published in England about
America, and to offer rousing proofs of American distinction to readers who
might still think it rustic or primitive.[20]

The habit in exploration narratives of comparing geological features
to architecture was probably imported from the picturesque. Meriwether
Lewis, for one, frequently made this type of comparison, such as his exalta-
tion of cliffs that resemble parapets and buttresses; Prince Maximilian, in
his 1833 *Travels,* indulged the same habit. The relentless transformation of
random natural settings into overdetermined landscapes found virtue in
nature only when it was acted upon by art. "Nature is worthwhile," notes an
art historian, "only if it astonishes through the intervention of human ingenuity." The art that picturesque viewers wanted most often to be reminded
of was usually the fashionable landscapes of Salvator Rosa and Claude Lorrain, whom Meriwether Lewis himself invoked at the Great Falls of the Missouri: "I wished for the pencil of Salvator Rosa . . . that I might be enabled
to give to the enlightened world some just idea of this truly magnificent and
sublimely grand object."[21]

The composition of such a painting would include standard effects: a
near-ground *repoussoir,* a planar recession, a horizontal frame, and a prospect. In other words, a small reflective pond or pool, a gentle series of lay-
ers that sweep back toward the horizon, a horizontal object (such as shrub-
bery or a row of cows) that establishes a "frame" for the backward sweep,
and a view into the vanishing point of the horizon. Claude Lorrain's style has
been broken down additionally into the "Claudian formula" of trees that
frame the picture's lateral edges, a dark foreground *coulisse,* a middle-ground
scoop of water, and a distant mountain. The Claudian formula, art historians acknowledge wearily, was endlessly repeated by painters and writers in
this period. The paintings were picturesque because of their insistent and
formulaic shaping of nature into art, what is generally called "composition"

but which here has specific meaning: the habit of framing with trees, for example, turns a random botanical specimen into a picture frame.[22]

The picturesque is as delightful as it is consistent. The picturesque traveler was devoted to scenes and landscapes, as opposed to nature in a scientific or empirical sense: this traveler would routinely "translate the political and the social into the decorative."[23] The scientific eye was often at odds with the picturesque, which has prompted one critic to designate the empirical eye as "vertical perception penetrative" and the picturesque as "horizontal imagination associative." This horizontal tendency is emphasized in one traveler's own definition of the picturesque as "intended to convey a general idea of the *surfaces* and *external appearance* of a country."[24] The implication of a cursory and superficial eye is strongly felt: the picturesque traveler did not demand, or convey, more than the formulaic impression of a landscape. The picturesque tone is characterized by ease, not the drive to discover; by gentle surprise, not the shock of the new. It is a prose style for "strolls" and "airs" and "sketches."

The literary picturesque, rather than focusing on specific paintings or painterly techniques or gardens, makes a display of the machinery of art that nature has become. Picturesque descriptions of landscapes contain likely comparisons, such as geology compared to architecture. Landscapes are cherished not only for their appearance, but for the aesthetic feelings their appearance provokes in the viewer. Such narratives resort to literary commonplaces in new landscapes simply as a matter of form. It is not the case that the picturesque is especially ingenious: it is only consistent. "The similarities among [picturesque travel] narratives stemming from entirely different countries and composed by persons of opposing temperament" amount to a "restricted number of spatial signs."[25]

The picturesque was thus an ideal tool for ordering discovery in America. Indeed, "the shaping and constraining legacy of Picturesque assumptions can be discerned [throughout] European accounts of North America."[26] It was the particular genius of this aesthetic to domesticate the wilderness for the nation, even more than in other movements in art. Romanticism, for instance, is unthinkable without nature poems and is an intellectual movement with strong interests in the business of representing nature. But Romanticism has seldom been characterized as an especially accessible or popular mode of representation; it is most interested in the individual response to nature. However predictable that response is, it is nonetheless a matter of the subjectively sublime, rather than the socially conventional. Romantic nationalism is thus concerned with the strong emotional demands of shared blood, rather than the "nationalness" of a landscape. Nature is a mystery, surpassing aesthetic and moral classifications, and can't be easily pressed into service as a means of national self-identity.

But mystery is precisely what the picturesque mode did away with. The picturesque imposed the discipline of national consensus and homogeneity on overly individuated experiences of nature. It offered a new nation a ready means of self-representation in a time when America had little idea what it looked like. The plot of the picturesque, notes one art critic, is "narratives of discovery, presenting pictures of things their writers have never seen before. . . . [Such] landscapes express the national mission of Euro-American settlement and cultivation."[27] Discovery, mediated through the national picturesque, was the shared imaginative pastime.

The picturesque, before it became a favorite of Whig writers and artists, also may have represented one last Federalist "compromise" (to use Irving's term) toward the literary marketplace of the early republic.[28] In a mood of mixed "accommodation and resistance," writers in the early nineteenth century found no ready and easy way of combining both commercial and artistic successes. Richard Chase has described the contradictory literary impulses of surrender and defiance and finds the particular genius of the American novel to be its elements of romance, full of these incongruities; Michael Gilmore has added to this set of contradictions by insisting on the power of the marketplace, over the individual artist, to dictate terms. Though neither of these studies examines Irving and the picturesque, their conclusions—that nineteenth-century literary culture can be imagined only through the competing conditions of culture and commerce, demand and supply, and tradition and novelty—offer a useful road map to the popular picturesque.[29]

The picturesque had, eventually, a relatively small presence in the nineteenth-century literary marketplace; it had little readership in the class whom Jacksonian Democrats courted in elections; it offered no serious counterpunch against this class among vintage Knickerbocker or new Whig readers; it supposed of itself none of the high seriousness of the novel form; its practitioners spurned professionalism and thus kept the picturesque in the realm of casual or polite letters; and its politics largely ignored the dominant issues of hard money, tariffs, immigration, banks, land speculation, and slavery. By the time of Emerson's *Essays, Second Series* (1841), the picturesque was synonymous with "quaintness," like prevalent Whiggish rhetorical appeals to history and tradition.[30]

Perhaps the key piece of evidence to the market-driven aspect of the picturesque is in its lifespan, which in significant ways resembles that of the Federalist party. There were simply fewer and fewer successors to Irving as the 1820s advanced. Pike's *Journals* are a case in point. They were virtually unread in the nineteenth century. They resemble most the sections of Lewis and Clark's *Journals* that were written by Lewis, but they lack the balancing presence of a Clark. Pike's style far outdoes Lewis's own and indulges the prolixity of the picturesque traveler. A critic of travel writing notes that "among the many 'tastes' available in the latter part of the eighteenth century, none was more congenial to the innovative desires of the age than that for discovery. It flourished . . . alongside the Picturesque."[31] But Pike, in 1806, was aware already of the threadbareness of his mode in the new century. In his *Preface* he acknowledges the literary culture his account joins, for, as he notes apologetically, "books of travels, journals and voyages, have become so numerous, and are so frequently impositions on the public" (xxiii).[32] These numerous books would have included Claude Étienne Savary's *Lettres sur l'Egypte* (1796), which Pike cites in his *Journals;* or bestsellers such as François Le Vaillant's *Voyage dans l'intérieur de l'Afrique* (1790), J. Hardy's *A Picturesque and Descriptive Tour in the Mountains of the High Pyrenees* (1825), or Jean Houel's *Voyage pittoresque des isles de Sicile* (1782), or indeed Irving's own *Sketchbook.*[33] Books entitled *Voyage pittoresque* were standard fare in eighteenth-century European print culture: a quick survey of imprints reveals more than two hundred such entries in French and English for the period 1760–1890.[34] (There is a noticeable drop-off after 1840.) Novels sold better, and the picturesque ephemera of the *Sketchbook* soon dropped from publishers' lists, giving way to character-driven, realistic fictions such as *The Spy* and *The Last of the Mohicans.*[35] The sense of being driven into the past, with which the picturesque is preoccupied, eventually was the genre's own fate.

Pike realized the restrictions and also the outmodedness of the picturesque tone, but he struck it consistently, even desperately, for a significant and practical reason. His expedition had been planned as a filibustering raid, aimed at breaking up the republic and overthrowing American sovereignty in Louisiana (and eventually Spanish sovereignty in the Southwest). When this experiment ended in Burr's indictment, Pike was naturally eager to bury the project under a sensibility of narrow, innocent, gentlemanly landscape savoring. The picturesque in Pike's journals, then, is an edifice (and a refuge) of exaggerated gentlemanly behavior, national devotion, and aesthetic excess. Pike did not mind seeming naive: it proved him innocent of imperial conspiracy. He was eager to explain his journey through the West as an experience of aesthetic responses and refined feeling, which made him see the canvases of Rosa and Claude, not the incipient provinces of Burr. And with him, the picturesque became an aesthetic—enfeebled in the ways I have described—of belated Federalism.

The picturesque lent itself to Pike's faux-naïf pose: the political tone of the picturesque is of politics that conceals itself, or the politics of being apolitical—"the effacement of the political and the social [into] . . . the spontaneously 'natural.'"[36] The effort in the picturesque is to escape ideology and to appear free of history; frequently this effort contradicts the supposed valor of subjective individual responses. Like the Federalist party itself, picturesque aesthetics in the early nineteenth century felt to its practitioners not so much an agreeable taste as received wisdom. Federalists tended to imagine themselves not as a party, but as a collective dissociation from party politics altogether, an oligarchy who were national and anything but local, in sentiment and destiny. (Once party politics became inescapable, the Federalists covered their change in policy by calling themselves a "party" and the Republicans a "faction.") [37] Likewise, the picturesque was imagined to be universally a way of seeing, predicated though it was on a (fairly tedious) set of artistic conventions, and the (fairly predictable) responses of the individual subject. Luckily, that subject would never drift beyond the limits that the picturesque imposed; travel narratives reproduced themselves effortlessly and identically, one by one. Just as all travel around the late 1790s amounted to picturesque voyages, all picturesque voyages contained predictable remarks alleged to result from an "individual experience" in nature —according to strict aesthetic rules. Hundreds of travelers trudged through thousands of miles of entirely unexplored terrain, only to be convinced of the same aesthetic effects over and over. Picturesque aesthetes may have thought they were merely encouraging an actual and repeatable cognitive response, but the picturesque is hardly daring enough to have contained more than the usual number of trees, much less accommodate an observer's raw psychology. (It was in part this gentility that Henry David Thoreau actively parodied in *Walden*. One of the raw items in that text is the woodchuck on which Thoreau threatens to dine.)

The picturesque, in fact, denied the anxiety it invoked. On the one hand, it represented a sharp departure from earlier, monarchical natural settings, such as the symmetrical style of the royal gardens at Versailles. "[The picturesque] was conceived," notes a landscape critic, "as wild and empty space to be enjoyed in solitude," as opposed to a public space of hierarchy, restraint, and display. But on the other hand, the picturesque sounds downright panicky about the radicalism it was supposed to permit: part of the original provocation of the picturesque landscape, despite its eventual formulaic quality, was its shadowy and irregular features, which posed for many observers "a visual emblem of all that was threatened by the new democratic politics." [38] The picturesque, then, was in its sensibility analogous to Federalism: shrinking from the democratic future, and prescribing a mode of genteel obsolescence that denied its own ideological particularity, the better to fade gently away.

Thus the political innocence that happens to be a specialty of the picturesque was achieved through nostalgia. William Gilpin, one of the three theorists of the English picturesque, offers a cheerful statement of this desire to dodge origins: "Enough has been said to show the difficulty of assigning causes: let us then take another course, and amuse ourselves with searching after effects. This is the general intention of picturesque travel." [39]

Marx was to point out how well this camouflage worked: "The function of ideology," sums up one of Marx's commentators, "is to conceal contradictions in the status quo by . . . recasting them into a diachronic narrative of origins. . . . One important structure of ideology is *an idealizing appeal to the outdated values of an earlier system,* in defense of a later system that in practice undermines the material basis of those values.[40] Irving's *Astoria,* for example, classicizes and romanticizes the fur trade in this way: it obscures the indefensible by casting it as nostalgically heroic. The nostalgia of the picturesque idealizes a pastoral or at least premodern mode of living, and attempts to incorporate the political present into that ideal. It is a celebratory aesthetic, one that lauds the vague glories of past civilization, and one that is, as we would say now, "in denial" of modernity. It is, as Tom Stoppard points out, essentially a touristic taste, imported into landscapes with a zeal for displaying strictly the refinement of that import. This denial encompasses both the fuzzy "pastness" of its paintings—what year is it, exactly, when the American Southwest resembles the ruins of ancient Rome?—and the equally fuzzy projected future of the landscape under scrutiny. The picturesque sought to turn the unknown future into a recognizable past by obscuring the specific details of both times. Pike's interest in the picturesque would have been fundamentally linked to this malleability of specific details.

PIKE'S TWO SOUTHWEST expeditions were initiated not by President Jefferson (as in the case of Lewis and Clark) but by General John Wilkinson, commander of the Army of the West. Vice President Aaron Burr, a longtime friend of Wilkinson's, was more ardent for American expansion into the West than even Jefferson had been. When his term of office ended in 1805, and after he was drummed out of politics for shooting Alexander Hamilton in a duel, Burr went west on what seems to have been a nefarious "tour of inspection" of the states west of the Appalachians.[41] He met Wilkinson at Fort Massac, Missouri, as Wilkinson was traveling to St. Louis to take up a position as military governor of Upper Louisiana. The four days the two men spent together at Fort Massac have been described as a "secret conference," perhaps spent in formulating their *coup d'état* in the American West. Burr then traveled to New Orleans, where rumors began to circulate about his dealings with foreign governments, from whom he had sought military aid in his takeover attempt. Wilkinson, fearing prosecution, was extremely displeased that the news had broken. Newspapers began to run stories about sightings of mysterious barges loaded with muskets drifting from Kentucky to New Orleans, and letters of credit being circulated in Philadelphia banks on behalf of Aaron Burr.[42]

Though tempted, both the British and the Spanish turned Burr down: his terms (half a million dollars and a fleet of warships) were difficult to meet. Some private funds were raised eventually, and Burr wrote confidently to Wilkinson in 1805 that they would seize Baton Rouge by Christmas. But the revolution hit a few snags. Over months of delays, the plans to capture the West languished, and Burr's imagination fixed instead on the annexation of

Mexico. Zebulon Pike was dispatched almost immediately to reconnoiter and map the Southwest. There is no evidence that Pike knew in 1805 of Burr and Wilkinson's conspiracy—but by the time of the preparation of his journals for publication he surely did.

Wilkinson was Burr's accomplice until 1806; he feared his own ruin and so turned Burr in, and in early 1807 the first treason trial in American legal history commenced. Pike, all this time, was in the field, alone with Wilkinson's instructions, his own professional ambitions, and his West Point code of honor. His skills as a geographer were, it appears, less than expert, and his company, mistaking the Rio Grande for the Red River, stumbled into Spanish New Mexico. The Spanish took him captive for his misstep, seized his papers, and sent the United States government an invoice for $22,000, the cost of retrieving Pike from the wilderness near Santa Fe and frog-marching him to Chihuahua. (The seized papers were returned to the United States only in 1910.) Pike himself was released after a few months. His success on the expedition, by all accounts, was mixed.

Upon return, with the Burr trial under way, Pike found himself in the disagreeable position of guilt by association. Newspapers called him "a parasite of Wilkinson."[43] Burr's trial was going disastrously even for Wilkinson, who eagerly testified against his old friend; Pike would surely go down too. Reasoning, we may suppose, that the enemy of my enemy is my friend, Federalists aided conspicuously in Burr's conspiracy and his trial, help that they imagined as a blow to Jefferson and his "faction." At least one Federalist senator was indicted along with Burr, another was chief defense counsel, and still another was jury foreman (who led the movement to acquit). Pike himself had no such support; he had only a Federalist literary mode at his disposal.[44]

Pike's defense in such a circumstance was to claim geographical error as his reason for roaming into New Mexico: he simply didn't know where he was. He denied the charges that he had deliberately provoked capture in order to spy for Burr on Spain's military preparations in Chihuahua. It was an embarrassing position for an ambitious military explorer to assume, but Pike had little choice: he could either insist on his expertise and seem an accomplice, or admit to lesser, still stinging, charges of error. In other words, in order to appear innocent, he also had to appear incompetent. He also had to dissociate himself from the conspiracy of a fallen Republican vice president by using a genre of Federalist writing at its most mawkish and nostalgic.

His expedition journal, therefore, takes pains of an extraordinary kind. Where most exploration journals will only reluctantly admit of error or misstep, and insist upon the generally triumphant sweep of the company through *terra incognita*, Pike's journal instead conveys the confusion and haplessness of his expedition and his own inclination for aesthetic asides and poignant ethical pronouncements. His sense of honor—he calls himself in his preface "a man of humanity and feeling"—exonerates him from the plot that launched his expedition in the first place. Sedition is not just dangerous, it is vulgar and far beneath him:

> There has not been wanting, persons of various ranks, who have endeavored to infuse the idea into the minds of the public, that the last voyage was undertaken through some sinister designs of general Wilkinson; and although this report has been amply refuted by two letters from the secretary of war, published with this work; yet I cannot forbear in this public manner, declaring the insinuation to be a *groundless calumny*, arising from the envenomed breasts of persons, who through enmity to the general, would in attempting his ruin, hurl destruction on all those, who either through their official stations or habits of friendship, ever had any connections with that gentleman (xxv; emphasis in original).

While the Mexican captivity episodes are unique to American exploration, the balance of Pike's *Journals* offers a set of general concerns about nature and nation that not only echoes Lewis and Clark, but predicts later explorers' narratives. Pike stands with Lewis and Clark as an inaugural figure in the exploration narrative, articulating the general themes of the genre while deploying, perhaps in the most nostalgic terms until after the Civil War, the idioms of European aesthetics. Pike conveys in his journals a learned sensibility, somewhat charmingly out of place—indeed, sometimes, during great ordeals, off on a sentimental journey—that cannot help but be tried by the western journey. And the greater the trials, the more effusively sensitive Pike becomes. Charged with stringent frontier duty (yet mindful of seeming too expert), Pike composes a journal that attempts to bring order to the American Southwest; but in addition to a military reconnaissance and Indian treaties, Pike has to carry out faithfully the demands of his code of honor and his artistic eye. Their failure is at least dignified.

RATHER THAN ENGAGE directly the accusations Pike knew were in circulation, his *Journals* conjure up an idealized, scandal-free landscape inhabited by an obsolete figure, the gentleman, who simply cannot possess any political savvy. (We may recall D. H. Lawrence's description of James Fenimore Cooper, another Federalist: "He was a GENTLEMAN, in the worst sense of the word.") [45] The fall of gentility into the rigors of exploration and captivity, furthermore, is Pike's way of representing his own fall into difficulties with Wilkinson and Burr. Pike claims his good intentions and the intervention of forces beyond his control, such as nature. His forward motion into unexplored territory becomes a retrograde march into lost principles.

This method is apparent in many of the early comments Pike makes about the landscape. His vocabulary is aesthetic; he frequently uses the terms *sublime* and *beautiful*. It is common in the picturesque voyage to invoke these terms, which does not distract from the governing picturesque idea, but rather establishes the general visual credentials of the traveler. It is often not the term itself but the way it is deployed that makes the effect picturesque. At times, the designation "picturesque" is simply a way of splitting the difference between the beautiful and the sublime. Pike himself seems to apply these terms in an automatic fashion, like a painter once again arranging the Claudian formula. He may note that "a prospect from the dividing ridge to the east and south-east is sublime. The prairie rising and falling in regular swells, as far as the sight can extend, produces a very beautiful appearance" (315). Or later, in the vicinity of Pike's Peak, he sees both sublime and beautiful at once and not only underscores the fact, but adds on for good measure a comparison to Eden:

> We ascended a high hill, which lay south of our camp, from whence we had a view of all the prairie and river to the north of us; it *was at the same time one of most sublime and beautiful* inland prospects ever presented to the eyes of man. . . . In short, *this view combined the sublime and the beautiful;* the great and lofty mountains covered with eternal snows, seemed to surround the luxuriant vale, crowned with perennial flowers, like a terrestrial paradise, shut out from the view of man (375; emphasis added).

In the field, Pike commonly transforms his experience in this way, dulling otherwise unremarkable events with moral observations. He often regards his enterprise as a moral trial for beauty. The artistic eye is rewarded for its suffering: "[We] were amply compensated for toil by the sublimity of the prospects below. The unbounded prairie was hung with clouds, which appeared like the ocean in a storm; wave piled on wave and foaming, whilst the sky was perfectly clear" (350). The motif of pain-reward appears often in the *Journals,* signaled by Pike's descriptions of extravagant episodes of agony followed by the determination to carry on, with the requisite homily or rationale to do so. This process of pain-reward is helpful to Pike in at least two ways. First, it mimics the process of picturesque vision; the pain-reward motif, in fact, may well be inherent in the picturesque. The picturesque dotes on the sensations and feelings that a landscape "prompts." Its larger goal, in fact, is to credit nature as the laboratory for human imaginative capacity. All along, of course, the transaction originates with the mind and ends with the mind; the landscape is simply brought to order. The picturesque is, in other words, a model for cognition. Thus, pain followed by a reward is structurally and conceptually analogous to sensations followed by aesthetic judgment. In each case, a moral evaluation takes place. And in each case, there is a drama of cause and effect: the role of nature is to "cause" the picturesque "effect," whether through the endurance of toil or the apprehension of beauty. As a literary habit, it is one of Pike's commonest. And to present moral evaluation, or a reward for suffering, in as natural a light as cause and effect is helpful to Pike, making his *Journals* rhetorically coherent, and his ultimate claim of innocence more credible. The redemptive end of all "toil" applies more generally to Pike and his own labors: the perils of accusations will also eventually be overcome.

The second use of the pain-reward motif indirectly reinforces Pike's credibility as a sentimental hero, another way of describing a picturesque tourist. This credibility is often related, in Pike's account, to his patriotism. For example, when a small party is separated from the main company for several days, Pike writes, "*Our sensations now become excruciating* not only for their personal safety, but the fear of the failure of the national objects intended to be accomplished by the expedition" (336; my italics). When one of Pike's men travels alone to Santa Fe, Pike notes that "we parted, but not without tears" (370). Later, while captive in Chihuahua, he meets two Mexican officers who are invalids in a hospital. His description of their decline suggests that all good men have the noble stature and the tragic frailty (whether from tuberculosis or syphilis, the two usual picturesque maladies) of the sentimental hero: "[I met] two officers, who were fine looking men, and I was informed had been the gayest young men of the province, who were mouldering away by disease, and there was not a physician in his majesty's hospitals who was able to cure them; but after repeated attempts had given them up to perish" (414). In another episode, while captive in Mexico, Pike meets an American soldier, David Fero, who had once served with Pike's father. The poignant account might have appeared in Mackenzie or Richardson:

> [A] countryman, an acquaintance, and formerly a brother soldier, in a strange land, in distress, had ventured to see me—could I deny him the interview from any motives of delicacy? No; forbid it humanity! forbid it every sentiment of my soul! . . . Our meeting was affecting, tears standing in his eyes. . . . I promised to do all I could for him consistent with my character and honor. . . . When I bid him adieu, [I] gave him what my *purse* afforded, not what my *heart* dictated (416; emphasis in the original).

Generally, descriptions of strong feeling happen concurrently with Pike's national pride, so that the two become, for him, the same impulse. America itself becomes a sentiment. Pike's insistence on his extravagant moral fitness can assure his readers of his innocence from political intrigue, if at the same time his geographic incompetence, while still demonstrating his patriotism. All along Pike insists, through ordeals and trials, that "we might not have made the tour, without some benefit to our country" (339). Pike's sacrifices are essential to his standing: the sentimental observer, as one critic notes, "is the non-hero of an anti-conquest. . . . Things happen to him and he endures and survives."[46] Thus the irony, that Pike's failure to explore properly (he is on an anti-conquest) is his basis for claiming successful disengagement from the Burr conspiracy, is built into his choice of literary modes.

The most compelling episode in Pike's journal occurs a few weeks before his captivity, and addresses, startlingly, his predicament with Burr and Wilkinson. In this section, Pike successfully turns an episode of sedition into a picturesque scene, offering a model to the reader for resolving the larger question of sedition hanging over Pike's own reputation. He commands a company of some twenty-five men, and one of these soldiers, named Brown, ragged from starvation and exposure, defies Pike's authority and protests violently the pains of service. Pike is faced with a field crisis (deep snows block their progress), as well as a crisis of morale and authority. "For the first time in the voyage," Pike remarks of this event, "[I] found myself discouraged" (371).

Following the recovery of the company in camp, when they at length shoot a buffalo and have their first meal in days, Pike turns to the matter of discipline. He records his complete speech to the seditious man in the *Journals*. The speech is unique in the *Journals*, which generally narrate spoken language indirectly. (Even a melodramatic encounter with Indians, in which Pike negotiates a transfer of their loyalty from Spain to the United States and a change of flags on their flagpole, contains no direct quotation.) The direct representation of the speech underscores its position as a performance, or at least as a verbal response that stands out prominently from the routine of the military reconnaissance. In an eventful journey, the episode of military discipline—and, of course, mercy—becomes the centerpiece. It is as if their expedition has been arranged entirely for the purpose of moral uplift, such as this episode provides: and so the literary picturesque finds Pike not only not guilty, but also positively innocent.

Pike's address to Brown, as with a monologue in a drama, has two audiences, the company and the reader. Both audiences would have had a similar interest in a sedition problem: the company in its immediate safety and morale, and the reader in national safety and morale. In the former setting, Pike is the judge, a role he would surely want his reader to favor over his latter role as the accused. And Pike was keenly aware of the importance of rendering judgment: in earlier months, squabbling with Indians over a minor theft of property, Pike notes that "if you have justice on your side, and do not enforce it, they universally despise you" (302).

Pike's decision to set off the speech with quotation marks is augmented by his emphasis in it on the consequences, not to mention the high moral stature, of good rhetoric. He underscores the villainy of treason, an offense that is moral and criminal but primarily linguistic: "it was the height of ingratitude in you," he tells the soldier, "to let *an expression* escape which was *indicative* of discontent. . . . Your duty as a soldier called on your obedience to your officer, and a prohibition of *such language*." Pike's emphasis on the perils of language and expression is striking, if precise by the code of law: the specific charge against Brown is that "you this day presumed *to make use of language* which was seditious and mutinous" (372; emphasis added).[47]

The speech transforms the crime, from bona fide sedition into loose talk provoked by distress and excess feeling. And this transformation is the basis of Pike's mercy: remarking on Brown's crime, he observes to the company that "I . . . passed it over, pitying your situation and attributing it to your distress, rather than your inclination, to sow discontent amongst the party."

Pike's largesse is based upon the general persona he assumes in the *Journals,* of a picturesque traveler with a surplus of feeling. Such a surplus would typically be devoted to country, and feeling often signals, on its own, that Pike has national motives in mind. Pike, in his address to Brown, sounds as though he must justify the charges to Brown, and he does so by appealing to Brown's feelings and Pike's own weakness:

> Had I reserved provisions for ourselves, whilst you were starving; had we been marching along light and at our ease, whilst you were weighed down with your burden; then you would have had some pretext for your observations; but when we were equally hungry, weary, emaciated and charged with burden, which I believe my natural strength is less able to bear, than any man's in the party; when we are always foremost in breaking the road, reconnoitering and the fatigues of the chase; . . . your ready compliance and firm perseverance, I had reason to expect, as the leader of men and my companions, in miseries and dangers (372–73).

The rhetorical surplus in this passage—Pike's overwrought phrasing such as "weighed down with your burden" and "the fatigues of the chase," and his elongated series of clauses—demonstrate, by the logic of Pike's performance, the correct use of language: as a necessarily excessive vehicle for noble feeling. Pike is calling Brown to account for sedition, but in effect is also correcting his forms of expression. Brown, Pike implies, is justified in having feelings of discontent, but must discipline his form. Sedition, then, becomes a crime of bad art. And Pike is uniquely qualified to correct it.

Pike admits his only frailty: his "natural strength is less able to bear" the burdens of the field than any man's. But whatever his physical weakness, his moral position is strong. The picturesque is vividly in force here, with all its moral implications and pictorial detail. Pike is revising a type of landscape (Brown's loose expressions) into a more appealing and more artful form. Indeed, the elegance, or at least the high artifice, of Pike's address draws our attention strongly to its picturesque effect, or "the intervention of human ingenuity" as described above. With sedition carefully revised into an aesthetic crisis, Pike is free to discuss its moral implications. The picturesque landscape becomes for him a site of mercy, just as earlier it was a site of sedition. Invariably, it is a site of moral trial. Just as he naturalizes a moral evaluation of Brown by continually posing it as a cause-effect relationship, Pike naturalizes his own ongoing moral evaluation—the one that the American public was busy deciding. His instructions to Brown not only confirm

Pike's military authority (and so demonstrate his patriotism), they also confirm his picturesque credentials. Enacting the two simultaneously, as I have suggested, is crucial to Pike's successes both as a commander and, by implication, as an unofficial defendant. His mercy is based upon the argument Pike would most like his readers to agree to: that treason, while villainous, can be forgiven.

Pike's joyous return to the United States, after a few months in Mexico, is in many ways a standard one for exploration journals. The few concluding lines incorporate the poignant contrasts of an arduous field tenure and the restoration to home territory. Pike resorts to a "words cannot express" formulation of wonder, a commonplace of picturesque travel report—and one that usually precedes a further surge of words. His ending displays the excesses of feeling and the love of country in a combination that his narrative has imparted all along: "Language cannot express the gaiety of my heart, when I once more beheld the standard of my country waved aloft!— 'All hail cried I, the ever sacred name of country, in which is embraced that of kindred, friends, and every other tie which is dear to the soul of man!!'" (447–48). Pike identifies nationalism here as a governing allegiance from which all other allegiances derive, a type of trickle-down loyalty. But surely also trickle-up: in his efforts to display his individual standing as a gentleman and a good heart, Pike also establishes his loyalty as an American. The kinds of "ties" exist dialectically in Pike's *Journals,* another picturesque habit of composition, in which the cause and the effect become impossible to differentiate. This shifting circulation of Pike's virtues, from patriotism to gentility to feeling, finally proves impervious to the accusations of sedition, as indeed Pike himself would prove to be. Never indicted, Pike went on to distinguish himself in further military service, gaining promotion to brigadier general, and dying a hero at the siege of York in 1813.

HUME'S REMARK, at the head of this chapter, offers one statement of the explorer's problem: that aspirations to be objective are generally mistaken for objectivity itself. Pike's writings, and their connections to the Lewis and Clark *Journals,* present again what seem to be a standard set of problems, both physical and metaphysical, faced by explorers. They are a pair of texts that, without recourse to each other, reached comparable conclusions about landscapes. In the case of Pike, his text urgently deploys the terms of European aesthetics and nascent American nationalism, both as principles of order in unknown lands—just as Lewis and Clark had done. These terms, for Pike, were political: they concealed his defensiveness about any implication in the Burr Conspiracy. Pike's reliance upon generalized aesthetic and moral terms in his *Journals* deflected attention from the details of his own possible involvement with Burr and onto the picturesque possibilities of the landscape and, by implication, the American political future. For

Pike, generalizing his wisdom like a seasoned party hack, landscape was anything but a local matter.

The problems of exploration take in the range of difficulties in westering, from exposure, illness, and starvation, to Indian attack, mutiny, and geographical and psychological disorientation. In Lewis and Clark's case, the general decline of enthusiasm and national pride in their *Journals* corresponds to the expedition's decline in fortunes and their distance and disaffection from their sponsoring government. Lewis and Clark's observations of landscapes changed over the course of this decline: exuberant aestheticism subsided into the fear of death. The collapse of ideals about landscape was traumatic, but the two were such competent field soldiers that the expedition was a thoroughgoing success. The Northwest Passage never did materialize, but Lewis and Clark were instant celebrities. The eighteenth-century taxonomic approach to nature failed them, but the scientific academies in Philadelphia absorbed the duo's findings with enthusiasm. In other words, Lewis and Clark had a problem en route that none of the American public—not even Jefferson, who badgered Lewis upon return to edit and publish the *Journals* and be quick about it—could yet appreciate. The failure that, in the view of Lewis's biographer and others, even prompted Lewis's suicide in 1809 was entirely private.[48] As a later explorer would lament, "The nation like the information obtained by [explorers,] but forget their sufferings."[49]

Zebulon Pike, unlike Lewis and Clark, *was* blamed publicly for his failure, a charge that still preoccupies historians. It seems from the historical evidence that Pike was unlucky in his associations, but not guilty of conspiracy.[50] He is remembered primarily for the Colorado peak that bears his name, sometimes for his tendentious standing after the Burr trial, and hardly ever for his *Journals*. Pike himself had named the mountain James Peak, after Dr. James Long, the first to reach its summit, but this name never stuck.[51] This hierarchy of Pike memorabilia—the Peak, the Burr Conspiracy, and the *Journals*—emphasizes the manner in which nineteenth-century America awarded fame: first, for discovery and conquest, such as the high mountain in the Rockies; second, for corruption, whether proven or not; and finally, for literature, which few read in Pike's own time, and fewer read now. Pike was not only not declared innocent, he also was not declared readable: the *Journals* gave Pike little vindication in the public eye. Vindication seldom has one literary formula, but in Pike's case, the picturesque might well have benefited from a William Clark or a Chingachgook, to balance Pike's over-gentlemanly posture and help him beat the rap.

3

The Land without Qualities

Stephen Long and William Emory

Texas has been absorbed into the Union in the inevitable fulfillment of the general law which is rolling our population westward. . . . It was disintegrated from Mexico in the natural course of events.
JOHN O'SULLIVAN, *Democratic Review* (1847)

They just want this Californy so's to lug new slave states in.
JAMES RUSSELL LOWELL, *The Biglow Papers* (1848)

This chapter assesses two exploration accounts, from 1820 and 1852, by explorers for whom the picturesque had become the aesthetic of choice: Stephen Long, who explored the "Great American Desert" between the Missouri and the Rockies, and William Emory, who surveyed the new southwestern border with Mexico following the 1848 Treaty of Guadalupe-Hidalgo. My purpose is to suggest how an aesthetic system such as the picturesque, when dedicated to American nature, tends to remove ambiguity and uncertainty about the appearance of nature and the conquest of land. The picturesque became quickly absorbed into the politics of gleeful westward expansion, or Jacksonian exploration narratives, so that the hesitancy of, say, Zebulon Pike from the early nineteenth century, however ineffectual, is gone. In its place is a buoyant jingoism, made respectable by aesthetic language.

The examples of the picturesque in the current and previous chapters are meant to demonstrate that American nature in the nineteenth century tended to sport its politics in aesthetic terms. Any reader of Kant or Wordsworth will not be surprised by this claim; but for the design argument to stir up a concerted Transcendentalist response (as I discuss later, in chapters 4–6), American nature will draw nearer to Emerson and Thoreau in part through exploration accounts—accounts that, in several cases, are picturesque. The picturesque is in part the background noise of Transcendentalist High Theory.

Transcendentalism, though, was not particularly interested in the picturesque, with a few exceptions.[1] The Transcendentalist view of nature was more precise and more willing to contain contradictions. As this chapter will narrate, picturesque exploration was both sloppy about its empirical claims (picturesque land masses all tended to look uniformly like ruined architecture) and univocal in its politics (picturesque America always looked discernibly American). The mid-nineteenth century was in part a drama of bringing under steady aesthetic control the appearance of a deserted, but still planned-looking, continent. To me it is clear that the stakes were quite high: I cannot account for Jacksonian rhetoric about nature in any other way.

Long and Emory were explorers who significantly misread their literary prototype—for whom the political misgivings and ambiguities in the Lewis and Clark *Journals* became explicit sanctions of national triumph. Long in particular made great, though spurious, use of the Lewis and Clark expedition as his source for patriotic optimism about American nature. That he also made over their legacy in picturesque terms tells us that exploration had evolved from its mixed "genre trouble" of the early nineteenth century to Long's univocal aesthetic reading of new land, or to Emory's shrill recital of our differences from Mexico. It is in part this monotony of picturesque exploration that may account for Emerson's and Thoreau's impatience to find nature interesting again, and more philosophically shrewd than explorers had let on.

STEPHEN LONG'S EXPEDITION of 1820 traveled between the Missouri River and the Rocky Mountains, and its mission, devised by Secretary of War John C. Calhoun, was to trace the Arkansas River to its source and to map the route of the Red River. Neither of these goals was accomplished. The expedition did have along the exceptional painter Titian R. Peale, who sketched wildlife and landscape scenes. And Peale's father, Charles Willson Peale, who ran the famous Peale's Museum in Philadelphia, accepted seventy-five animal and plant specimens from the troupe for his natural history collection. For these mixed successes, the Long Expedition has been judged kindly by a Western historian as not only "bridg[ing] the gap between Lewis and Clark and John C. Frémont, but also . . . symboliz[ing] a young nation's ambition to learn about itself and its potential."[2]

The *Account of an Expedition from Pittsburgh to the Rocky Mountains, under the Command of Major Stephen H. Long* was actually written by Long's fellow explorer Edwin James; Long approved it for publication.[3] Some of the controversy of the *Account* is in its perpetuation of the error of Zebulon Pike, namely that the fine grazing land west of the Missouri was arid and infertile. Pike had compared it to the Sahara. For his part, Long described its "hopeless and irreclaimable sterility." One observer marvels that "such learned men could see [a desert] in a land that supported the Plains Indians";[4] historians have generally found in this error an impulse by both explorers to "hem in westering Americans and thus insure the unity and strength of the

Young Republic, which was in some danger of stretching itself too thinly in its incessant westward drive."[5] But the theory of "ruinous diffusion," as it is called,[6] is inaccurate, given the unmistakable buildup in Long's account for patriotic expansion and progress, which he proclaims, in a near-miss of the century's greatest phrase, as "the manifest propensity . . . to remove westward" (66).

No reader of the Long account, in other words, has imagined the desert error to be innocent; it represents an aesthetic choice on the explorer's part to shape and fashion the Great Plains. Rather than speculate on Long's anxieties about ruinous diffusion as an explanation—speculations which, frankly, are not borne out by the *Account* itself—I would like to focus instead on the role of desert landscapes in picturesque exploration, a literary model that maps well onto Long's narrative, and for which the *Account* provides ample evidence. The desert in this literary context solves the problem of how Long and James could have made, and then insisted upon and popularized, the mistaken and long-lasting designation "desert." The desert was of special interest in the travel literature of the late eighteenth and early nineteenth centuries in part because of the newspaper coverage of Napoleon's conquests in Egypt, which introduced Western Europeans to vast stretches of sandy terrain for the first time, and in part because, in a landscape tradition that focused chiefly on the cultivation of plant life and the artful arrangements of nature, the desert provided the ultimate challenge. It had nothing in it to cultivate or arrange; it was the land without qualities.

Picturesque travel writers were generally unfazed by this challenge, and the accounts of desert travel appeared regularly: for example, Claude Étienne Savary's *Lettres sur l'Egypte* (1796) and François Le Vaillant's *Voyage dans l'intérieur de l'Afrique* (1790). Far from concern over "ruinous diffusion," Long focused on the possibilities of cultivation. Apparently, then, "within the Picturesque aesthetic, the term *desert* simply indicates the absence of husbandry or conspicuous management."[7] And it was the picturesque traveler's purpose to supply the signs of management or order, even if he had to invent them.

Long's insistence on the word *desert* to describe what really wasn't one may simply have been literary vogue; but the word also provided him with an exaggerated opportunity to impose the terms of order in a disordered environment: to erase an irrational landscape and make it into a rational one. There was a political purpose to this effort, too. In Long's "Preliminary Notice" to the *Account,* he remarks that "the time will arrive, when we shall no longer be indebted to the men of foreign countries, for a knowledge of any of the products of our own soil, or for our opinions in science" (4). Long probably had Alexander von Humboldt in mind, who had mapped the American Southwest in 1811. (Emory, discussed in the second half of this chapter, took Humboldt similarly to task.) The discovery of the "desert" west of the Mississippi had been accomplished, according to Long, by an American, and furthermore, this American had utilized the European picturesque in the process, evidently a payment against the foreign intellectual debt. Long's insistence on an essentially fictitious landscape term permitted both scientific and political triumphs.

It is the *Account*'s fundamental scientific error—calling the Great Plains a desert—on which the balance of the narrative capitalizes, creating a fiction of the expedition. When I describe Long's desert as fictitious, there are at least two fictions operating. The first is the picturesque itself, which, like all aesthetics, belongs to the world of pleasing untruth. We may agree that a picturesque landscape is not, strictly speaking, representational or "true": we may say, accurately, "The Great Plains don't look like that." But while an incorrect usage of the word *desert* may well discredit our standing as scientists, on the other hand, the sheer fictiveness of *desert* sanctions our ability to make aesthetic judgments. It is not surprising, in fact, that Long's picturesque narrative tends to get things wrong; we are trafficking here in the beautiful, not the true.

Second, even within an aesthetic system that already has made over the standards of truth in representation, the desert is an extreme case of falsity. The desert Long claims to have seen simply is not one, so that his use of the term is contrary to observation, a contradiction about which the expedition was largely untroubled. In fact the blame for the error has recently been placed on one of the mapmakers on the expedition, the nineteen-year-old William H. Swift, who inscribed the words *Great American Desert* across the Great Plains.[8] Long did not dispute the assignation—though he easily could have—and it is even possible that he requested it. This map was published with the official report. Long merely notes in the early pages of the *Account* that he is not a historian, but is providing a "sketch true at the moment of our visit" (3).

The final fiction, therefore, is the *Account* itself, which uses the expedition as an occasion for literary invention as much as for scientific observation. As a fiction about exploration, the *Account* fits neatly into the genre of picturesque travel writing; Long's term *sketch* to describe his technique places him with Washington Irving and other picturesque "sketch" writers of the early nineteenth century. (A quick review of "sketch" titles in this period reveals, besides Irving's 1820 *Sketchbook,* this partial list: James Kirke Paulding's 1822 *Sketches of Old England,* the anonymous 1833 *Sketches and Eccentricities of Col. David Crockett of West Tennessee,* Anne Newport Royall's 1826 *Sketches of History, Life and Manners in the United States,* Sarah Joseph Hale's 1829 *Sketches of American Character,* and Theodore Dwight's *Sketches of Scenery and Manners in the United States* of the same year.) As in Irving's *Sketchbook* or his *Tour on the Prairies,* in these works "America itself was designated a literary form," a nice phrase that suggests the importance of the frontier West to sketch literature.[9] In Long's case, the literary form dictated the scientific conclusions.

The sketch is a neglected genre. It is one of the most favored picturesque (and also Romantic) literary forms, because of its tendencies to convey impressions over meaning, to render grand scenery and themes on a small scale, and to offer portraiture in outline rather than in depth. Larger than an anecdote and smaller than a short story, the sketch is apparently spontaneous and effortless in its (usually first person) composition, and unpretentious and light in tone. ("A brief account, description or narrative giving the main or important facts and not going into details; a short or superficial essay or study," notes the *Oxford English Dictionary*.) As with the picturesque in general, the sketch does not demand hard facts or everlasting moral resonance, but rather offers appearances, surfaces, and exteriors. And both modes announce to us their interest in specifically *visual* appearances: a picture in the picturesque, a sketch in the sketch.

With the coincident literary modes of the picturesque and the sketch, then, Long's *Account* presents the Great American Desert. The most important of the picturesque habits of description is the enthusiastic comparison between nature and art. And the purpose of these comparisons is to contain and control in the lexicon of images the somewhat sprawling and random encounters with nature. Long notes of a geological formation called the Great Tower, for instance, that "its form and situation strongly suggests the idea of a work of art" (27). And, later, of another striking view, Long points out that "Castle Rock" possesses a "striking resemblance to a work of art. It has columns, and porticoes, and arches, and, when seen from a distance, has an astonishingly regular and artificial appearance" (340). (One of the troupe, Samuel Seymour, duly made a *sketch* of Castle Rock.) Long's sketch, as he claims, actually "embraces the permanent features of nature": clearly, Long found his picturesque vocabulary suitable for fixing ephemeral observations to permanent form.

It is not surprising, then, that Long cites the most famous of ruins poems —Shelley's "Ozymandias," where

> Round the decay
> Of that colossal wreck, boundless and bare
> The lone and level sands stretch far away.

Passing the ruined dwellings of Indians, Long notes that such scenes "never fail, to produce an impression of sadness" in the observer (38), and he credits "Ozymandias" for stirring this response. (It would be fascinating to take a quantitative survey of the American ruins located only with the assistance of Shelley.) Long's interest in archaeology in the *Account* works along these lines: the desert, it seems, will yield up its picturesque historical proofs when proper aesthetic training is brought to bear on it. Archaeology provides Long with a science that deals in picturesque history, and one that can readily make sense of a desert.

But if Shelley provides training in nostalgic sadness in "an antique land," then other writers contribute different models in order to make this picturesque landscape more cheerful than Shelley's. If the argument of "Ozymandias" is the impermanence of all human enterprise over time, then the argument of Long's *Account* plays more loosely with this liability of culture. In other words, where Shelley saw a memento mori, Long saw a cooperative, essentially prelapsarian effort between the landscape and the expedition mapping it to invent (and not ruin) America.

Thus, the picturesque offered Long what Romanticism could not: a way out of the sadness that "never fails." It is difficult, perhaps, to imagine cheerful ruins, but Long saw little else besides excessive optimism in the landscape, still retaining its romanticized archaeological emphasis but not its associations with loss and death. This bizarre cheerfulness may finally be the distinguishing characteristic of the picturesque sketch.

On the banks of the Ohio River, for example, Long discovers a prism of an unidentified mineral. He responds with a set of references that place the object not in geological but in specifically archaeological terms. The prism, he notes, is like "tubes of very hard stone" mentioned by the Jesuit priest Venegas in Alta California (19). Long seems to have regarded the Spanish record of exploration as an authoritative if antique source, as other nineteenth-century explorers frequently did.[10] (Indeed, traces of the Spanish presence often constituted ruins in themselves.) The effort to place the unknown mineral in some useful scientific context simply heightens the specimen's resemblance to other romanticized discoveries by the Spanish. Near the unidentified prism, a clay riverbank reminds Long of a collection of artifacts in Charles Willson Peale's museum, collected also from California: "in the Philadelphia museum, are many Indian pipes, of that red indurate clay" (19). In other words, the geological makeup of the uncharted river on which they were traveling was *already* an artifact, precataloged in the museum owned by the father of the expedition sketch artist. These two small specimens indicate that Long was a good observer of detail and that, when he didn't know something, he would make a series of comparisons to describe the item anyway. They also indicate, however, that those comparisons tended to be cheerfully nostalgic, making associations with the mellowing California missions and making contributions to quaint historical collections in the East.

Long also relied on the history of American exploration to fill in the landscape—which, as he insisted, was barren. Lewis and Clark make appearances in the *Account,* as do Marquette, Joliet, and Zebulon Pike. The Council Bluff site in Missouri, where Lewis and Clark had held a famous conference of Plains Indians, receives a lengthy commemorative description of its position, beauties, and advantages. The description is prompted by Long's interest in providing in his account (in the bitter words of one of his colleagues) "amusement of the publick": [11]

> The Council Bluff, so called by Lewis and Clark, from a council with the Otoes and Missouris held there, on the 3rd of August 1804, is a remarkable bank, rising abruptly to the brink of the river, to an elevation of about one hundred and fifty feet. This is a most beautiful position, having two important features, security and a complete command of the river . . . [with] a view of a most extensive and beautiful landscape. The river is here and there seen meandering in serpentine folds. . . (94–95).

Long was interested in the Bluff in part for its specific picturesque interest or "amusement" (serpentine rivers, parklands, and so on) but also for its historical associations, which placed his expedition in the heritage of westering. Lewis and Clark themselves had the prestigious patronage not only of President Jefferson but also of the American Philosophical Society (another "Philadelphia museum"), a relationship Long mentions to establish the pedigree of his own journey. Citing Jefferson's *Notes on the State of Virginia,* Long associates an incident on his own expedition, involving a Lakota chief, with Jefferson's story of Logan, the defeated chief, as likewise "one of the most affecting incidents in history" (12–13). Long's landscapes are always heavily associative in this way. Likewise, the journey to Pike's Peak prompts Long's meditations on the significance of the place to the many disciplines that influence him: "We bivouacked for the night, surrounded by the grandest and most romantic scenery I ever beheld—what a field is here for the naturalist, the mineralogist, chemist, geologist and landscape painter" (171).

It turns out, in fact, that Long's excesses of description, and shortage of science, were noticed. One of Long's colleagues on the journey eventually grew exasperated by their rapid transit through the amusements of the Plains, which led, he insisted with frustration, to no discovery at all. In a letter to his brother, the explorer complained:

> We have travelled near 2000 miles through an unexplored and highly interesting country and have returned almost as much strangers to it as before. I have been allowed neither time to examine or collect nor means to transport plants or minerals. We have been hurried though the country as if our sole object had been, as it was expressed in the orders which we received at starting "to bring the Expedition to as speedy a termination as possible." [12]

Long meanwhile was recording the difficulties he had in judging distances, scale, size, and age—a confession of some scientific incompetence. "Nothing is more difficult to estimate by the eye," he wrote, "[than] the distance of objects seen in these plains" (275). He continued: "Three elk, which were the first we had seen, crossed our path at some distance before us. . . .

For a moment we thought we saw the mastodon of America, moving in those vast plains." And Long finally admitted the limits of his aesthetic framing when he confessed, late in the expedition, that "we feel the want of ascertained or fixed points of reference" (411). Perhaps, from his colleague's complaints, we can imagine a rate of travel that did not permit close scrutiny, and conjured elk into more-romantic mastodons. We can also discern from the literary clues in Long's *Account* the associated effort to resist scientific observation as such, and to rely instead on the literary and historical values of the picturesque desert.

These picturesque values—favoring a succession of ruins over present-day inhabitants; focusing on beauty instead of fact; playing loosely and impressionistically with science—mark out an effort by Long to accomplish his exploration strictly within picturesque terms. (From the complaints about too many "amusements" we may wonder whether the designation "Great American Desert" was even the very worst of Long's errors.) One of the purposes of this picturesque narrative, as I have mentioned, was Long's sense of the glories backing his expedition and the confirmation of national merit on the basis of his descriptions.

The Eastern press was quick to pick up on the national implications of the venture, whether prompted by Long's account or by the romantic nature of the expedition itself. The *Niles Register* of 1824, for instance, mistakenly noted that the Long expedition had explored the terrain of the "colony of the late lord Selkirk." The reference is to the Scottish Thomas Douglas, Earl of Selkirk, who arranged for Scottish immigration to North Dakota, until boundary disputes ruined the enterprise in 1816.[13] (A former colonist of Selkirk's wanders widely afield through another journal of the Long expedition.)[14] Selkirk's fame in America was also due to his ancestor's contribution to the literature of discovery and survival—Daniel Defoe's *Robinson Crusoe,* which was inspired in part by the adventures of Alexander Selkirk, a sailor left alone on an island for four years. The *Niles Register* seemed to find in the Long expedition the occasion for both a convoluted literary succession (Selkirk inspired Defoe *and* Long) and a national succession, so that the Scots were repelled and the American claim solidified. In North Dakota, to be sure, but the enthusiasm of the *Niles Register* was more sweeping.

Likewise, the *North American Review* of June 1825 devoted several pages to the Long expedition and used its successes as an occasion to rail against the dawdling of the U.S. government in mapping western boundaries. The article grumbled:

> It is mortifying in the extreme for an American to reflect, that while the British government, pursuing an expanded and magnanimous policy, are sending its bands of explorers to every region of the earth . . . *and even to the borders of our own United States;* . . . it is mortifying, we say, to witness these great acts of enterprise and spirit in a foreign country, and then come down to our own

pitiful contrast. . . . Three fifths of our wide possessions are to this day a complete *terra incognita*.[15]

The *North American Review* recognized the picturesque impulse toward providing cultivation and husbandry in blank spaces, and blamed the United States for only slowly exploiting this possibility in its explorations.

Long himself was in too great a hurry to add much nationalistic flourish to the conclusion of his *Account*. His colleague, John Bell, however, more than made up for this omission by concluding his own journal of the expedition with swoons of national fervor. His scene is Washington, D.C. He makes an explicit comparison between survival on the Long expedition and the survival and triumph of the United States following the late war with the British:

> The Star-Spangled Banner [was flying]. . . . I halted and dismounted from my horse to contemplate the scene. Six years ago, I had witnessed the Capitol in flames [during the War of 1812] fired by the hand of my country's foe; Phoenix-like it had risen from the ashes with tenfold splendor. Four months ago, I had turned my back to the snow capped mountains . . . [and] since then, I had encountered many hardships, fatigue, privations, and famine . . . [but] thanks to the Great Spirit have returned home.[16]

Bell, speaking for the troupe, suggests that the real purpose of the expedition has been to reflect positively on American history. The restoration of the national capitol after the War of 1812 is a commemoration of the explorers' restoration after their arduous field duty. Long, throughout the *Account*, has insisted on as much by filling a barren landscape with beauties prescribed by, at turns, the Philadelphia Museum, landscape painters, Thomas Jefferson, and the American travel writing of his own time.

Occasionally the fatuousness of manifest destiny is made specific and plain in an exploration journal, and Long's ideological contribution may well be that he was untroubled by fatuity. Long's desert is, after all, great, and American. His *Account* certainly makes the ideological puzzle simple: America will invent itself according to terms that appear immemorial, but which are actually contingent and occasionally random.

BY THE LATE 1840s, the aesthetics of manifest destiny were concentrated not so much on the unknown lands of the Far West as on national boundaries, established during the Polk presidency, that would describe and delimit American from non-American territory.

Oregon, negotiated from the British in 1846, reached north to the fortyninth parallel. In Francis Parkman's *Oregon Trail* (1849), the main text about the region from mid-century, the narrator is described as cheerfully "unpuzzled" about his observations of Native American life and the succession of nations. The attraction of Oregon for Parkman was not in the glories of its recent diplomatic acquisition from Great Britain, nor even its cosmopolitan mix of tribes and settlers, but rather the chivalric excitements of buffalo hunts and Parkman's own sense of Indians as the colorful but doomed inhabitants of the last frontier, who would give way inevitably to Americans, "that race of intrepid and restless pioneers."[17] The politics in *The Oregon Trail* take place strictly inside U.S. boundaries: Parkman does not mention the recent (difficult) border settlement, nor the vast British territory north of Oregon.

Such notions of tranquil isolation were not an option along the thirty-second parallel. A more contentious borderline, and one that would attract from its first advent in American politics quite a different portion of the public's attention, was the one with Mexico. This borderline was unimaginable in the nineteenth century without the vast attendant literature of American geopolitical transcendence, and in an international context. Henry Thoreau was part of New England's conscience on the subject of the Mexican War, and later I review his fury against, particularly, the 1847 Battle of Buena Vista, assailed in *Walden* as a deep villainy. But in general, the Mexican War enjoyed some considerable (though far from unanimous) domestic approval fed by the romantic figure it cut in the popular press: Mexico was America's Agincourt. It is no wonder, then, that the two border surveys of Mexico in 1846–47 and 1854–57, led by Lt. William H. Emory, found their voice in the tone of euphoria and prophetic conquest; nor any wonder that Emory's southwestern version of Parkman's *Oregon Trail* was a government-sponsored border survey that sought to fix this international question for good.

The border survey itself, a document that appeared regularly during the busy mapmaking era of the 1850s, was a new literary form in U.S. exploration writing.[18] Concerned less with *terra incognita* than with the holy writ of American national identity, the border survey, in Emory's case especially, was a response to the uncertain terrain of the Southwest, especially following a controversial war. Acquisition of Oregon had been negotiated despite well-known international tensions ("54°40' or fight!"), and evidently Polk chose not to fight two expansionist wars at once; the decision to strive for a southwestern empire meant that the northwestern border did not require a similar battle. (One Congressman accused Polk of avoiding a real foe and attacking an easy target, thus "cringing to the strong and oppressing the weak.")[19] The negotiations with the British for Oregon, moreover, had never quite approached the diplomatic breakdown prompted in Mexican-American relations by the annexation of Texas. As with the pro-Mexican-War U.S. journalism of the 1840s, Emory's border survey would find in the landscape the rationale for an American victory, and go to some trouble (averting mutiny at one point) to document it. It would be Emory's claim throughout his report that American lands look self-evidently American, and indeed have waited for centuries for the error of Spanish (and then Mexican) possession to be corrected. That he claimed visible geographical proof in an extraordinarily featureless and barren landscape was of no importance: when in doubt, he simply (and literally) hoisted the flag.

Emory's survey was also to borrow from the picturesque the convention of landscape as proof of the viewer's own moral excellence. Emory left out, though, the ambivalence still detectable in the earlier picturesque—the mood of occasional misgiving that had prompted Irving's ringing defenses, late in life, of Federalist respectability against Democratic corruption; or Pike's concerns in his *Journals* that even during a military enterprise, nothing was worse than offenses against good form. Border surveys could dispense entirely with those niceties; as unreconstructed hallowings to American greatness, they would no sooner admit ambivalence on questions of national virtue than they would admit uncertainty about where America stopped and Mexico began.

The border survey, then, was a case of mid-nineteenth-century literary "development" in the subgenre of exploration writing, and one that, examined alongside the writings of the Transcendentalists, tells us several things. New England was busily engaged with the problem of the expanding continent, and was putting up at least generic resistance to the bad form of manifest destiny offered in border surveys. Thoreau was a surveyor himself; mapmaking and landscape description seemed to New Englanders a vivid mark of conquest, in the way that mere politics did not. (Emerson's biographer notes that in the 1850s he eschewed the writings of Karl Marx, finding more interest in the exploration narratives of André Michaux, Bayard Taylor, John Frémont, and Parkman, which he read instead.) [20]

We may also observe in the unapologetic nationalism of Emory the shadow text of Jacksonian Democracy—the popular ideology that Emerson and Thoreau could not abide, but which they could not ignore or entirely refute. Finally, Emory tells us where the intellectual complexity of exploration, at least for actual explorers, had finally terminated: in unreconstructed triumphalist history. As his second border survey shows, Emory was not interested in the view from the southern side of the border; looking from the south toward *el norte* was an unthinkable condition. Such an outlook was not the interest of New England, either: their change in perspective was to be far different, focused on the borderlands of the inner life.

Emory's second survey (1854–57), then, represents a high phase of manifest destiny, one that adopted freely and somewhat unsystematically the literary conventions of previous exploration writings, and one that proudly offers redemption to Americans (from being Mexican, perhaps; or simply from being nationally indeterminate). This border survey, as I review it, is of interest because it narrates a border, but also because it narrates a specific border, that with Mexico. Though borderlands have tended to be, in the words of Gloria Anzaldúa, zones of hemorrhage rather than safety,[21] Emory relied on the contemporary imagination about Mexico as well as on ancient conceptions of mapmaking that composed, organized, and settled empty spaces; he found in borderlines the uncomplicated comforts of limits and boundaries and applied them to the case of Mexico.

The old idea of *translatio imperii,* or of a westward-moving civilizing force led by one great nation, found ready expression in the border survey, as it does in world maps generally. The ideological work accomplished by maps, described by critics interested in the visual rhetoric of empire, is evident even in so basic a question as this: why is the New World always placed on the left side of global maps?[22] The answer is that the "natural" movement of exploration was understood to take the explorer from the inhabited east to the uninhabited west, and never (say) eastward across the Pacific. Exploration simply couldn't happen meaningfully if the trek were not westward-moving, although some explorers, unmindful of the literary perils of ignoring this theory, did reach North America from the west. The construction of space in this manner—by no means the only example since 1492—tells us that maps place a section of land into a new, separate context, one that carries assumptions of ownership and comparative civilization. Unsurprisingly, maps invent space more than they represent it. Such an approach was fine by Emory, for whom borderlands were there to be conscripted in the historical drama of manifest destiny.

Mexico was a specific episode in this drama. While Henry Thoreau staged his poll-tax protest in July 1846 and then denounced the annexation of Texas, the territory under dispute was already being surveyed for the first time by Emory. The Mexican War was in some manner as stagey as a Transcendentalist's one night in jail: Thoreau's view of the poll tax was locally known, and his incarceration forced the Concord jailer to enforce the letter of the law so that Thoreau might theatrically draw a moral lesson.[23] President Polk, for his part, campaigned over several months for Texas annexation and then sent U.S. troops to provoke a Mexican response along the border; the war acquired its tone of moral outrage according to the Polk script for territorial expansion. Political theater about Mexico provided a venue for Thoreau and Polk both to announce predictions about a destiny that was becoming increasingly manifest. Emory's Mexican survey, a text written as these dramas unfolded, makes similar displays of American geopolitical prophecy.

Emory's second survey of the U.S.-Mexican border, following the Gadsden Purchase, was undertaken with the purpose of determining the geographical limits of the late American conquest.[24] Its aesthetic, as in the earlier case of Zebulon Pike's *Journals,* is usually the picturesque. Just as Pike had acquired political innocence from Aaron Burr's conspiracy by representing himself as a *voyageur pittoresque* and not an agent provocateur, Emory likewise recognized the advantages of an aesthetic system that could transform political facts into natural wonders. The picturesque offered a descriptive mode that ignored the significant issues behind the war (slavery, the annexation of Texas, the drive to take California) and instead confirmed the redemptive American ownership of newly won territories. Emory also took up, in the 1850s, the necessary assessment of limits upon the illimitable, and his survey became the means for deciding borderlines—those between America and Mexico and (correspondingly) those between the politically quick and the politically dead.

The picturesque, as I have suggested, provides an educated observer with a means of description that avoids issues of human agency and promotes certain historical fictions. The picturesque also permits an agent-free, historicized landscape to relieve the observer from anxieties over loss and ruin, or indeed, protests about aggressive wars: rather than prompting odes to dejection, the picturesque often inspires and informs the cheerful travel "sketch." Emory stares at an empty landscape and sees not decline and fall but, instead, soaring land values and European envy.

The fall—signaled by the poor land management of the Spanish and the Mexicans, and their cultural failures in general—is reversed in Emory's survey by Yankee accession. Emory's border survey settles the important question left after the war: it specifies where the redemptive American zone begins. The drive to establish national difference in the survey is the reason it is so copiously, but unconvincingly, illustrated—unconvincing, because in those illustrations each side of the border looks much the same as the other side. Emory ignores this fact, and the possibility that the reversed fall is a myth, by distracting his readers with complaints about his funding problems. The American presence along the border would, in Emory's view, transform the area to one of prosperity and cultivation, a set of possibilities the picturesque uniquely provides for a desert landscape. But the U.S. government frequently thwarted the best impulses of Yankee ingenuity by withholding funds, so that for Emory the landscape really did promise more than his mere government could deliver.

But the funding delays were, finally, not a crisis. In addition to promoting an absence of human agency and an eccentric historical sense, the picturesque in Emory's survey also redeems an incompetent government: Emory had no need to cover up the funding problems (as Pike did the Burr Conspiracy); he could use them, ultimately, as a marker of what was not yet redeemed, but inevitably would be. Indeed, Emory finally makes the picturesque case that an unresponsive government was not a hindrance to his efforts, but rather *proof* of an exceptional nation.

EMORY'S SURVEY WAS requested by President Franklin Pierce in 1854 following the completion of the 1853 Gadsden Purchase. The Gadsden Purchase itself was made on the basis of Emory's earlier surveying work in the Southwest, the 1846–47 survey that included his recommendation for a railway route in the vicinity of the Gila River, territory subsequently specified in the 1853 purchase.[25] Emory was appointed commissioner "to run the boundary line between the United States and the Mexican republic according to the treaty."[26] His *Report* was to provide documentary evidence for an already consolidated conception of American expansion in the Far West. The location of the border was a fairly dull matter of railway routes and topography, along with a vague desire to punish the Mexicans for the war and for impeding the sweep of the American continent, and it was this latter sense that would dominate Emory's work. His endeavor was one of interpretation, not observation. Throughout the *Report* his surveying skills focus on the physical site of the border—the illustrations almost outnumber the pages of narrative—while endowing it with qualities the illustrations would not possess without Emory's claims that they do.

It is fortunate for Emory that his border could play loosely with facts, because his work was the culmination of a controversial war, and there was much to recast in picturesque terms. The Mexican War had been denounced in New England literary circles, by Northern abolitionists, and by other interests as well. The Whig party, led by Daniel Webster, repeatedly criticized Polk's flimsy pretexts for the war. Horace Greeley, in his influential *New York Tribune,* compared the war to Napoleon's ill-fated campaigns in Spain. The *National Intelligencer* regularly praised Mexican soldiers for their fortitude. The Whigs started rumors about Polk, claiming he reaped a deluxe sixty-eight dollars a day and entertained dreams of conquering all of Mexico, while his soldiers earned pennies in the field. And if the president was opposed by the Whigs, he was often on no better terms with his own party. The Democrats were so riven with factions—united only in opposition to Polk—that in 1847 Polk confided gloomily in his diary that he was "in a minority."[27]

Sectional differences added to the crisis. In the controversy over the Wilmot Proviso, an amendment on a bill for funding U.S.-Mexico border negotiations that prohibited the extension of slavery into any new territories, Northern and Southern antipathies interfered with the attention the Mexican War then required simply to keep soldiers equipped and fed and negotiations continuing. The Proviso was lost and won many times during Polk's efforts to continue to fund the war and Congress's efforts to decide the slavery question; at most times the conduct of the war was entirely dominated by the associated politics of slavery.

Emory, a West Point graduate and career officer, called "a picturesque cavalry officer" by historian William H. Goetzmann, had participated in a few of the California campaigns of the Mexican War in the course of his first survey, including the conquest of the Pueblo of Los Angeles on January 9, 1847, with the Army of the West.[28] (Los Angeles had put up little resistance.)

His second survey, in the 1850s, was conducted under official terms of peace, but it was not easy work. Largely unrecorded in the *Report,* but noted in an autobiography of one of his colleagues, Emory's troupe was plagued by mutiny, famine, and the inattention of the U.S. government in funding the enterprise.[29] Not only was the border in question controversial, but Emory's exploration itself was marked by difficulty and delay. Nonetheless, Emory persisted (and finally succeeded) in his campaign to describe the natural features, historical interest, and picturesque appearance of the borderlands, in the interest of a redemptive myth of America.

The natural features of the Mexican border were recorded under the aegis of then-authoritative scientific discourse. Emory first mentions, and disputes, the exploration narrative of Alexander von Humboldt, whose 1808 *Views of Nature* (translated into English in 1850) had become one of the primary sources on American nature in the nineteenth century.[30] In 1811, Humboldt had mapped the region Emory was reconnoitering, and Humboldt's maps were still in use by the United States Army. Emory claims Humboldt's methods of citation in *Views* were sloppy: "The system of borrowing without acknowledgment, hitherto adopted, has tended very much to obscure and distort the history of explorations and surveys of the [West] . . . and has led Baron Humboldt into grave errors, and to commit personal injustice" (p. xiv). Humboldt's "personal injustice" remains unspecified, but Emory's refutation of a major European treatise on American nature, placed conspicuously in the opening of his *Report,* is a gesture similar to Thomas Jefferson's refutation of Georges Buffon in *Notes on the State of Virginia* (1784). Jefferson's interest was in disproving Buffon's theory of dissipation: that all species in the New World tended toward decline and extinction, a tendency evident in their smaller size. Humboldt's *Views of Nature* appeared during the continuing controversy over the Buffon thesis, a moment when, as Antonello Gerbi notes in *The Dispute of the New World,* it was the obligation of every thinker to comment on the question.[31] Humboldt's claims in *Views* effectively reinvented (in the words of one critic) America as nature: the continent was alive and "ripe," as it were, to European interpretation. (And ripe to economic exploitation. Humboldt became rich from South American mining.)

Emory's interest was in heading off a Humboldt-style set of assumptions about the border region. As with Jefferson's Virginia, Emory's landscape was a microcosm of American virtues, and he had to defend it, as Jefferson's generation had done before, from European influence and domination. The only other scientist named in the *Report* is the American astronomer A. D. Bache, Emory's father-in-law and the grandson of Benjamin Franklin. (West Point, Emory's alma mater, had a curriculum designed by Franklin, eschewing classics and instructing students in science and mathematics.)[32] Bache had taught Emory a system of surveying through the use of astronom-

ical observations; father- and son-in-law corresponded frequently when
Emory was in the field.[33] Where Humboldt's influence might have introduced the landscape as a continuum in a European narrative about America, Emory specifically rejects this possibility and claims the area as one that
Humboldt and his like cannot map, describe, or conquer.

Emory portrays the border as the natural tableau for the national drama
lately played out in the Mexican War: nature confirms the recent develop-
ments of politics. He claims that "the border is embraced in the zone separating the tropical from the temperate, more northern regions" (39). His
nature lexicon immediately announces a liability of the Mexican side, which
is tropical while the United States is temperate. The charge of too much
"tropical heat" recalls the Buffon thesis refuted by Jefferson. "It is fortunate," Emory continues, "that two nations, which differ so much in laws, religion, customs, and physical wants, should be separated by lines, marking
great features in physical geography" (39). Emory's theory of the border
is that it has only been placed where nature dictated, and will only enhance
the natural order by separating two immiscible cultures. Emory sums up
these differences in his comments, earlier in the *Report*, on regions not gifted
with the "temperate" personality of the north. Stranded on the Isthmus of
Panama before the survey, Emory observes a place crammed with hopeful
miners on their way to the California gold rush, and an example of northern and southern temperaments:

> The state of Panama, with its mongrel race of Indians, negroes and Spaniards,
> with their intellects obfuscated by bigotry, and *their bodies enervated by a tropical
> climate*, was wholly unequal to the task of receiving [the influx of miners]. For-
> tunately, the mass of them was *the self-governing race of the whites of North Amer-
> ica*, and when disorder and confusion seemed inevitable, propriety resumed
> the sway, and a germ of civil liberty and self-government was planted for the
> first time in that mis-called republic (2; the emphasis is mine).

Emory's sense of national difference was based on the idealization of
Anglo-Saxons then current in American and European race theory. Certainly his views on race are unsurprising for the 1850s, but in terms of his
border survey, these views prevented him from keeping nature separate
from history. Emory does note that the border exists in "a neutral region,
having peculiar characteristics, so different as to stamp upon vegetable and
animal life features of its own" (39). But that peculiarity was provided by
the ideology that propelled the Mexican War in the first place: manifest destiny. Indeed, Emory announces that the border exists precisely as a function
of that ideology, which must come from nature: "The boundary is a good
one; and if the United States is determined to resist what appears to me *the
inevitable expansive force of her institutions and people*, and set limits to her territory before reaching the Isthmus of Darien, no line traversing the conti-

nent could probably be found which is better suited to the purpose" (39; the emphasis is mine).

Like the promising western vistas of Virginia described by Jefferson (which pointed to California), the border was not merely a treaty line but a reassuring sign of American "force," which, Emory notes, the United States was curiously "determined" to restrain. His tone here is difficult to characterize —a triumphant joke, or disagreement with any Mexican treaty at all?—but Emory invests the border with enormous symbolic power, and he draws it to restate certain self-evident truths from the era of Jefferson. And the border itself is not characterized as a made-up line, the product of politics, when Emory describes it as a line to be "found" (not placed) across the continent.

Historical succession, then, provides a justification for Emory's observations along the border. The central theme of this history is the decline of Spanish civilization to a point of ruin, owing to its inherent weaknesses, thus facilitating the American takeover. And the landscape says as much. A series of ruined water reservoirs, left by the Spanish, prompts this reflection: "The remains of these wells were found, and they form one of the many external objects to be seen throughout the extent of the frontier which convey the impression that the country has steadily gone backwards since the days of the Spanish rule" (57–58). Further scenes prove that the Spanish never deserved the territory, because they were incapable of making it prosper:

> This town [El Paso], although built in the sixteenth century, and possessing a very considerable trade, does not contain a single stone, brick, or wooden building. The houses, of one story, are built of adobe (mud and straw), and the tops covered with tile, grass, or mud. . . . They resemble very much the ruins of the houses described in the oases of Syria, and particularly in the dimensions of the rooms, which are accommodated to the rude carpentry of semi-civilized nations (92).

Emory's interest in ruins, specifically those found in Middle Eastern desert oases, marks out his picturesque point of view—a convenient aesthetic system for filling the desert with meaning. In this sense, a desert was a useful means of conveying the vintage of a landscape that was, after all, entirely new to Emory's party, and moreover a parcel of the "new" world. If America had a desert, then perhaps, like Syria, it would also have ruins, and history: it was part of the picturesque endeavor to find them. Picturesque values— preferring ruins to the present; defending the rights of fancy; dealing slackly with science—mark out an effort by Emory to accomplish his exploration strictly within picturesque terms.

One of the nagging problems of travelers' views of America was always the scarcity of ruins, a deficiency that had to be recuperated through the overemphasis on such ruins as there were.[34] It is a frequent paradox of American writing: if ruins prompt in the observer a sense of historical succession, then the privilege of the American historical present, for an American observer of ruins, is to confirm that decline and fall are in evidence, but do not obtain for the observer's American empire. The observer should, by the sense of his historical position, be observing also from a position of decline, but somehow he is not; rather than observe after the fall, the picturesque traveler observes, evidently, after the redemption. In a landscape that will only just permit a railroad passage, Emory nonetheless focuses on the possibilities of cultivation.

Emory's picturesque view likewise provides the somewhat arbitrary boundary line (decreed, after all, in order to run a railroad line) with national history and national promise. The sense of promise, to be fulfilled now that American "force" can be unleashed in the new land, is a by-product of a picturesque aesthetic that sees potential cultivation in every scene. Emory's Hispanic history is organized around patterns of steady decline, even as his natural history denies the Buffon thesis and rejects European scientific expertise altogether; decline will be transformed by the providential American arrival. Where there was nothing, Americans will create—just as in the picturesque, where there was only random nature, a picture will appear.

Emory's picturesque accomplishes this feat by focusing on just one of the features of the picturesque: irregularity. As I described previously, the irregularity of the picturesque was not extraordinarily challenging to viewers, but rather provided only comparative roughness and range to otherwise "pretty" scenery. The principle of irregularity—typically expressed in picturesque paintings and gardens by an irregular set of shrubs, or a serpentine brook, or a ruined monument or grotto—signaled that nature could be appreciated for its asymmetries and imperfections, rather than for its subjugation into formal gardens or unrealistic ideality. The imperfections, after all, were minor and unthreatening, and ultimately subject to the requirements of the picture. The imperfections of nature represented in the picturesque—which are not to be thought of so much as flaws, but as variations in natural form—simply threw into high relief the overall harmony of the scene as a whole. Indeed, the irregularities ultimately were proof that the scene *was* harmonious.

Thus the chief irregularity occurring in Emory's *Report,* the mysterious delays in funding from the government, can be regarded as a picturesque variation on form. They do draw the viewer's attention, but only in the interests of proving the transcendent harmonies and promise of the scene overall. Historians have reviewed the circumstances of Emory's survey frequently with an eye toward theorizing about government exploration funding in the 1850s, but have not made the connection between Emory's narrative in the *Report* and the way he presents the funding crisis.[35] Just as Emory notes that "nodules of more durable [sandstone] project beyond the weather-worn surface of the softer sandstone, producing picturesque appearances" (66), so he can observe of financial difficulties that they prove the presence of an overriding merit and virtue. In one case, the delays occur when the entire company might have decamped for the gold rush to make their fortunes ("the field of gold was spread before them" [6]), but not one man leaves, despite the government's "failure." Like any other hardship in picturesque travel writing, this failure is minimized by its subjugation to the larger themes and impressions of the *Report*.

Some of the illustrations from the *Report* meant to verify that the American Southwest was different, redemptive, and picturesque actually provide a case study in this effort of Emory's. Indeed, the illustrations went to some pains, despite the scarce material proof at hand, to confirm the assertions of the *Report*. For example, in *View on the Prairie between San Bernardino and the San Pedro, Looking West along the Parallel 31°20' (No. 2)*, we observe a desert landscape: a foreground plane with Joshua trees and cacti, a rolling middle plane, to the left a large hill, and to the right an infinitesimally sized flag (see figure 7). We are to imagine the scene bisected by a border. Like figure 8, below it *(View on the Prairie between San Bernardino and the San Pedro, Looking West along the Parallel 31°20' [No. 3])*, the representation of what Emory has claimed as an obviously differentiated pair of climatic and political zones does not really reflect this difference. It is difficult, for instance, to see where the alleged tropical and temperate zones are. It is even more difficult to imagine where the borderline is. In *Near View of the Initial Point of the Boundary Line on Parallel 31°20' Looking South along the Meridian* (see figure 9) and *View from Initial Point of Boundary Line on Parallel 31°20' Looking North along the Meridian* (see figure 10), the lack of difference is even clearer: if we reversed the captions on these illustrations, it would not matter, because the northern view looks almost identical to the southern.

But the artist faithfully observed the formulaic picturesque style, so that even in so dull a picture as *View on the Prairie* we can find our way through receding planes from foreground to background while enjoying some of the irregularities of the scrubby foliage. The flatness has successfully been composed into a *scene*. The flag, too (which in other views is larger, and is in fact an American flag), typically appears at a vanishing point in the horizon and occupies the point where, in a more eventful landscape, the eye would naturally be drawn. With little overwhelming physical evidence that the United States looks very different from Mexico, the flag offers a symbolic object to contemplate. Like the character in Molière's play who was shocked to discover he had been speaking in prose all his life, the viewer may also be surprised to find a barren region now endowed with Americanness.

The tedium of this landscape is relieved in later views, when another artist introduces charming foreground botanical illustrations to enliven the flatness of almost-undifferentiated desert. In *View from Iron Monument No. II*,

VIEW ON THE PRAIRIE BETWEEN SAN BERNARDINO AND THE SAN PEDRO, LOOKING WEST
ALONG THE PARALLEL 31° 20′ (Nº 2)

Figure 7. *View on the Prairie between San Bernardino and the San Pedro, Looking West along the Parallel 31°20′ (No. 2)*, from William H. Emory, *Report on the United States and Mexican Boundary Survey*, vol. 1.

VIEW ON THE PRAIRIE BETWEEN SAN BERNARDINO AND THE SAN PEDRO, LOOKING WEST
ALONG THE PARALLEL 31° 20′ (Nº 3)

Figure 8. *View on the Prairie between San Bernardino and the San Pedro, Looking West along the Parallel 31°20′ (No. 3)*, from Emory, *Report on the United States and Mexican Boundary Survey*, vol. 1.

Near the Edge of the Colorado Desert Looking East towards Monument No. IV (see figure 11), the flag, used as a distance marker and vanishing point in earlier views, is now in the foreground. *View from Iron Monument* is almost comic in its inclusion of posed desert props, such as the animal skull and the rattlesnake. Animal bones often provide a memento mori, and if that is so, the death must surely be Spain's (it occupies the "southern," or right side, of the scene). The skull is an artifact of both science and art, to be incorporated into the American sense of history—a transaction made especially conspicuous by the flag having been planted right into the skull. The foreground tableau in figure 11, as in figure 12 *(View from Iron Monument No. II, Looking South West towards the Cordilleras of Lower California)*, is a vivid example of the sometimes-strained quality of the picturesque, attempting to frame and

NEAR VIEW OF THE INITIAL POINT OF THE BOUNDARY LINE ON PARALLEL 31°20 LOOKING SOUTH ALONG
THE MERIDIAN

Figure 9. *Near View of the Initial Point of the Boundary Line on Parallel 31°20' Looking South along the Meridian,* from Emory, *Report on the United States and Mexican Boundary Survey,* vol. 1

VIEW FROM INITIAL POINT OF BOUNDARY LINE ON PARALLEL 31°20 LOOKING NORTH
ALONG THE MERIDIAN

Figure 10. *View from Initial Point of Boundary Line on Parallel 31°20' Looking North along the Meridian,* from Emory, *Report on the United States and Mexican Boundary Survey,* vol. 1.

comment on the vista in the receding planes even at the expense of aesthetic gravitas.

Military artists in America worked largely in the picturesque tradition, and struggled, as Emory's artists did, to depict the vast scale of American scenery within a European aesthetic more suited to modest-size views.[36] (This problem of difference in scale, had it been introduced, may well have refuted the Buffon dispute.) The illustrations in Emory's *Report* do not entirely dispel the sense that the territory in the Gadsden Purchase is arid and uninteresting, try though they do to present that aridity in as high an aesthetic as was then available.

The imaginative interest of these scenes is supplied by Emory's claims in the *Report,* visually symbolized by the flag, that the purchase of the Gila River

VIEW FROM IRON MONUMENT Nº II. NEAR THE EDGE OF THE COLORADO DESERT LOOKING EAST
TOWARDS MONUMENT Nº IV.

Figure 11. *View from Iron Monument No. II, Near the Edge of the Colorado Desert Looking East towards Monument No. IV,* from Emory, *Report on the United States and Mexican Boundary Survey,* vol. 1.

VIEW FROM IRON MONUMENT Nº II. LOOKING SOUTH WEST TOWARDS THE CORDILLERAS
OF LOWER CALIFORNIA.

Figure 12. *View from Iron Monument No. II, Looking South West towards the Cordilleras of Lower California,* from Emory, *Report on the United States and Mexican Boundary Survey,* vol. 1.

area was part of a drama of American ascendancy, to which even unsuspecting desert scenes were subject. His readers will note the heroic triumph of America in the Far West, represented both by Emory's specified historical succession and by the triumph of the picturesque illustrations to make sense of random nature. The two not only overlap: they are the same triumph.

The capacity of the picturesque to reign in a disordered landscape is appropriately figured in a survey of a border—itself a means of limiting and controlling space. These physical descriptions, though, are inanimate without the spark of national expansion behind them, an energy with its own inner tensions. The survey provides a prospect of inevitability and infinity, alongside a description of limits and controls. Although Emory endorsed the program of continental expansion that began with Jefferson, the borderline with Mexico must have provided, as a painting provides, a more congenial means of organizing and comprehending the vast space of that continent, and justification of the place of the republic in it.

4

Emerson's 1830s

In 1881, Oscar Wilde, on tour in California to lecture about aesthetics, summarized the perils of nature worship in the United States. A ladies' luncheon
club and artistic society had proudly exhibited its work to him, including a
set of china painted with landscapes. Wilde advised: "I do not see the wisdom of decorating dinner plates with sunsets and soup-plates with moon-
light scenes. . . . we do not want a soup-plate whose bottom seems to vanish
in the distance. One feels neither safe nor comfortable under such conditions."[1] Wilde, speaking a year before Emerson's death, was addressing a nation deep into its gilded epoch, in "safety" and "comfort" after war and re-
construction, and one that sought in pictorial nature—mistakenly, as he
pointed out—the assurances of uncontroversial good taste.

In the bourgeois leisure regimen of decorating one's china with natural
"scenes," American nature had come a long way from the comparatively ecstatic 1830s, when Emerson wrote about nature not as if it were parlor decor
but our primal source of enlightenment about the mind of God. His *Nature*
(1836) specifies quite a different view of nature and art. One feels neither
safe nor comfortable: "*Nature*, in the common sense, refers to essences unchanged by man; space, the air, the river, the leaf. *Art* is applied to the mix-
ture of his will with the same things, as in a house, a canal, a statue, a picture." This *Nature* is difficult to picture on china plates. Emerson's interest
in these "essences unchanged" began in the late 1820s and (as with Wilde's
audience almost sixty years later) shows national interests at heart. Emerson
imagined the American continent not only as the culmination of westward
movement and exploration, but as a bequest from nature on loan to history.
It was a way of describing nature and nation in the same breath. He came to
this conclusion, as it happens, by thinking about the primal Americaniza-
tion of nature: the expedition of Columbus.

Early in 1827, Emerson had written in his notebook from Washington Irving's *History of the Life and Voyages of Columbus*. He had found a favorite text suddenly puzzling. He copied down dates and places from the voyage, noting that Columbus returned from his discovery "not quite seven months & a half from the time when he sailed thence."[2] The journal indicates that, days later, he was still working out—arithmetically if not philosophically— the significance of Columbus's voyage: in the margin he subtracted 1492 from his own year, 1827, with no comment on the result.

The Columbus sum, though, seemed to come back to Emerson frequently. As with many such hints in the universe that implied to Emerson cosmic planning (such small episodes of wonder are a common feature of his prose), the Columbus figure seemed powerfully suggestive. In a habit of mind that readers of Emerson will find familiar, we see him redouble his confidence in the universe by moving evenly from faint traces to ringing metaphysics. Drafting his Sermon LXIII in 1829, for instance, he wrote a paragraph resolving the difficulty of understanding Providence, which was admittedly "too vast for human optics" (*JMN* 2:176). The solution, he mused, was to use small clues to infer great notions, or "to pick up here & there a pebble contrivance, & say see! a God! as Newton thought." Emerson was repeating (and appropriating) Newton's own biographical metaphor of himself as a child on the beach collecting pebbles; he also was sketching the intellectual processes of the argument from design.

The argument from design is a line of thought that constitutes a significant part of Emerson's philosophical activity in the 1820s and 1830s and culminates in *Nature*. The journals tell us that in this period, Emerson reverted frequently to design arguments, in moods good and bad. In fact design was never so savagely depicted by Emerson as in 1829: "see! a God!" seems to take enthusiasm for design to a new imbecility. But despite his skepticism toward it, the logic of the argument from design seemed to validate for Emerson a long series of momentous ideas, such as the purpose of the Columbian discovery. Columbus's purpose, for Emerson, was not to discover America (which, coincidentally, he did), but to overcome intellectual routine: "Five or six facts independently of almost no value, made the discovery of America in Columbus's mind & it took as many centuries to accumulate them. One man sees a fact & secures it which is to him altogether frivolous but inestimable to the race when seen in connexion with another fact that not known for 100 years after" (*JMN* 3:176).

The virtue of Columbus, for Emerson, was in his synthesis of the frivolous, miscellaneous observations of other men. To discover not a God that made the world, but a new world that needed to be discovered—the teleological argument for Columbus held America as the endpoint, not God as the starting point. Emerson perceived Columbus's genius in his mental fitness, not in his discovery. And design had taught Emerson this style of reasoning. Design for Emerson was "not a proof," observes Jonathan Bishop, "of the existence of an anthropomorphic divinity, but evidence of the human mind in its natural action of finding patterns."[3]

Some patterns, of course, were better than others. Explorers in general struck Emerson this way, as achievers whose minimal equipment made their discoveries seem the result of having superior minds. Indeed, Emerson admired Columbus elsewhere for having a "mind as solitary and self-subsistent as any that ever lived" (*JMN* 4:107). (Walt Whitman, writing for the *Brooklyn Daily Eagle* in 1847, shared Emerson's devotion to Columbus as the progenitor of American political genius and called Jefferson "the Columbus of our political faith.")[4] And finally: "Columbus came almost in an open boat. Throw in mind against matter; an energetic purpose is as good as a century of improvements. And the planetary system," concludes Emerson with a flourish, "was ascertained by Copernicus without telescopes" (*JMN* 3:325).

America and its discovery was a mental exercise for Emerson, one to which he became increasingly devoted in the 1830s—in part as the natural development of his intellectual system in *Nature,* and in part to respond to the expansionist politics of Jacksonian Democrats. As Carolyn Porter observes, Emerson's America was western-facing: "Jefferson's step beyond the Constitution's dictated powers [to purchase Louisiana] was to . . . create the America in which Emerson found himself in the 1830s and 1840s."[5] The American continent suddenly had to answer questions about private theories of ecstatic nature as well as broadly public ideas of manifest destiny. The answers it provided to both queries were difficult to tell apart, a problem against which Emerson struggled with limited success.

In this chapter and the next, I place the design argument in its 1830s American context: the discourse of nationalism. I discuss the natural history lectures that form the basis of the best-known of Emerson's essays, and after a fashion, I sneak up on *Nature* and its claims for national exceptionalism that so far have not been critically described. I also discuss the intellectual motives for Emerson's choosing such a mixed philosophical endeavor—that is, his interest in the antiquated design argument, despite its growing political associations with Jacksonian America. Although the discussion of nature and Emerson seems familiarly and automatically one of imported Romanticism, with only various "influence" questions left to settle (Coleridge or Carlyle? Goethe or Wordsworth?), the veneration of nature was not only a matter of Romantic formula for him. Nature for Emerson was animated in American exploration journals and in the accounts of the westward expansion of the continent.

The somewhat unexpected means to this Western exploration "influence" is through the knotty theology of the argument from design, and the seriousness with which Emerson tried to apply it to America without its conversion to a similar, but debased, version of the argument—namely manifest destiny. Under the direction of national design logic, the idea of Columbus *must* have suggested to Emerson the solution to the vastness of Providence: to fail to see this equation of discovery and destiny would be to deny the truth of the senses and the fitness of the mind. But such conclusions about a fine American fate were available to more than one mind at a time; indeed, they were the sport of Jacksonian Democracy. The next chapters will trace the previously unobserved connection between Emerson's interest in nature and his qualms about colluding in the nationalism of Jacksonian rhetoric and with the party he conceded was simply "more magnetic" than its opponent.[6]

THE NATURAL HISTORY years in Emerson's career have attracted attention for a number of reasons—reasons that have not fully defined the importance of the period. First, the lectures are described familiarly as finger exercises to the ecstatic outburst of *Nature:* they reflect Emerson's desire to synthesize the logical conclusions of science with the intuitive, visionary mode of Romantic nature worship. Stephen Whicher offered this view of the career in 1953 in *Freedom and Fate,* and it has proved resilient, appearing again in Robert D. Richardson, Jr.'s most recent biographical account of the 1830s.[7]

I find the limits of such an assessment in the biographical fallacy that *Nature* was inspired by Emerson's epiphany in the Jardin des Plantes in 1832, and thus strictly in a European context; and, similarly, that Emerson's understanding of landscape and natural science was a French import. The recent *Emerson Museum,* by Lee Rust Brown, is the best of these Jardin des Plantes studies, and admirably situates Emerson in the world of French natural science.[8] Brown is excellent at conjuring up those Parisian cabinets and gardens, at showing what they looked like to Emerson, and why. But the centrality of Emerson's American sources—mainly exploration narratives, such as those discussed in earlier chapters—tell a different story about Emerson's naturalism, and perhaps about American nature. The lectures of the 1830s have a quality not typical of French natural science, namely nationalism. Indeed, natural history for Emerson took place primarily in America: the discipline of natural science and the United States possessed a common philosophical lineage and purpose. French scientific sources, and indeed cosmopolitan Romanticism itself (as Brown acknowledges), are not an explanation of Jacksonian political turbulence, nor of Emerson and the West; at most they offered Emerson an intellectual model that he would transform—and sometimes simply ignore.

Emerson's natural history lectures have a second critical charm, in that they offer evidence for reading him as a secular and an inchoate modern, even as the forerunner of various poststructuralist schools of thought. Julie Ellison and Richard Poirier, for example, have found in Emerson a proleptic history of twentieth-century literature and criticism. Both of these readers find in the 1830s the origins of Emerson's use of "theory" as well as an identifiable Jamesian Pragmatism.[9] Robert Weisbuch has updated the post-dated Emerson even further, and declared him postcolonial.[10]

In my view, all these studies miss the religious content of Emerson's scientific curiosity. Kevin Van Anglen has offered a corrective to this "myth of secularization." Rather than begrudgingly admit that Transcendentalism had simply a "religious dimension," he argues, we might avoid the very un-Transcendental error of separating careers into "secular" and "religious" components at all—components that were perfectly fused, after all, for Emerson himself.[11] The natural history lectures and the years preceding *Nature*—imagined so frequently as a secular career move by Emerson, as if the ministry had been a temporary repression of his "real" affections for science—might better be seen for the ways they continued, rather than severed, his religious training and faculties. "What is really astounding," Perry Miller reminds us, is that "most of the ardent celebrators of natural America serenely continued to be professing Christians."[12] The tenor of New England liberal Protestantism provided that mental possession by nature was not "secular"; getting into the mood of nature was to fall into line with one of the most devout religious sensibilities of the times.

Another imprecise view of Emerson's 1830s has been of his political dispassion. Although the Jacksonian strains of his individualism and idealism already have been theorized (in, for example, Sacvan Bercovitch's 1993 *Rites of Assent*), Emerson's actual politics, for many critics, did not commence until the 1840s, when he began to take abolitionism and women's suffrage seriously, or until 1850, with the painful passage of the Fugitive Slave Law—in other words, until Emerson became recognizably "liberal" or, sometimes, "progressive." Maurice Gonnaud's estimable study, *An Uneasy Solitude*, offered a superior engagement with the available evidence on Emerson's politics and also concluded that the 1830s represented his "flight away from social commitments." Len Gougeon finds even the 1837 address on slavery simply derivative of W. E. Channing's book on the same topic; the entire decade was mere "prologue" to Emerson's "public commitment" to abolitionism years later. John Carlos Rowe dates Emerson's awakening to 1844, when he delivered the "Address on the Emancipation of the Negroes in the West Indies." Emerson's "intellectual schizophrenia," Rowe alleges, also surfaced in this moment: *Nature* has no serious politics and thus eventually, "when [Emerson] endorses a liberal political position, he must abandon transcendental principles"; he must trade youthful idealism for real issues. Robert Milder has found a way to declare Emerson a radical, but only during the years 1837–42; *Nature* still resolutely "predates open ideological involvement with the times."[13]

Aside from using the vexing anachronism *liberal* to describe the reform movements and progressive causes of the 1840s, the understanding of *Nature* as somehow a prepolitical essay suggests that its jaunty metaphysical propositions about merging with the godhead have only an antipolitics, or perhaps a meliorist politics, built into them.[14] But as David Van Leer points out in his superb analysis of Emerson's philosophy, "idealism is not a naive doctrine"; "one does not stumble on it by accident, without calculation," nor by disregarding the world of politics that surrounds one.[15] Given the deep theological origins of *Nature,* as well as its interest in the rhetoric of continental exploration, I cannot agree that the 1830s were "prologue": theological debate, as the Puritans would attest, leads seldom to the "blessed fruits of sweet communion," and 1830s America, of all times and places, was hardly free of national politics.[16]

We might better see the 1830s, and the natural history lectures, as Emerson's trials of method, philosophical as well as political. I have described the ways that national meaning in the early nineteenth century was contested in aesthetic terms, and that those aesthetic terms were burdened, as they had been since Romanticism began, with moral gravitas and a jumpy political pulse. The story of a moment of origin always begins to sound like fighting words; but let us say that, conservatively, at least as early as William Blake's desire to build Jerusalem in England's green and pleasant land, the description of a national landscape was no longer settled, was no longer nonpartisan, and was no longer individual or harmless. In America, itself aspiring (or perhaps slouching) toward Jerusalem, the stakes were higher. No man, observed Emerson, "owns the landscape" (*CW* 1:10). But who controls it?

THE DESIGN ARGUMENT states that from the manifest design of the world we can infer the presence of a designer.[17] Such an intellectual habit, as I have suggested, is well fixed in exploration writing; while explorers had no particular interest in theological issues, their struggles with landscape resemble the intellectual processes described by the design argument. That is, to talk about the design argument, you posit an observer, who ranges through nature and perceives order in it and draws conclusions from that perception; this observer is, by any other name, an explorer. The design argument in America, then, is intact in a genre quite distant from theology, namely in the literature of exploration.

If design did not inspire "enthusiasm," or piety of an exuberant and irrational sort, it did please many Deists, whose sober tracts on the argument from design were standard works of the period and were well known to Emerson from his reading at the Harvard Divinity School. The design argument was also a form of argument that tended to be popularized, so that its appearance, unacknowledged, in American exploration narratives should not surprise us. It was formulated among theologians and shaped by philosophers, but the design-argument habit of mind is cardinal in Western literature—from the Nineteenth Psalm, where "the heavens declare the glory of God, and the firmament sheweth his handiwork," to William Wordsworth's sermons in stones (borrowed, of course, from Shakespeare).

Design arguments frequently advert to national destiny. The New England Puritan conception of Providence, for instance, is an argument that closely resembles design. Providence, or providential history, had been ascribed to the New World continuously since 1492, particularly by the religious refugees who arrived in New England in 1620.[18] For Providence, like design, infers divine intentions from observable phenomena; but its scope is the entirety of history, and its objective the apotheosis of a nation.

In the eighteenth century, Thomas Paine, not known for his defenses of divine planning and intention, made a claim in *Common Sense* that was already a commonplace of Dissenting historiography: "The Reformation was preceded by the discovery of America: as if the Almighty graciously meant to open a sanctuary to the persecuted in future years, when home should afford neither friendship nor safety."[19] Paine's description of America as the divinely intended haven for refugee Protestants, though a bit tepid around the phrase "as if," reiterates the logic of finding in a random series of events, or in the chaos of nature, the orderly design of God. And in Emerson's own time, the rhetoric of American providence had been taken over by Andrew Jackson and the Democratic Party and reformulated as manifest destiny, so that the nation was ordained for our possession and prosperity.

The tendency for the design argument to sound like national history is a frequent liberty taken with it, especially in narratives of American history. The record of the confusion between design and providence is worth reviewing, so that we can appreciate Emerson's attempt to make sense of them separately.

The Puritans' emigration to Massachusetts was, by their own descriptions, "providential." This general term announces the presence of divine planning in an otherwise undistinguished series of historical events. The Puritans also held a belief in "special providences," or miracles. "Providences" are individual events that deviate from expectations, but which can be accounted for, somehow, as God's will. The singular "providence" is broader in scope: it is the theory that from the entirety of a history, we can discern God's plan. "One should bear in mind the contrast," notes a critic of Emerson and science, "between the religious concept of immutable law and that of . . . fickle and capricious 'illustrious providences.'"[20]

Providential history, like design, proceeds analogously: from observation, we infer divine intentions. The two arguments are often taken to be identical. Perry Miller's analysis of Puritan design, for instance, presents it as a species of providence: "The record of humanity was to [the Puritans] a chronicle of God's providence, *exactly as* occurrences in nature . . . were significations of His governing will."[21] Sacvan Bercovitch reviews the co-existence of providential history and natural theology, linking them first to Cotton Mather's and Jonathan Edwards's textual hermeneutics; then, in Emerson's *Nature*, he finds the combination of "the terms of Puritan and Romantic salvation," a line of continuity that "demonstrates the sustained influence of Puritan secular hermeneutics." This continuity is certainly intuitive, even if the history of ideas might not bear it out: "[it] follows logically," notes Bercovitch, "from the Puritan concept of errand."[22]

Design prompts our study of nature to discover its laws and systems and is best understood as a basis for "pure science," or the inquiries that simply increase our knowledge of nature. The Enlightenment motto, "study nature," assumed that from right observation, right conclusions would follow. Providential history also encourages the discovery of laws and systems and then declares, from the explication of historical narratives, their completion and fulfillment in the future. (Puritan typology, for instance, is a practice in providential history.)[23]

But as a quick survey of Newton or Paley will suggest, for every law of design, there is a corresponding admission of imperfect observation. Indeed, for Paley, writing after Hume, our inability to make perfect observations is not couched as an "admission," but rather as another proof: "If there were but one watch in the world, it would not be less certain that it had a maker." Paley argues not that a chain of evidences leads to the proof of divine agency—which then relies on the strength of every link of the chain for success—but rather that design "is an argument separately supplied by every separate example." The conclusion is foregone; the individual observations may be false or simply eclectic: "the eye proves [design] without the ear; the ear without the eye."[24]

Typology and providential history rely, by contrast—and with some urgency—on the correctness of *all* examples and the accumulated chain of proof. There were no eclectic details in providential history, amusing though we may find them today. For instance, Increase Mather once famously noted that the shape of an unusual cabbage, in its resemblance to a scabbard, prophesied the future outbreak of the French and Indian War. (He was writing after the war.) Augury from a cabbage may strike us as comic, but in the strict economy of Puritan providence, it was unthinkable to let such evidence go to waste.

Puritan theology, in advance of Newton's *Principia Mathematica* (1687), did not separate design from providential history, so that the rationales look similar for both. The natural theology read in Puritan textbooks endeavored above all to assert orderly laws of nature, so as to insist upon their being broken when miracles occurred: the solidity of natural laws gave weight to all contrary natural occurrences, namely miracles or "special providences." Miracles, or disorderly natural occurrences, were always a theological problem. The problem was solved, in Miller's account, by some Puritans "proclaim[ing] their cessation with what looks suspiciously like relief;" natural law could not otherwise prevail. The hush-up, as it were, did not go unnoticed. Finally, "insistence on special providences in late seventeenth-century New England is the most noticeable response of its theologians to the new science." Providential history, Miller shows, generally makes its case as natural theology does: "proof of God's existence is [in] the ordinary and constant course of things."[25]

Thus, science (namely Newton's mechanics) contributes to design its crucial difference from providence: design, fully articulated, accommodates—and usually welcomes—deviations from the course of things. Design is a more bizarre account of human life. But whether or not design and providence share a similar "hermeneutics" is a conclusion, then, that shifted over the centuries. The shifting state of the argument is significant because of Emerson's own view of the problem in the 1830s, and his attempt at a new synthesis.

In Miller's and Bercovitch's formulations, providence and design (on the one hand) make possible the interpretation of divine will and (on the other hand) are themselves made possible by the Puritan practice of interpreting divine will. Either design and providence provide tools of analysis, revealing the order in random phenomena, or they are the philosophical results of an analysis that seeks order. The sum of these two postulates—Miller's and Bercovitch's—offers providence and design the identical cause and effect. The two theories are no doubt as hermeneutically based as Bercovitch suggests. However, this account does not consider, particularly in the case of Emerson, the historical development of design quite apart from providence, and thus the real interest of Emerson's fusing them. Emerson's use of design—which is, finally, a skeptic's argument—signals his departure from the skeptical limits posed by the eighteenth century.

EMERSON'S NATURAL HISTORY essays from the 1830s took up the recombination of two philosophical positions, design and providence, into one theory of animated American nature.[26] Emerson's hope was to preserve design (and, surely, America) from the debased form of the theory that the Jacksonian Democrats had brought into currency. Emerson's efforts were primarily philosophical; his endeavor in this period was to deploy the best metaphysical formula of nature imaginable as a spur to moral action, namely as resistance to the slipshod and empty "individual" that the Jacksonians had created. This individual was proclaimed the inheritor of the American landscape, and Emerson was outraged by this individual's thin philosophical and moral content. The natural history lectures, focused strongly on landscapes, eventually brought Emerson's celebratory prose back to the individual who could perceive and reclaim those landscapes.

The philosophical affinity of design and providence had been weakened by the starvation diet of rationalism in the eighteenth century, so that refulgent analogies between historical providence and the design of nature were increasingly called into question, as in David Hume's *Dialogues Concerning Natural Religion*—Hume was a thinker whom the Harvard Unitarians, for one, found "terrifying."[27]

Emerson's response to this growing estrangement was not skeptical analysis, but instead buoyant and apparently counterintuitive accounts of the dazzling abundance of nature, no longer proof of Christianity for Emerson, but of American exceptionality. Design, bearing the accumulated weight of philosophical controversy, was finally to be established in *American* landscapes. Emerson's interest in American landscapes was eclectic, sometimes referring to real places he knew and revisited, but more often invoking imagined regions such as "the Far West." His references, if of unspecified location, are nonetheless quite specifically American, and generally anti-Jacksonian. The nature essays resolve old arguments not only about natural order, but also about the historical succession of nations.

The decision by Emerson to take up design and make it over was an unusual one, given the options in the early nineteenth century. But the period preceding the 1836 *Nature* is a rewarding one for observing Emerson's quick synthesis of science and philosophy, and it can begin to account for his reverting to design. Inaugurated by his declaration in the 1833 *Journals* ("I will be a naturalist"), the 1830s and the preambles to *Nature*, his series of natural history lectures ("On the Relation of Man to the Globe," "The Naturalist," and "The Uses of Natural History"), reveal that Emerson's attention was more and more drawn to the possibilities remaining in the design argument. It was already an antique by the time Emerson took up natural history. Design was structurally intact (and, from accounts, still widely accepted),[28] but lacking the centerpiece of a cosmic first cause.

On the other hand, there was little of commensurate philosophical rigor to take its place. The Unitarian Church, the most liberal form of Christianity open to Emerson, still instructed divinity school students in design—even though Unitarian minister William Ellery Channing, in an 1821 sermon, had declared its stringency "atheistical and at war with all sound philosophy."[29] Daniel Walker Howe has reviewed Unitarians' devotion to design and their misgivings toward it: he corroborates Unitarians' basic conservatism (the Unitarians were a "safe and comfortable" class), which rejected the potential radicalism in, say, Kantian Idealism, and opted for the comparative prudence of an antique theory such as design. Given the Unitarian interest in science and technology, moreover, it is no wonder they welcomed a theory that found its proofs partly in botany and geology.

But finally, Howe concludes that, as with Channing's worries about an overmechanized cosmos, Unitarian confidence in design may have been "whistling in the dark."[30] Given the range of intellectual options, it was by no means the clear winner when the Unitarian conscience, Howe shows, was candid with itself. For one thing, it seemed both a bit retrograde (even for Unitarian Cambridge) and also a bit radical. Harvard moral philosophers occasionally voiced an interest in a theory that was more up to date, but they sensed the danger to religion in moving too swiftly: "There is nothing in the scientific study of nature," promised one preacher, feebly, "to hinder men from . . . becoming religious."[31]

Emerson's theory of nature, then, solved a problem Unitarians had, but never solicited help in solving; he offered a version of design and providence that was not nostalgic but innovative, fusing the two after their long estrangement and making science the instrument of religious ideas. In the natural history lectures (and in *Nature,* as I argue chapter 5), Emerson recapitulated—and then recommenced—a lengthy polemical background to design and providence. It took him eventually to the ecstatic national amour propre of his essay *Nature.*

Emerson was quick to see the aridity of some statements of design, as his natural history lectures indicate, but was cautious, at first, to discard them for other available counterclaims. One of the variations on design that intrigued Emerson for some time was Emanuel Swedenborg's theory of correspondences. Perry Miller has puzzled over Emerson's attachment to Swedenborg, when similar philosophical conclusions might have arisen for Emerson from reading Puritan divines. Miller's confusion suggests, again, the imprecise contemporary equation of providence with design: "It is strange that the generation of Emerson and Alcott should have had to go to Emanuel Swedenborg for a doctrine of 'correspondence,' since *something like it* had been embedded in their own tradition for two hundred years."[32] Emerson's decision to go to Swedenborg was a discovery of what was then the most coherent philosophy to combine design and providence. For Emerson, it had not been done before. And to judge by his eventual disaffection with Swedenborg, it had not been done right.

The doctrine of correspondence delighted Emerson during his first encounter with Swedenborg, communicated to him through Samson Reed.[33] *Nature,* in 1836, at the height of his enthusiasm, contains numerous Swedenborgian echoes.[34] Swedenborg, a geologist and engineer turned theologian and mystic, suggested in his writings of the 1740s that "correspondences" were manifest throughout the universe, linking the spiritual world to our material world. His theories were based in the scientific observation of phenomena, as design theory often is, and were also as comprehensive, historically, as providence often is. His mechanistic model attempted to reconcile scientific hypotheses with Christianity, and the Swedenborgian cosmos was constantly in the process of being simplified by the explication of correspondences.

As two biographers of Emerson have shown, his interest in Swedenborg was short-lived. The account of Swedenborg in "The Poet" (1841) restates the doctrines ambivalently: "I do not know," observes Emerson, "the man in history to whom things stood so uniformly for words" (*CW* 3:20). By the mid-1840s series "Representative Men," the essay on Swedenborg lays to rest the possibilities of correspondence: "Swedenborg's system of the world wants central spontaneity. . . . All his types mean the same few things. All his figures speak one speech. All his interlocutors Swedenborgize" (*CW* 4:74–75). The central flaw, for Emerson, lay in Swedenborg's fear of doubt and a system that too urgently sought to allay it: "He thought," laments Emerson, "as large a demand is made on our faith by nature, as by miracles" (*CW* 4:63). Swedenborg, it seems, did not distinguish carefully enough between the reassurances of providence and the eclectic beauty of design. Emerson's own theory of correspondences would focus entirely on this distinction.

The effort at apologetics sometimes precedes disbelief (as with the weak protestations of the Unitarians that science was nothing to fear), but in the case of Emerson, the design argument needed only a removal from theological stalemate into a theory of nature that would get us somewhere, namely the promising landscape of the Far West.

TAKING UP DESIGN is of interest to Emerson's thought not only *because* he did it, but because of *when* he did it. The oscillating careers of design and providence arrived in Emerson's writing to be reconnected in his nature essays. And it is useful to note that, given the options, such a reunion was not philosophically inevitable.

As an introduction to this process, it is interesting to discover that among Emerson's lectures on the topic of design was a poem on design, "The Rhodora," composed just as the natural history lectures were completed.[35] The elaborate philosophical responses contained in the lectures meet the claims of previous thinkers on their own ground; that is, Emerson deployed prose to refute writers of prose. "The Rhodora," however, is an extended sonnet of sixteen lines, and as verse it is not a thundering refutation of Swedenborg or Paley in their own polemical terms. The poem offers a strong critique of design and sets forth a series of problems that the lectures and *Nature* address.

The attack on design in verse form was probably also meant to meet and reply to the other contenders in the business of nature theory: the Romantics and their shared devotion to design, or "sermons in stones." Emerson's strategy in "The Rhodora" was to improve upon the monotony he found in Romantic nature reveries and to broaden a modest individual space or landscape into transcendent national nature. It is a sign that such expansion, for Emerson, was intellectually legitimate, even if it did unwittingly lead him to endorse the expansion then taking place in the Far West.

In the 1820s Emerson recorded in his journal frequent excerpts from

Byron's poetry and meditations on the Romantics, all of whom, somehow missed the mark: "A Romantic age, properly speaking, cannot exist," he declared in 1823 (*JMN* 2:194). The effort by Byron and others to restore dignity to the individual by freeing and even cultivating his spontaneous responses to nature seemed to Emerson programmatic. The man who memorized long sections of *The Prelude* during college was still sneering, in 1822, at Romantic "sepulchral grottoes" and "Gothic ignorance" (*JMN* 2:75). Emerson saw the exuberance and liberty of Romanticism already cramped by its repetitious landscape and architectural metaphors. The fetishization of ruins in Wordsworth and Byron particularly became, for Emerson, the process of "desolate and disgusting corruption" by "the worm and the reptile" (*JMN* 2:75).

One of the mottoes Emerson transcribed into his journal in the early 1820s was Byron's line from *Childe Harold's Pilgrimage,* "Pass not unblest the Genius of the place." The phrase was the unofficial motto for an idealized union of mind and landscape. But by the end of the entry, asserting "another prospect," Emerson had altered Byron's language and dedicated his journal to "the Genius of the Future" (*JMN* 2:74–75). *Place,* changed in this early journal entry to *Future,* is a typical and ongoing conceptual change. The nature essays eventually would bear out this tendency in Emerson to include in an idealized landscape the historical procession represented, for him, by America.

The landscape of "The Rhodora" is not especially Romantic. There is no single Romantic nature poem, but one feature of Wordsworth's and Byron's landscapes is their preoccupation with ruins (as in *Childe Harold* and "The Ruined Cottage," and in Percy Shelley's "Ozymandias"). The Romantic ruins poem, in one view, "substitutes nature for culture. . . . Wordsworth interrogates the landscape politically."[36] But "The Rhodora" lacks the commonplace ivied ruin; the landscape is notable instead for its freshness and color. The ambivalent view of design contained in the poem is couched, in part, as a rejection of Romantic interest in decay, because those features, like design itself, were becoming increasingly formulaic. The potential political interrogation of landscape in "The Rhodora" is also rejected, because the ruins poem offered minimal satisfactions to Emerson. "The whole of it," he shrugs over Byron and the decaying Romantic landscape, "amounts to what?"

Here in full is "The Rhodora: On Being Asked, Whence Is the Flower?":

> In May, when sea-winds pierced our solitudes,
> I found the fresh Rhodora in the woods,
> Spreading its leafless blooms in a damp nook,
> To please the desert and the sluggish brook,
> The purple petals, fallen in their pool,
> Made the black water with their beauty gay;
> Here might the red-bird come his plumes to cool,

And court the flower that cheapens his array.
Rhodora! if the sages ask thee why
This charm is wasted on the earth and sky,
Tell them, dear, that if eyes were made for seeing,
Then Beauty is its own excuse for being:
Why thou were there, O rival of the rose!
I never thought to ask, I never knew;
But, in my simple ignorance, suppose
The self-same Power that brought me there brought you.[37]

The poem rehearses the principles of design in a tone that can barely rise to the occasion. A single flower is meant to verify the spiritual truth of the senses: "if eyes were made for seeing, / Then Beauty is its own excuse for being." The strongest impression of the poem is its skepticism, indicating that design was far from a settled question for Emerson in 1834. The subtitle is our first clue. Emerson evidently was offering the poem as a real answer to a real question, a view his biographer supports, linking its composition to an exhilarating moment of "extraordinary vision" in the Mount Auburn cemetery that Emerson had experienced the month before.[38] As with Paris in 1832, nature had posed its questions and Emerson had hurried to record the answers in his journal. He evidently felt a rush of natural coherence that prompted his poem—the same feeling that made decay and ruins, for Romantics, the paradoxical sign of restoration.

But we cannot read "Rhodora" as a ringing defense of design. (One would not fully emerge for Emerson until 1836.) The poem expresses skepticism by duplicating, in part, the formal logic of Christian apologetics—the analogical reasoning and the straightforwardness of faithful questions that always lead to faithful answers—while sloughing off its logical conclusions. The logic of a defense is evident in the question-answer structure of the poem, which raises an issue, and elaborates it theologically. The poem's ending, linked syntactically with the meditations of the speaker ("in my simple ignorance, [I] suppose[d] / *The self-same Power that brought me there brought you*"), also stands on its own as an answer to the question in the subtitle. The previous fifteen lines of the poem, then, are simply a series of steps in the "proof" of the final line. Like William Blake's "The Lamb"—

Little Lamb who made thee?
. . . Little Lamb I'll tell thee.

—"The Rhodora" speaker is someone for whom design is an insight from daily observation, not an arid scholastic conclusion. The pedantic charge of the question-answer is diffused over the course of the poem, as, say, a parable successfully makes its point without a *basso profundo* moral pronouncement.

On the other hand, the question-answer structure begins to eat its own tail: it introduces doubt about its efficacy. Emerson, like Hume, had already expressed his exasperation over the use of Christian "evidences," the proofs that subjected universal truth to merely local argumentation. He described in his journal in 1832 a "teacher, when once he finds himself insisting with all his might upon a great truth," then blunders, and settles for simply "a cautious showing how it is agreeable to the life and teaching of Jesus" (*JMN* 4:45). His complaint concerns the enfeebled quality of a backward proof: we might better believe in the grandeur of "truth is truth" rather than the workmanlike defenses of truth as a "vehicle" for Christianity, complete with the endorsements of Jesus.

It is likely, therefore, that a poem from 1834 would itself bear the weight of this complaint. Thus the question, "On Being Asked, Whence Is the Flower?" appears, from the viewpoint of a poet skeptical toward logic, to be parodic of that same logic. The bizarrely hypothetical "occasion" for "Rhodora" is more obvious when we extend Emerson's implied subjunctive in this way; we can hear not just the sense of "When I was asked . . ." but instead "*If* I were asked." If the speaker were asked, he would conventionally answer: design. But noting the reprimand in the *Journals* from 1832 toward any "cautious showings," the poem fails to convey its conventional answer successfully. If the question may be read as disinterested or skeptical, the answer comes across as deliberately platitudinous.

We see this quality, in part, in Emerson's logical diction, the "if-then" statement that constitutes the central assertion of the poem: "*if* eyes were made for seeing, / *Then* Beauty is its own excuse for being." Here the buried subjunctive of the title is stated outright in the "if" half of the sentence, and as with the title, the mood suggests the meagerness of the available terms. That is, Emerson hypothetically entertains the full argument of design, and pursues the logical steps design entails, but evidently cannot posit them in declarative certainty. Design is offered, literally, for the sake of argument.

The vocabulary of logic in the poem is a kind of landscape terracing, a technique that attempts smooth transitions between levels, but only draws attention, here, to its own changes in elevation, changes that can cause logical missteps. Design, it seems, is nobly intuitive, but intellectually suspect. The overt naïveté of the "Beauty" couplet compliments our logical faculties while it parodies the conclusions the logic of design offers. Perhaps Beauty is not Truth after all.

THE LECTURES EMERSON offered during 1833–34 were devoted to the problem posed by "The Rhodora." That problem—namely, how can we discard design when it is so gratifying to the spirit? and how can we save it when it is so malnourished by logic?—would culminate, in part, in the 1836 *Nature*. The natural history lectures attempted to synthesize Emerson's contemporary reading in science and his long-standing frustrations with "certain theological expressions" (as John Ruskin would archly call the design argument) while recasting the history behind both the science and the theology.[39]

The lectures are conventionally read as the product of Emerson's fascination with natural history, botany, geology, zoology, and taxonomy. His journals, his reading, and his book borrowing during these months confirm as much. But those three sources also tell us where else natural history unfolded its meaning: in the exploration of the New World.

In addition to enjoying Romantic favorites of travel such as Byron's *Childe Harold* and Goethe's *Italian Journey,* Emerson often read exploration narratives and reports. This interest began in approximately 1819, at Harvard. *The Quarterly Review,* which he read regularly, was to provide Emerson with a number of fascinating discovery articles; these items caught his eye, and in the following list I indicate where they cropped up in his lectures from the period (titles in parentheses represent lecture titles):[40]

1812   "Lichtenstein's Travels in Southern Africa" ("On the Relation of Man to the Globe")

1817   Robert Southey, "Accounts of the Tonga Islands" ("Permanent Traits of the English National Genius")

1819   "De Humboldt's Travels" ("On the Relation of Man to the Globe")

1826   "African Discoveries" ("On the Relation of Man to the Globe")

1830   "Life and Public Service of Sir Stamford Raffles," governor of the East Indies ("On the Relation of Man to the Globe")

Alexander von Humboldt was a particular favorite: Emerson borrowed often in the 1830s from at least two volumes of the adventures of Humboldt (which he took out of the Boston Library Society in 1831) to add details to "On the Relation of Man to the Globe" and his introductory lecture on English literature from 1835.

Here are more exploration texts we know Emerson read before the publication of *Nature* in 1836:

1821   Captain Cook, *Voyages*

1823   Louis Simond, *Switzerland; or, A Journal of a Tour and Residence in that Country*

1830   Sir William Edward Parry, *Journal of a Second Voyage for the Discovery of a North-West Passage from the Atlantic to the Pacific* (1821–23)

Sir William Edward Parry, *Journal of a Second Voyage for the Discovery of a North-West Passage from the Atlantic to the Pacific* (1824–25)

1832   Joseph de Acosta, *Naturall and Morall Histoire of the East and West Indies*

> Captain Basil Hall, *Fragments of Voyages and Travels*
> Thomas Jefferys, *A Description of the Spanish Islands and Settlements on the Coast of the West Indies*
> 1833   Washington Irving, *History of the Life and Voyages of Columbus*
> Mrs. Christian Isobel Johnstone, *Lives and Voyages of Drake, Cavendish, and Dampier*
> 1836   William Bartram, *Travels through North and South Carolina, Florida, the Cherokee Country . . . with observations on the Indians*
> Hermann Pueckler-Muskau, *Tour in England, Ireland and France*
> Sir John Ross, *Narrative of a Second Voyage in search of a North-West Passage (1829–1833), including reports of Capt. J. C. Ross and the discovery of the northern magnetic pole* [41]

We know also that the record of Emerson's book borrowing, from which the preceding list derives, logs his reading only partially: for example, the *Journals* reveal that Emerson purchased, in 1845, John Charles Frémont's *Report* on the exploration of the Rocky Mountains, a text that does not appear in the records of his Cambridge and Concord library borrowing, nor in the list of books in his own library. (His *Journals* show an ongoing interest in Frémont.) He wrote familiarly in his journal in 1826 about Walter Raleigh's *History of the World* and habitually, in the 1820s and 1830s, about Columbus's *Letters,* although their acquisition from a library or a bookseller was not recorded until 1842 and 1851, respectively.

There is also evidence in the bibliographical record of Emerson reading other exploration accounts but without a definite date. Because Emerson usually read exploration accounts soon after they were published, it is safe to assume that the following texts would have come to his attention by the mid-1830s:

> 1804   Jean Jacques Barthelemy, *Travels of Anarchasis the Younger in Greece*
> 1828   Frederick William Beechey, *Proceedings of the Expedition to Explore the North Coast of Africa*
> 1761   Pierre Francois Xavier de Charlevoix, *Journal of a Voyage to North America*

Then there is a third category of exploration reading by Emerson—books on the subject in his personal library. Again, we cannot determine when he read many of them, but I list here those that would have been available by 1836: [42]

> 1792   Jeremy Belknap, *A discourse intended to commemorate the discovery of America by Columbus . . . [celebrating] the third century since that event* (owned by Emerson's grandfather)

1769   Jean Bernard Bossu, *Nouveaux voyages aux Indes occidentales . . .*
        du grand Fleuve Saint-Louis, appelle vulgairement le Mississipi
1830   Hall Jackson Kelley, *A geographical sketch of that part of North*
        American called Oregon

And, finally, Kenneth Cameron has pointed out that in the Emerson household, one brother's borrowing from a local library frequently meant the
book was read by all the brothers.[43] Here are three exploration writings
from the household's lists of books borrowed:

1825   John Churchill, *A Collection of Voyages [to Hudson's Bay]*
1829   John Franklin, *Narrative of a Journey to the Polar Sea*
1820   Edwin James, *Account of an Expedition* (That is, of the Stephen
        Long expedition described in chapter 3.)

This inventory tells us a few things about Emerson's interest in the subject. The number of books indicates that exploration was more than merely
a casual interest for him; while they were always outnumbered by books on
science and theology, exploration accounts vied at times with history and
biography for Emerson's attention. It was also a lasting interest: in the 1840s
the numbers of exploration readings approximately doubled, and he kept
reading in the genre until the 1860s; the 1830s, in other words, were the
initial, enthusiastic phase of his interest in the subject. Emerson also seems
to have read about the minor local dramas of exploration—whether in the
polar regions or the tropics, in Oregon or Florida—in something like the
global spirit, of the larger campaign to map unknown territory and to carve
out, in most cases, the land that would comprise America. He read exploration accounts the way that others might read a serialized novel.

The *Journals* back up this view of the matter, and record an intense and
abiding concern on Emerson's part toward exploration and explorers as
episodes of national expansion and triumph. In the ten years before *Nature*,
Columbus is a perpetual topic in the *Journals*, encapsulating for Emerson all
the smaller efforts by, say, Parry and Ross in the poles, Bartram in the South,
Acosta and Jefferys in the West Indies, or later Frémont in the Rockies. Columbus was so important to Emerson, in fact, that he can hardly contemplate a human feat without mentioning the explorer. Emerson frequently
flatters the heroism and greatness of Columbus—he was one of the two
"gifts of the Old World to the New" (Lafayette was the other); he was a "divine man," a "preferrer of the still voice within"; he was the model for all
bold actions—to "launch out from the ignorant gaping World, & sail west
for a new world." In a trial of the later roll call of *Representative Men*, Columbus in the *Journals* is the equal of Wordsworth, Goethe, Newton, Handel, Ra-
phael, Shakespeare, Luther, Watt, Fulton, Washington, and Wren.[44]

Indeed, for Emerson, the greatness of discovery and exploration feats was more than simply the evidence of the smooth functioning of the cosmos: "men become *causes* . . . what is Columbus but Columbia?" he asks in 1833 (*JMN* 4:360), seeing in the personality of his favorite explorer the achievement and historical destiny of the nation. Discoverers and explorers simply returned from *terra incognita* with the evidence for claims that hardly needed proving—chiefly, that America was bound for glory, because its lands gave great men a chance to vaunt their exploring talents. He writes in 1836, perhaps as a memorandum of requisition to the universe: "Columbus needs a planet to shape his course on" (*JMN* 5:236).

Columbus also furnished for Emerson a beloved metaphor, one that could soar cosmically and also spread locally toward the American West. If Columbus was teleologically Columbia, then Columbia is God's plan for the land mass occupied by ever more restive Americans. In recognizably Emersonian terms, which might easily pass for Jacksonian fanfare about Western settlement, Emerson asks when we will embrace the American territorial prerogative: "Can we not trust ourselves? . . . Dare we never say, this time of ours shall be the era of Discovery? The morning twilight is grey in the East; the Columbuses, the Vespuccis, the Cabots of moral adventure are loosening their sails & turning their bowsprits to the main . . . the heart sails ever forward in the direction of the open sea." Andrew Jackson himself had averred, in his *Farewell Address* of 1837, that "if you are true to yourself, nothing can impede your march to the highest point of national posterity."[45]

The explorers Emerson mentions were well chosen: Columbus for his familiar place in the pantheon; Amerigo Vespucci for giving America its name; and Cabot—John, whose discoveries in North America ushered in the British presence there, and Sebastian, who sought the Northwest Passage. Such adventures were, for Emerson, the vanguards of "moral adventure," a phrase not strictly a matter of conscience, given the intricacy of his geographical language and his insistence on discussing real lands and real men. Discovery and exploration were the necessary work of the awakened heart let loose, as it happens, on real American territory.

The recurrent theological hints about exploration as a "moral adventure" lurk in Emerson's reasoning about it. He found exploration a powerful rite that he wanted to restore to its actual, animated substance. Just as transubstantiation is commonly misunderstood as a mere symbol of sacrifice and not the flesh itself, so with exploration; exploration dealt with a type of "real presence" for Emerson, as the communion wafer is the real body. (Of course, he had given up on performing communion for his parish in 1832, rejecting it as "absolutely incredible."[46] But the theory seems to have stuck.) Exploration in America verified that the divine was present in the American landscapes reported in discovery. Indeed, such elaborate and wildly successful enterprises could hardly be the product of chance: exploration in America had an oddly, but rationally, designed-looking history for

Emerson. So he would conclude a decade later that for Americans to aspire to the mind of Columbus meant we must take over more and more territory: we shall take "up the universe into [ourselves]. . . . Yonder mountain must migrate into [our] mind." The "design" of the universe would be mastered with the help of "Columbus, [and] Jesus" (*JMN* 9:441).

The natural history lectures, composed in this period of concentrated interest on explorers and morals, contain a lengthy and technical series of quarrels with the design argument, as if the only way to take up the universe into ourselves is to give eighteenth-century theology a good thrashing. It was not an inevitable route to the national apotheosis that Emerson had in mind. But theological technicalities were in many ways a saving quality to differentiate him from any other Western-dreaming Democrat, whose notion of taking up the universe was to exterminate the Cherokee, to seize California from Mexico, and to countenance a broadly imperial mode of federal expansion. Emerson focused on natural history and design because he could do no less when describing America; as chapter 5 discusses, he could take seriously the winning notion of a national "destiny" only by conferring on it a lengthy philosophical and theological history.

The natural history lectures, then, theorize about how to do design properly. Attacks on William Paley's theory of design, for instance, are a prominent feature. Emerson includes in "On the Relation of Man to the Globe" a vividly "Rhodora"-like meditation on the design of the body ("The eye is a miracle. The hand is another") that proclaims the "strict relation" between the senses and the body that carries them. As an example, he describes "the art of throwing a stone . . . studied" by young boys: "I well remember my own vain endeavors to make the stone hit the mark, by all the nicety I could use in carrying the hand skillfully, until, by chance, I one day forgot to attend to the motion of my hand at all, and looking only at the mark, the stone struck it. . . . If the eye is fixed intently on the mark, the hand is sure to throw truly" (*EL* 1:40).

The famous example of the stone and the watch that, as Emerson well knew, opens Paley's *Natural Theology* is here under significant revision. Paley had described the enigma of a watch found upon the ground and "the inference we think is inevitable, that the watch had a maker," and had contrasted it with the undesigned and unsuggestive appearance of a stone.[47] His argument emphasizes, in its anatomization of the watch parts ("coiled spring . . . elastic chain . . . series of wheels"), that complexity evokes design. The watch is Paley's real model; the stone is a mere counterexample, and by itself could not prove anything. From a conclusion about design, *Natural Theology* asserts a method for proving the inevitable inference.

Emerson's example, which reverses Paley's terms and finds sufficient proof of design, instead, in a stone, replaces the usual method of design. The efforts by the "hand" to hit the mark are hindered, evidently, by too much "nicety" in technique, which recalls Emerson's earlier complaints about the misuse of "evidences." (Even Newton, Emerson coolly observed in 1832, became a Unitarian [*JMN* 4:26].) More obvious, though, is the implied critique of the classic design argument, one that had deployed, evidently, the wrong item in its pair of objects. In Emerson's version, the stone, well thrown, is all that is required to hit the mark. "I will not stop," declares Emerson, "to draw the fine moral which speaks from this fact" (*EL* 1:40). That fine moral might be: a watch would be required as religious proof only by a thinker of too much nicety. The extravagance of the watch stands, in some manner, for a deeply overintellectualized position. The problem with design is not in its conclusion, but in its argument.

The attack proceeds again in "The Naturalist." In that lecture Emerson endorses a program of science education as a means of appreciating "the works of Creation": "Recur to Nature," he insists, "to guard us from the evils of Science" (*EL* 1:71). His chief example of an evil of science is our dependence upon the clock and our corresponding alienation from "a day as an astronomical phenomenon." The recurrence of the watch example in the lecture—repeated from its notable reversal in "On the Relation of Man to the Globe"—proclaims that the gloves, so to speak, are off. The lecture is not only a polite adjustment of Paley's example but a direct dispute: the watch stands for all the "crutches [that] destroy the use of the limbs they are meant to aid." "We are so enslaved by art," grumbles Emerson, "that we always know it is about half-past four or twenty minutes of five." Instead, we ought to relearn the natural signs, the "solstices and equinoxes." Paeans to the day lead to repeated wordplay on "daylight": a country walk will allow a man to "see a day perhaps in a light in which he never regarded it"; he will see "the pines glittering . . . in the light every breath of air will make audible." The strictures of too much science are cast off by Emerson's incantatory tone in the lecture: "'It is Day. It is Day.' That is all which Heaven saith" (*EL* 1:71). Design is increasingly verified by the evidence of the eyes—eyes now, it seems, made for seeing. Emerson's well-known habit of aphorism in his essays has as its target here the specific logical aridity of Paley. These two lectures not only inveigh against Paley's bad logic, they suggest a counter-method that better suits the design argument, because that counter-method need never first deny design in order then to prove it.

Indeed, Emerson's growing frustrations with old design arguments cohere around this point, that skepticism is not always its own reward. Favoring the stone over the watch, and then blaming the watch for its power to alienate us from the day, Emerson rehearses the elevated claims in his lecture "The Uses of Natural History" and its assertion of an "occult relation" between man and nature. Paley, for Emerson, had been too content to show design with merely the logical minimum required for its proof. Design merits more. The closing lines of "On the Relation of Man to the Globe" proclaim its superabundance: "Design! It is all design. It is all beauty. It is all astonishment" (*EL* 1:49).

While he posits a more ecstatic design argument, Emerson also allows another line of thought, namely nationalism, its say in design. Emerson's journals during these years contain repeated entries indicating his concern with national issues. The natural history lectures, although nominally devoted to science, also contain asides on the topic of America, so that this period of composition, leading up to 1836, seems one of growing interest on Emerson's part in the philosophical uses of America. He was at some pains, here as later, to reject going national concerns in the politics of his America—specifically, the figure of Andrew Jackson and the Democrats, who evidently did not rank as representative men. (Not a single American would make that 1850 roster.) Emerson shared some of Jackson's exceptionalist rhetoric about the nation (as the "era of Discovery" journal passage suggests), but he was usually baffled and more often offended by what the Democrats did. Emerson's nationalism instead made America the historical heir to the accumulated philosophical controversy about design, where this old argument could at last be settled and its promise fulfilled.

Emerson was not alone in his sense that Jackson was leading Americans to bad ideas. W. E. Channing observed in his letter to Henry Clay on the annexation of Texas (1837) that "we must all admit a change. When you and I grew up, what a deep interest pervaded this country in the success of free institutions! And now," he lamented, "who cares?"[48]

In Emerson's "Relation of Man to the Globe," navigation and exploration voyages are examples of the "strict relation" between man and nature: our skills at seafaring, such as those displayed by Sir Francis Drake, suggest the achievement of that narrow interval "between perfect safety and total destruction" (*EL* 1:37). Proportion in nature means that "man is made just strong enough to keep his place in the world;" he is led by his wants "to the possession of the globe" (*EL* 1:37). Emerson's interest in navigators and explorers from the late 1820s to this, his first public lecture, suggests that the Columbus equation from 1827 continued to fascinate, and reminds us that the discovery of America would become one of Emerson's most frequently used metaphors for describing the course of providence.

In "The Naturalist," Emerson's criticism of Jackson is explicit. The program of science education outlined in that lecture possesses certain "intellectual influences," namely that the study of nature "restrain[s] Imitation, the vice of overcivilized communities" (*EL* 1:74). "All American manners, language, and writing are derivative," laments Emerson; "we wish to state facts after the English manner." The American indenture continues, even though "we are exonerated [from England] by the sea and the revolution." If we ignore the call to study nature, which inevitably "leads us back to Truth," the possibility remains only that "Time will certainly cure us [of Imitation], probably through the prevalence of a bad party ignorant of all literature and of all but selfish, gross pursuits." The bad party here is certainly Jackson's, whose defects qualify as "the vice eminently of our times, of our literature, of our manners and social action." Starting here what "The American Scholar" would complete in 1837, Emerson casts the national plight in terms of the landscape: American genius is evident only when it refuses servility to English models and resorts instead to its native and "permanent forms of Nature." American culture may yet achieve the radiant good of American nature, but only if Jackson and his bad party do not interfere.

The logic in "The Naturalist" and in "Relation" asserts that America, as Jackson himself might claim, has a manifest destiny in its landscape, and that it is only a matter of correctly reading the landscape to fulfill it. As with the complaint about Paley's design in the natural history lectures, the American continent confirms sound conclusions, but bad methods. Nationalism comes in for a similar critique: it is right that Americans long for a national culture, but that culture is, so far, put wrongly to use. Emerson concludes "The Naturalist" by intoning Jefferson: "No truth can be more self evident than that the highest state of man . . . can only coexist with a perfect Theory of Animated Nature" (*EL* 1:79).

"The Uses of Natural History" (1833) rounds out this set of lectures aptly, for it begins the questions raised by "Relation" and "The Naturalist" and marks out the areas that *Nature* will soon inhabit. As in "Rhodora," Emerson regards with skepticism the promise of design, and "Uses" is singularly terse on the subject of God. Indeed, Emerson would never again revert to design for the purpose of invoking the conventional "evidences" argument of the Unitarians. Instead, his philosophical efforts display exasperation at the very idea.

While design, as an intellectual edifice, is complex, Emerson in "Uses" deploys it for purposes that shrug off the scholastic tendencies that might necessarily accompany such complexity. Emerson begins asking apparently naive questions, such as the one that eventually launches his 1836 manifesto: *To what end is nature?* In "Uses," this naïveté is still expressed cautiously, compared to the unreserved ingenuousness of *Nature.* The opening sentence sets the tone: "It seems to have been designed, if anything was, that men should be students of Natural History" (*EL* 1:6). Like the eyes in "Rhodora," the aptitude and innate interest we show in the sciences, although they profit us in the manner that the lecture goes on to describe, are at best only a possible result of design. Evidently, other explanations obtain; but Emerson does not even approach this set of possibilities, as the lecture focuses instead on the meditative process that brings a perceiving subject (perhaps the "Man thinking" of "The American Scholar") toward the rewarding inquiries of natural history. Thus the skepticism evident in "Rhodora," which blames design for some of its faulty conclusions, is attenuated, and similarly,

Emerson announces not his expertise and authority, but his novitiate status: "I will be a naturalist." Design, which had had to be resuscitated from its Unitarian liabilities with some shrillness in other lectures, is fully accommodated in "Uses" to a new reasoning about nature. The real reward of design, as Emerson shows, is in obviating the need for skepticism at all.

Thus the nascent vocabulary of *Nature* in "Uses," as many critics have shown, celebrates the "occult" features of immersion in the natural sciences.[49] To be sure, the manifest structure of the lecture, which arranges the uses of natural history in an ascending list, does not strike us immediately as mystical or intuitive, just as the if-then language of "Rhodora" has been read as a straightforward display of formal logic. Emerson's uses for natural history are five: good health, practical uses, delight in contemplating the truth, salutary effects on mind and character, and as a means of explaining man to himself. "Uses," as a conspicuous departure from a sermon, makes use of a conventional lecture style while never approaching the conclusion that a lecture about design might well be expected to reach: it never shows that God exists. ("The most tedious of all discourses," Emerson would note in his journal in 1837, "are on the subject of the Supreme Being" [*JMN* 5:305].) This absence, in a lecture that nonetheless stages a gratifying crescendo in its list of "uses," reflects back, as "Rhodora" does, onto the uses, as it were, of proof. The more insistently logical Emerson's structure, the more self-satirical it appears; it does not thunder a proof of God, but rather alights on the gentle image, repeated from "Rhodora," of "the leaves of the lightest flower" (*EL* 1:26).

Another way of describing this self-satirical effect is to remind ourselves that the natural history lectures were Emerson's first secular career move, and as such were at some pains to make over the usual authoritative gestures present in sermons. The copious critical work on Emerson's lectures and sermons has yielded conclusions as uncertain as the border between these two genres. But the sermons remain, in the view of Emerson's biographers, relatively undistinguished among his literary and philosophical productions, while the lectures were his livelihood.[50] Emerson's secularity was not only in the process of dodging theology, but of adverting to his own kind of nationalism. The "challenge and the practice of skepticism in Emerson's early career," notes a critic, "turned him from the outer world to the inner, [but also] forced him to turn again and confront the world around him."[51]

Because Emerson insisted upon the amateur status of his knowledge of natural history in these lectures, and because their textual details display his refusal of the most erudite defenses of design, the alleged naïveté of the natural history lectures, and in particular *Nature*, continues in the criticism: the essay may never shake its nickname, "the Happiness Pill."[52] Emerson's discovery in the early 1830s that skepticism was not inevitable coincided with his trials of method, particularly the methods that design might retain after its skeptical component was removed. Indeed, if design did not permit a skeptical analysis of the cosmos, such as the type evident in Channing's sermons, what good was it? [53] But how could design, which asserted only the vacancy of nature without God's presence to infuse it, be worth the trouble? As with other philosophers after Kant, Emerson recognized that design, to be useful at all, must not lapse into the archaic claim of mysterious and occult causality. Nor could Emerson tolerate the extravagant "Ideal Theory" of Bishop Berkeley (whom he would especially target in the "Idealism" chapter of *Nature*), where reality was *all* subjective ideas. Emerson's method in 1836, for which the essay *Nature* is termed naive, transformed design into a tool of revelation—of discovering "uses" for nature that did not rely upon mere teleology.

5

Emerson's *Nature*

West of Ecstasy

I read nothing in St John or St Paul concerning the planting of America or the burning of Anthracite coal. Yet as I sit here in America by my anthracite coal fire, I cannot help thinking that there has been somewhere a design that one should be inhabited and the other burned.
RALPH WALDO EMERSON, *Journals* (1835)

Manny Schwartz and Andrew Jackson—it was hard to say them in the same sentence.
F. SCOTT FITZGERALD, *The Last Tycoon*

The conviction that nature is always American is most evident in Emerson's writing when, as in the journal excerpt above, philosophical possibilities are converted into natural facts. Lumps of coal are designed for burning, just as America is designed for planting. (It is only a minor oversight of the Gospels to neglect trenchant geological and agricultural comment.) [1] The proofs in this comparison of coal and America are analogous, if not interchangeable; Emerson sees the same plot everywhere.

Nature is probably the best statement of this plot. It is also the work that so encapsulated Emerson's genius and speculative boldness that, in the opinion of one critic, it was "never afterward surpassed." [2] *Nature* is the most popular work in the Emerson canon, and it has been read theologically, philosophically, ecologically, biographically, psychologically, and (enigmatically) as "the Happiness Pill." [3] It has seldom been read politically.

That reading, which is the project of this chapter, relies on Emerson's interest throughout the 1830s and 1840s in discovering an alternative politics to the increasingly repugnant program offered by Jacksonian Democrats. Born into Federalist Boston, which became Whiggish Boston in the 1830s, Emerson wanted a party called "Democrats" to be democratic; he was quick to see how little they were. Rather than consent to the logic of continental expansion, whatever its costs—a program with a primary assumption of an American exceptionality and a manifest destiny—Emerson instead looked for another version of this Jacksonian design argument, one that retained intellectual rigor but avoided political misstep. Correcting perceptions is a process that has its best trials (and successes) in nature: nature could restore the blind man "to perfect sight."[4] Nature, therefore, would also permit Emerson to correct political perceptions at the same time.

Nature is not the obvious vehicle for this politics, and in part the problem is terminology: even the title *Nature* does not announce nationalism the way (say) *The American Scholar* does.[5] If, however, we can imagine a methodology in which America is an assumed term—a sort of philosophical given, a question always posed rhetorically and formally for Emerson by nature—then we may find in *Nature* a peculiar but vivid set of proofs for American exceptionality. These proofs are organized around the critique of what philosophy might accomplish in *Nature* and the call, advanced also in *The Method of Nature,* for a method based on "ecstasy." The presentation of this critique would have been a topic of some national interest, in part because of the flaws in Jacksonian democracy, which for Emerson were primarily epistemological. If Emerson could show that skepticism and Idealism both failed to account for nature adequately, he could then posit a new method for contemplating nature: a method, similar to the argument from design, that just happened to present a resistant position to the Jacksonian Democrats.

Nature, then, is usually the last of his great works to suggest a politics. Chapter 4 reviewed some of the explanations offered for Emerson's devoting the 1830s to natural history, a period and a topic that strikes many readers now as the disinterested preliminary to his later political seriousness. I described my objections to such a view, in its misreading of Emerson's religious and scientific vocations; its understanding of his natural history as the product of European training; and its insistence that his natural history must be ideologically neutral. Given the centrality of *Nature* to American letters (Richard Poirier has even suggested that "Emerson . . . *is* American literature") the political reading seems crucial indeed.[6]

Emerson usually had to award topics, even political ones, a philosophical lineage and purpose simply in order to take them seriously; and conversely he had to match up the philosophers he liked against the plangency of local color. The writer who called wild mushrooms "these little Vegetable Self-conceits [that] front the day as well as Newton or Goethe" also pointed out that "Fichte, Kant, Schelling and Hegel . . . lack the confirmation of having given piggy a transit to the field."[7] The designs of anthracite coal and of America confer on each other not just rustic values, but also philosophical gravitas. It is possible to imagine even the Democratic Party, when taken seriously, similarly decked out in philosophical colors.

It is also possible to see it that way in Emerson's journals and letters. Even as natural science took its imaginative hold for Emerson, the other topic he wrote about frequently in the 1830s was national politics. Even on the way to Europe, he wrote that he hoped to catch a glimpse of its spirit of place, or its animating principle, something he could best describe as "the America in America" (*JMN* 4:106). He wrote exasperatedly to Thomas Carlyle in

1834 about Andrew Jackson: "a most unfit man in the Presidency has been doing the worst things."[8] His journal entries on politics often complain about the moral inadequacies of presidents and parties. In 1834, after Jackson's reelection, Emerson was relieved that at least Jacksonian rhetoric had not yet taken on board "the depravity that says, 'Evil be thou my good.'" Jacksonians, he suspected, may even reform: "the patriot will still have some confidence in the redeeming force of the latent i.e. deceived virtue that is contained within the . . . party." In the same year, he denounced Jackson's "unmixed malignity . . . withering selfishness . . . [and] impudent vulgarity," which were quite enough to cure Emerson "of his appetite for longevity." In 1838, as the Democrats won a third term in the White House, he wrote the well-known "Vanburenism" entry about "one wholly reversing my [moral] code," and facetiously terming the local party boss a "philosopher": "I hate persons who are nothing but persons. . . . All the qualities of man, all his accomplishments, affections, enterprises except solely the ticket he votes for, are nothing to this philosopher" (*JMN* 7:99). In all, the errors of the Democrats seemed to Emerson not strictly political but also epistemological, or even simply cognitive: lacking Transparent Eyeballs, the party simply didn't see things the right way. These are Emerson's recurring themes: first, that nature could correct errors of perception, even those by a "Bad Party," and second, that politics was really just a vulgar case of philosophy.[9]

Thus *Nature* generally proclaims its American politics in the form of corrected perceptions, even if the uncorrected (vulgar) case is not (vulgarly) identified. Emerson found both the fondest reaches of Idealism and the worst excesses of populism in his America, and *Nature*, his "little book," is a polemic to reclaim the one without the other. His strategy was to identify and glorify design—the theological argument that infers a divine purpose from local observations of nature—and to carefully protect it from Jacksonian design, or what would eventually be called manifest destiny.

The first section of this chapter reviews the status of the argument from design as Emerson inherited and revised it. His view of the design problem in *Nature* requires this background. In the second section I discuss the politics in *Nature* that arise from the logic of design. Finally, the third section discusses the elaboration of these ideas in Emerson's later essay *The Method of Nature*.

EMERSON'S ORIGINAL TITLE was *Nature and Spirit,* but in 1835 he changed his mind; he took out the second term in a move that mildly shocks one Emerson critic: "it is as though Lévi-Strauss had decided to call *The Raw and the Cooked* simply *The Raw.*"[10] But removing *spirit* didn't mean that the topic was gone from the work. On the contrary, it must have occurred to Emerson that spirit already was redundantly there, part of the cosmic assurances offered in the world, and that *nature* was the term that needed overspecifying.

And in the Introduction, Emerson (in order to overspecify) makes the first of many counterintuitive claims, that "nature" also means "art." Philosophy says so: "Philosophically considered, the universe is composed of Nature and the Soul. Strictly speaking, therefore, all that is separate from us, all which Philosophy distinguishes as the NOT ME, that is, both nature and art, all other men and my own body, must be ranked under this name, NATURE" (*CW* 1:8). On the one hand there is (immaterial) spirit, or Soul; on the other hand there is nature, which includes everything else. The case has been made for spirit, or Soul, so often and so thoroughly for Emerson that not only will the title omit it to avoid gauche philosophical overstatement, but the unfamiliar case, Nature, will be described instead.

Several points follow from this arrangement of the two terms in his Introduction. The first is that nature is the philosophical headquarters of the work. Natural science, therefore, is a philosophical technique: mushrooms, for instance, can lead us to Newtonian physics and German Idealism and, in the end, to a new sort of American politics. Second, nature is large—larger than just the usual range of sex, sunsets, and springtime—and its purpose is as a kind of aide-mémoire for spirit. Third, nature's capacity to remind us about spirit is its central benefit to us. Emerson would claim throughout *Nature* that the depth and variety of spiritual associations in nature are its chief merits, as if the cosmos existed in order to shout *"spirit!"* to us on a regular basis.

This logic, that specific terms are *implied* by other specific terms (*spirit* by *nature*, mainly) may need reiterating, because it is a philosophical gesture that would also inform his politics. "Nature always wears the colors of the spirit" (*CW* 1:10), notes Emerson in chapter 1, a claim that can shake off its bad-taste saccharinity when we imagine not just pretty and vaguely spiritualized landscapes (perhaps more sunsets), but instead the more insistent point that nature has no being without some kind of *a priori* spiritual assent. In this light, the rules are fairly strict.

These rules of being in nature are the sort that the design argument provides. If we take William Paley and his 1803 *Natural Theology* as the representative case of design for nineteenth-century American readers, then in *Nature* Emerson is fairly faithful to it, with a few significant exceptions. Paley's argument, introduced in chapter 4, runs this way: when we observe how designed-looking the world is, we draw the inevitable inference that it had a designer. If you found a stone on the ground, it would suggest nothing to you about its origins; but if you found a watch on the ground, its complexity and intricacy would cause you to infer logically that it had been made. The central features of Paley, for Emerson's purposes, are first that *nature looks made:* nothing about it ever strikes Emerson as unsuggestive or negligible or random. (Emerson's term for this condition is that nature is "emblematic.") Second, *nature has a purpose:* in *Nature,* its purpose is to remind us of spirit. Its "emblematic" quality makes these spiritual reminders possible.

Paley, it is true, was less interested in this second part of the design argument. Deists in particular, uninterested in divine commands, found in design a specific and useful proof of God's existence: He was the passive hat stand on which morality and meaning could be hung, and not the definer of ends and purposes. So in the early eighteenth century, especially as science demonstrated more of the delightful complexity of the world and the fact that purposes were often complex, the "physico-teleological" argument became a commonplace; it had its formal statement in Paley, among others. We see in the universe an intricate order that allows things to function not so much toward a specific end as precisely in accord with one another. Such order is evidence of an orderly architect, and cumulatively, it proves a universal God. The obvious metaphor for this argument from design was clockwork: God engineered the cosmos, set it ticking, and had no need to intervene again. But the real difficulty of the argument from design was that few skeptics would agree to it: in order to declare telos it was necessary to put one's faith in an orderly appearance of nature, which struck many thinkers instantly as both superstitious and uninformed. Thus, Emerson's antiskeptical reinvestment in the teleological aspect of design is his significant deviation from Paley and the form that the argument from design had acquired by the 1830s. Despite everything philosophy had determined by then, and all evidence to the contrary, Emerson turned to design.

In *Nature*, the evidence of this position is partly in Emerson's philosophical naïveté, a rhetoric of (for instance) old-fashioned teleological questions such as, "To what end is nature?" The work does not stake out the far reaches of skepticism; it does not wield Occam's razor; it does not evangelize for doubt. Instead, it reviews possible arguments from design in its chapters and finds not a careful and selective set of proofs, but a superabundance of them. Emerson described the technique this way: "Design! It is all design. It is all beauty. It is all astonishment."[11] This superabundance appears later in his lecture *The Method of Nature* as a voice behind your head (and, incidentally, it appears in the Columbus diaries as a voice from the heavens[12]) that you heed but may never see.

Nature does appear as though it could have been written by a skeptic, or at least a logician. It is structurally suggestive, like a watch found on the ground. It even alludes merrily to skepticism, under the mock-solemn phrase, "that Appearance we call the World" (*CW* 1 : 29). Its chapter headings advance us logically from small topics to large ones, presenting "Commodity" and "Beauty" for early treatment and reserving "Idealism," "Spirit," and "Prospects" for the end. And indeed, the thesis of *Nature*, that nature corrects errors of perception and reorients the mind toward spirit, is enacted in these headings, which begin in the material and end on the ideal.

In this way, the four material chapters "Commodity," "Beauty," "Language," and "Discipline" fulfill the plan announced in the first chapter, to show that the world is "transparent with . . . design" (*CW* 1:8). But most likely not Paley's design: Paley, a skeptic, had devoted only two pages of *Natural Theology* to the material suggestiveness of the watch on the ground, and the rest to its implications. (Perhaps his own example impressed him, at some point, as a little too much based on appearances.) By way of comparison, each of the material chapters of *Nature* multiplies examples like the watch in order to emphasize just *how much* the structural suggestiveness of nature can suggest. In other words, where Paley had sped from his example from nature to its theological implications, Emerson loiters over nature like a priest-botanist, pausing for some time in every episode of proof. It does not bore him; sometimes there seems no point in moving on in the argument. The possibility of arriving, many times, at the same sacred conclusion seems to Emerson a singular privilege, not to mention an inevitable human function: "Man is never weary" of it (*CW* 1:9).

The disappearance of nature altogether in "Prospects," then, has less of a sense of logical advance than of grammatical liberty. Nature does not so much disappear as change cases. Already in "Commodity" it had become both noun and verb: "Nature, in its ministry to man, is not only the material, but is also the process and the result" (*CW* 1:11). By "Prospects" there are still nature-verbs like "snow-banks *melt*" and "wind *exhale*," but "we learn to prefer imperfect . . . sentences" (*CW* 1:45).

Nature takes on skepticism, then; but it also makes an explicit attack on Idealism. This attack seems to have the same shape as Emerson's rejection of skepticism. Its proofs seem to Emerson flawed in the same way. Skepticism simply does not get you anywhere, nor does it present the case correctly: Paley's skeptical methodology had asked us to believe nothing at all about the material world and then, on the basis of one example, to believe one thing only. *Nature* asks instead for more matter, with less art. The conventional Idealist, figured primarily in *Nature* by George Berkeley, errs along similar lines, denying that "things are ultimates" or that nature has "an absolute existence," and instead insisting that nature is "an accident and an effect." This view Emerson finds a philosophical burlesque, only for the frivolous. It asks us for hostility to nature: to believe nothing that we already know through "instinctive belief" about matter—namely, that it exists—and instead to posit only what Berkeley would call "certain traces in the brain."[13]

It was announced by the subsidiary position of *spirit* in the title that *Nature* would not be an idealist's text. The "Idealism" chapter admits of Idealism only to the extent that *Nature* itself admits of skepticism. In the latter case, skepticism is only a means to an end: that is, skepticism can partially provide the argument from design. The limits of skepticism, for Emerson, are visible at all those points in *Nature* (they are frequent) that insist, anti-skeptically, on a teleological universe, which is design's real purpose.

And in the case of Idealism, Emerson refutes Berkeley simply by point-ing out that the Ideal Theory, whether intellectually frivolous or not, makes no difference to our experience of nature, and also (significantly) no differ-ence to nature's existing only for us—to nature's having a telos. The smooth and elegant functioning of nature, whether Ideal or real, is "alike useful and alike venerable" (*CW* 1 : 29). In fact there is even something in Idealism that must lead to teleology: it is unlikely, Emerson points out, for the universe to be both Ideal *and* meaningless. The mind would not posit nature in order *not* to comprehend it.

This philosophical critique in *Nature* places Emerson finally in a position of partly reconstructed skeptic-idealist, or some other half-measure of Ro-mantic intellectualism. My purpose in reviewing it is to show how the design argument serves him when nature is under scrutiny—there are rules and ordering principles, and from them nature acquires its philosophical gravi-tas and we our "occult relation" to it. I also want to emphasize to what ex-tent the survival of teleology preoccupied Emerson. When the topic is Amer-ican nature, the precision of that teleology will be essential, lest he fall in with the Jacksonians.

PERRY MILLER POINTS out that in the 1830s and 1840s, Americans were en-thusiastic about nature almost to the point of apostasy: "If here and there some still hard-bitten Calvinist reminded his people of ancient distinc-tions between nature and grace, his people still bought and swooned over pseudo-Byronic invocations to nature. It was a problem, even for the clear-est thinkers, to keep the orders separate." This enthusiasm was a condition of which *Nature* is a key symptom: "We get nowhere with Thoreau, Whitman or Melville, until we recognize how they revolved around, or struggled with, the propositions of *Nature*." The mood, according to Miller, was national-Romantic.[14]

But not uniformly. There were different versions of—perhaps the re-mains of "ancient distinctions" within—this mood. If it was nature's nation, it was also Jackson's age. The period was one, New Englanders said, of vul-garized politics: the rise of the Democrats was accompanied by a transfor-mation of tone, if not also overtone, of the democratic process. Jackson cashed in on rustic origins; his party was referred to by the Whiggish *Boston Gazette* as the Philistines.[15] Primarily an economic position, though—based on antiaristocratic preferments for the common man, hard money, and support of industrial development with minimal government regulation—Jacksonianism commented on land, to be sure (the age was a bacchanal of real estate speculation), but not land*scape*.[16]

Instead, Jacksonian enthusiasms about the American continent were re-

Figure 13. *American Progress, or Manifest Destiny,* by John Gast. Oil on canvas. Courtesy of the Autry Museum of Western Heritage, Los Angeles.

served for its potential for fulfilling political aims, particularly through western expansion. And although Jacksonians did insist on America the beautiful, they also continued to describe the continent as a beautifully empty one, requiring settlement and cultivation by a vast cadre of rugged individuals. This land would have no particular character until it was occupied. An example of this view is in John Gast's *American Progress, or Manifest Destiny* (see figure 13). Painted in 1872, it depicts westward movement by settlers and farmers, who urge forward the railroads and helpfully eliminate the obstruction of progress by removing Native Americans. In the center is the gigantic female figure of Progress herself, named "Star of Empire," draped (barely) in a neoclassical white frock, stringing telegraph wire as she goes. The land in front of them is being emptied of Native American occupants and buffalo as they advance; the drama of progress occupies the central pictorial space.

The Jacksonian method of filling the continent with Progress was only one option in the nineteenth century, and was an expedient one. Jacksonians might as easily have taken up, say, the picturesque, and filled the landscape with ruins; or turned to Southern sectionalism, and filled up unincorporated western regions with slavery. The variety offered by a dominating nature ideology created less of a single national mood than a national discourse, frequently in contradiction with itself: Jacksonianism was only one of the strains.

It was a strain that Emerson specifically resisted, however. Attuned to the political habit of making over transitory policy into everlasting principle, or of confusing nature with grace, he was to emphasize in *Nature* how nature clothes history, not the other way around. The "Beauty" chapter insists on it, and makes the Columbian discovery into a proof of the permanent exceptionality of nature in America:

> Are not these heroes entitled to add the beauty of the scene to the beauty of the deed? When the bark of Columbus nears the shore of America;—before it, the beach lined with savages, fleeing out of all their huts of cane; the sea behind; and the purple mountains of the Indian Archipelago around, can we separate the man from the living picture? Does not the New World clothe his form with her palm-groves and savannahs as fit drapery? Ever does natural beauty steal in the air, and envelop great actions (*CW* 1:15).

The important distinction here is that for Emerson, American nature was not just an adornment of Columbus's arrival, but had a kind of preexisting, pre-Columbian genius, one that Columbus fortunately happened upon. It was lucky of Columbus to perform an action *great enough* to merit nature's adornment. Columbus, as I discussed in chapter 4, was Emerson's favorite explorer, whose mental competence Emerson claimed made heroics possible. Here, the genius of American nature is the central and enabling fact of the Columbian discovery.

The Jacksonians would miss this point entirely in their effort to make nature's "adornments" available democratically, and likewise in their view that nature would *only* come to life when heroics like western settlement took place; otherwise it had no genius of its own. A New Jersey Democrat, speaking at the state's convention in 1844, formulated the acquisition of land as a way for every American to flex his muscles, and to get what was his. Land was a prerogative, and nature merely a means of describing that right:

> Make way, I say, for the young American Buffalo—he has not yet got land enough; he wants more land as his cool shelter in summer—he wants more land for his beautiful pasture grounds. I tell you, we will give him Oregon for his summer shade, and the region of Texas for his winter pasture. (Applause.) Like all of his race, he wants salt, too. Well, he shall have the use of two oceans —the mighty Pacific and turbulent Atlantic shall be his.[17]

To describe Texas in 1844 as "pasture grounds" makes an extraordinary leap, transforming the Annexation (which took place that summer) and the war that followed into inoffensive pastoral scenery. Oregon border disputes with the British, also a dominant issue of 1844, are similarly made over. The

Democrats could regard nature as the dependent clause of political action, a useful rhetorical device but not "emblematic" in the Emersonian sense. Instead, at the most, nature was a crude allegory—as in Gast's crude painting—and its specific details were unimportant to the conquering American Buffalo.

In one example of dispute with this political position, "Commodity" in *Nature* describes progress along the brisk lines that Jacksonian America was moving. But Emerson does not credit manufacturers or bankers or even senators; nature instead has provided that "[a]ll the parts [of nature] incessantly work into each other's hands for the profit of man. . . . [Man] no longer waits for favoring gales, but by means of steam, he realizes the fable of Aeolus's bag, and carries two and thirty winds in the boiler of his boat. . . . The private poor man hath cities, ships, canals, bridges, built for him" (*CW* 1:11–12). While this passage might sound like Jacksonian propaganda (and that is surely intentional), there are a few crucial differences. If nature does work teleologically, then we may still hear a distinction in the qualitative difference between, on the one hand, nature's submission to conquest —a position evident, for instance, in the exploits of the American Buffalo in Texas and Oregon—and on the other, nature's active provision of profitable commodities, like steam. Andrew Jackson justified the annexation of Texas by pointing out that it "will give our Union strength in the same manner that Louisiana and Florida did so. In the same manner, also, it will extend our agricultural, manufacturing, and commercial resources."[18] Jackson was drawing a direct line from the Lewis and Clark expedition, which explored the Louisiana Purchase, to his own aggressive theft of Florida and the annexation of Texas: each endeavor was to our greater national glory, allowing us in turn to take over more territory. But Emerson reverses Jackson's logic—that conquest makes nature belong more to us—and claims in *Nature* that, in fact, conquest makes us belong more to nature. (Henry Thoreau would feel only irritable in this position: he sarcastically observed that men had become more punctual since the invention of railway timetables.) Emerson's distinction, which may also be one Romantic's ambivalent tendresse about how to describe a steam engine, is borne out in the first pages of *Nature,* where Emerson describes the natural world as almost comically friendly: it is "kindred," never "mean." And thus its "profit" to us is to be described politely, if not also from a rather different philosophical position. The "kingdom of man over nature," then, is not a pasture in the state of Texas (*CW* 1:9, 1:45): it is instead a perfected state of the mind, one Emerson would describe in *The Method of Nature* as "ecstasy."

Emerson's suspicion of progress as a means of describing American nature lasted at least until 1847 and his "Ode: Inscribed to W. H. Channing," in which Emerson lists a gamut of progressive causes that carry on without Channing's benevolent influence. All causes strike Emerson as the work of "blindworms" and "jackals."[19] (A blindworm, "a small, limbless, burrowing European lizard with eyes so tiny it was popularly believed to be blind," Barbara Packer notes, is "the symbolic obverse of *Nature*'s famous Transparent Eyeball.")[20] The poem apportions the blame for the failures of politics, such as "the negro-holder" and our "harrying Mexico." These failures are the fault of the "little men," and not of the "God who made New Hampshire." To a New Englander, it must have been obvious that only fallen man made Texas. The "Ode" points out that our sins, liberal or conservative, are a "taunt" to the "lofty land" given to us. We fail to be worthy of New Hampshire, much less of Texas. Again, the "Ode" registers what must have been the greatest regional insult Emerson could imagine: to be unworthy of a southwestern desert state.

The "Ode" also commends to us the higher law, a "law for man" and not for things. Under the aegis of this exalted metaphysical condition—but only then—there are unlimited "fit" conquests, as Emerson's list makes clear:

> 'Tis fit the forest fall,
> The steep be graded,
> The mountain tunnelled,
> The sand shaded,
> The orchard planted,
> The glebe tilled,
> The prairie granted,
> The steamer built.

The famous lament in the "Ode" that "Things are in the saddle, / and ride mankind" conveys Emerson's sense of an inverted perceptual condition, one with vivid political consequences to be sure, but primarily a problem of how we see. The politics of the "Ode" circulate around this point, that the purpose of America is to exercise our best cognitive skills: all else is cant, rant, or "a trick."

Not only, then, does the critique of Idealism and skepticism compel Emerson to a philosophical position that endorses the design argument. It is also the case in *Nature* that design provides a riposte to Jacksonians; it describes their impoverished notions of conquest; it states the case for nature in specific contrast to theirs. The final "Prospects" chapter, in particular, takes on this problem.

Emerson complains in "Prospects" that we apply to nature "but half our force," using only our understanding. This faculty permits us to apprehend spirit only in the prosaic and vulgar details of our contact with nature "as by manure; the economic use of fire, wind, water, and the mariner's needle; steam, coal, chemical agriculture; the repairs of the human body by the dentist and the surgeon" (*CW* 1:43). Emerson reiterates his own earlier catalog of technological wonders (i.e., steam), but adjusts the decorum downward by adding manure and dentists. These details are not only trivial and comic in themselves, but also illustrate for Emerson the trivial and comic means by which the continent was being settled and cultivated. It is as if, he claims, "a banished king should buy his territories inch by inch, instead of vaulting at once into his throne" (*CW* 1 : 43). The sweeping notion of a monarchical "vault" into power would surely have appealed to Jackson, who was after all called "King Andrew" in the Whig press. But Emerson points out in this passage that Texas and Oregon, for instance—territories got by inches —are not only self-evidently the projects of dentists fiddling with manure and steam; they are the result of an error of cognition about what territory —that is, nature—is for. Nationalism, along Jacksonian lines, is not only wicked, but represents the sadly partial force of mind on matter. "Build, therefore," Emerson concludes famously—in terms that might easily have graced a Jacksonian pamphlet luring settlers westward—"your own world" (*CW* 1 : 45).

The politics in *Nature* are somewhat unmanageable and perhaps anti-democratic, because Emerson's interest in something beyond the Democrats never does seem transcendentally available to more than one mind at a time. The critique, though, is clear enough, and the use of "America" as a substitute for "nature" quite insistent.

Contemplating nature often became for Emerson a matter of noticing and appreciating the ways in which America looked designed for our occupancy. Some ways were better than others; manifest destiny was worse than design. There is little else in the way of methodology in *Nature* outside of this approach; the Jacksonian position required a fairly intense and univocal response.

Emerson's habit of conflating America with nature, then, is not simply part of the rhetoric Miller identifies as universal to all post-Calvinists in the nineteenth century. It is a strategic use of teleology (or, the argument from design), one that insists that America be used, as nature is used, but underscoring the extent to which both of them use us. Our nationalism is, it seems, a bequest from nature, a cognitive faculty that makes possible our mastery of our world—while encouraging at the same time, in lesser men, merely Annexations and Purchases.

It seems methodologically useful, then, for Emerson to fail to distinguish nation from nature. We are improved by our discourse with both nature *and* America, and not just materially: our perceptions are perfected, our strife eased, our spirit stirred. That is the purpose of both, as in the journal entry about burning the coal and planting the nation. (Emerson was sometimes mistaken about this process of improvement: it is, of course, the strangest claim of the "Ode to Channing" that racial successions, or blacks being exterminated by whites, simply *happened,* with no accompanying sense of its evil.) And while *Nature* has typically been read as a guidebook for exiting from history into spirit, Emerson found the historical fact of America a proof of claims, both lofty *and* modest, about nature. To claim that nature didn't belong to the Democrats—because after all, "none of them owns the landscape"—was the least he could do.

THE NEED TO restore philosophical coherence to his own claims on Idealism and nationalism would probably have been enough to prompt Emerson to take up the design argument and reinvent it in the 1830s and 1840s. Added pressure from the Jacksonian quarter gave the endeavor its occasion and shape. The resemblance of manifest destiny to design, so that the telos of America was to be settled by Americans, was proof to Emerson that, although debased in form, the design impulse was an innate one, containing dignity and truth. It only required release from the facile political logic that ruled it.

The Method of Nature (1841) continues the inquiries of *Nature* to disinter design from its Jacksonian fellow travelers. The "method" in the essay, described simply as "ecstasy," works etymologically: ecstasy means "outside the self," and so the essay demonstrates the difference between nature and the self that perceives it. Nature is definitionally *ecstatic,* outside, Not Me. The essay inquires, what is the method of nature? Or, in other words, what does it mean to be outside it? Unlike the naive question that commences *Nature* ("To what end is nature?"), *Method* has a more skeptical opening, positing not an idealized communion between Me and Not Me, but only an analytical possibility, Me analyzing Not Me.

This analytical distance, with the assumption of separation between subject and object, seems to represent something of a resignation for Emerson, the inveterate idealist. On the other hand, though, one of his central examples of a Me scrutinizing a Not Me is in the American West: "Who shall think he has come late into nature, or has missed anything excellent in the past, who seeth the admirable stars of possibility, and the yet untouched continent of hope glittering with all its mountains in the vast West?" (*CW* 1:136). This description of the West remedies the subject-object separation apparently in force in the essay. It also begins to illustrate the method of nature. In a minor advance from the logic of *Nature,* Emerson suggests in *The Method of Nature* that nature is not only a realm of meaningful ideas—that it is, in fact, our chief meaningful idea—but it can also be geographically specific, a feature absent from nature in *Nature.* The West is not just an analogy (a rhetorical term that emphasizes conceptual distance) for the optimism of the Me toward the Not Me; it is the actual site where this optimism can take place. The West is not *like* a region of hope; it is one. And nature is not just a construct of language (subject, perhaps, to grammatical mood); it is real.

Method asserts this immediacy early, when Emerson observes how language fails us and is not nature's proper medium, "whether it take the shape of exhortation, or of passionate exclamation, or of scientific statement. These are forms merely. . . . Language overstates. Statements of the infinite are usually felt to be unjust to the finite, and blasphemous" (*CW* 1 : 123–24). We fail when we resort to linguistic forms and assume their efficacy, which we must then inevitably mistake for their primacy. The purpose of ecstasy, in this sense, is to permit the Me to contemplate the Not Me, while at the same time averting that contemplation from linguistic idolatry. Ecstasy is an improved subject position, or a thinking man's Idealism.

Furthermore, it is in the West, as Emerson observes, that nature replies to all queries, saying, "I grow." Surely arguments about nationalism could be silenced in exactly the same way. Neither "foolish nations . . . [nor] great and wise men" distract us from American nature; and neither can persuade us of one particular end, or telos. In a reversal of his gambit in *Nature*, Emerson finds in *Method* that there is no end to nature, only ends: an emanation, "to be represented by a circular movement, as intention might be signified by a straight line of definite length" (*CW* 1 : 126). The Jacksonians in 1841 were continuing the squabbles over straight lines of definite lengths, or the national borders of the United States; there was some urgency to adjudicate exactly what America meant by "I grow." Such disputes struck Emerson as the distractions that always follow from errors of cognition: if there was a case in philosophy or politics in which nature looked less promising than planned, clearly one was reading the case wrong.

Berkeley himself had exulted, "Westward the course of Empire takes its way." The West, for Emerson, suggests (in a national riposte to Berkeley) that American nature in particular is not just an agreeably coherent set of ideas. Even Andrew Jackson could have ideas. Instead, the vast continent of hope answers the lingering doubts from the time of Lewis and Clark, when the buoyant Idealism of American explorers regularly failed them. That is, where explorers had found America frustratingly impervious to a great many philosophies, Emerson decodes it. Nature, as Lewis and Clark kept insisting in the latter half of their *Journals,* is an extraordinary epistemological problem. That problem, Emerson was quick to see, could easily be idealized into a matter of spirit—except that nature itself, especially in the American West, didn't easily renounce its materiality. The synthesis is that American nature exists, and our doubts about its existence are salutary, especially to Americans.

It may strike us as eclectic that part of Emerson's philosophical endeavor was to prove that America existed, but of course his precision on this question was intended to prove that Jacksonian America did *not* exist.

He visited the Far West only once, late in life, so that his musings on the subject in the 1840s were as nonperipatetic as those of most New Englanders, the sort who never got out of the dining car. He subjected even the California gold rush to his design argument. A lecture he gave on the Forty-Niners claimed: "I do not think very respectfully of the *designs* of the people who went to California in 1849. It was a rush and a scramble of needy adventurers.... But *nature watches over all,* and turns this malfeasance to good. California gets peopled and subdued, civilized" (*JMN* 13:440; emphasis added). Californians, as it happens, had themselves long imagined their territory as Emersonian: one editorialist urged a visit in 1869, for "a strange, new type of national character is waiting to be analyzed by Emerson."[21] And when Emerson did finally go to California for a month in 1871, presumably passing through that city named for George Berkeley, he was visited in San Francisco by an admirer, Miss Carrie Augusta Moore, who performed in a roller skating exhibition in town. She and Emerson exchanged admission tickets to each other's performances. He probably did not attend this roller skating show, but he did find the attentions of such visitors charming.

For Emerson, even great men could not justify nature's "enormous apparatus"; they were as "spotted and defective" as anyone else. The dubious native character of the Westerner, the people whom Emerson had claimed a few years earlier possessed bad designs, was probably as defective. Emerson was not aware that Miss Moore, the roller derby queen of San Francisco, was a native of Concord, Massachusetts, and possessed the same native character as he.

6

Thoreau and the Design of Dissent

My days were not days of the week, bearing the stamp of any heathen deity; nor were they minced into hours and fretted by the ticking of a clock.
HENRY DAVID THOREAU, *Walden* (1854)

The nation may go their way to their manifest destiny which I trust is not mine.
HENRY DAVID THOREAU, in a letter (1853)

Theological design, made over politically in the 1840s, is a key metaphor in three major works by Henry Thoreau: "Walking," *Walden,* and "Slavery in Massachusetts." America, as I have argued, was for Thoreau's mentor Emerson where design was fulfilled. The lessons of exploration were to remind us that we had to look at American nature differently: Emerson's corrective to Jackson was to see design without brutal conquest, or fulfilled promise without repugnant political programs like Cherokee removal and the Mexican War. Both Emerson and Thoreau grasped the limited scale of their exultation about nature: it was available to only one mind at a time. Both writers, too, saw that design, in political terms, was the thrown gauntlet.

Thoreau, of indifferent beliefs but never downright irreligious, mentions "god" hundreds of times in his major works and journals; perpetually disappointed by the Democrats, he was given to sounding like a Jacksonian. While hostile to the Democratic Party itself, he was schooled in the same religious rhetoric that had prompted John O'Sullivan, in the *Democratic Review,* to praise the American continent as the gift of God's providence. Thoreau, like O'Sullivan, looked to nature for confirmation of design and found it; but unlike O'Sullivan, Thoreau was uneasy, because it suggested that the best challenges to contemporary politics were to be made from a position of orthodoxy.

Not just any orthodoxy. Thoreau, after all, reserved his greatest hatred for the habits of mind that resorted, out of promiscuity or malice, to foolish consistency. And nature itself seemed, at times, foolishly eager to justify Jacksonian projects: there were, for instance, Democrats who praised the terrain of the Mexican War for its obvious sympathies to the Yankee cause. Instead of confirming political facts in natural facts, Thoreau sought for nature a role of positive critique, one that would redeem the politically expedient and intellectually sloppy design argument known, by 1845, as manifest destiny.

Thoreau's most powerful political writing, "Slavery in Massachusetts," ends famously on a redemptive pastoral image, the lily. The still-disputed possibilities of this text, ranging from pastoral retreat to blistering jeremiad, are more straightforward after a reassessment of Thoreau's design argument, the intellectual position he most wanted to rehabilitate. Particularly when it came to America, Thoreau wanted the logic of design, but not its fellow travelers.

In this chapter I describe first what kind of nonreligious, but still, in their way, pious design arguments interested Thoreau. I consider the methods of political critique in both "Walking" and *Walden* that Thoreau redeployed in "Slavery in Massachusetts" and then examine Thoreau's persistent use of design logic in the essay to reclaim two fallen abstractions, namely abolitionism and the pastoral. Finally, based on the evidence surrounding "Slavery in Massachusetts," I offer a reformulation of Thoreau's views as a case study for nineteenth-century anti-Jacksonian thought, characterized by strict religious training without piety, and a mass politics that would take effect only one mind at a time.

My reading proposes a middle way between two positions: first, the traditional criticism of *Walden* as a symbolic poem, unrelated to real nature and indulging in pastoralism for the sake of rhetoric; and second, the recent skepticism about what Thoreau constructed as "natural" in the first place, or that criticism which disputes the capacity of a text like *Walden* to present a genuine attack on its culture, because of the dominance of that culture in the terms, ideology, and imagery of the text.[1] *Walden,* I argue, is neither fully abstractable as the former school held, nor fully culpable as the latter claims. Thoreau came to like a design argument of his own that borrowed its logic from theologians, and he tried to keep this argument free of its vulgar relation, the ideology of manifest destiny.

Any keen nature observer in the 1850s would be expected to express doubts about religious faith: the sciences were steadily dismantling the traditional supports of belief by revealing, for instance, the real age of the earth in the fossil record. (This geological heresy prompted Clement Moore to grumble, "Whenever men speak of mountains, there is bound to be impiety going on.") Thoreau's steady use of a Christian proof with the vintage and pedigree of design offers an example of the nineteenth-century mood of declining faith. In Thoreau's case, a Christian proof in the service of unbridled non-Christian views indicates his rejection of contemporary religious doubts as newfangled and vulgar, even while simultaneously his nonbelief places him in the same modern camp, philosophically, as Tennyson. (Or William James. Or Darwin.) Thoreau's design shows a joy in argumentation, and not much in specific devotion to God: "Slavery in Massachusetts" is a rather mixed jeremiad in rhetoric and aims, not in its calls for renewed belief. The politics that follow from Thoreau's position are, in this light, somewhat unmanageable: by turns democratic and then warmly antidemocratic, Thoreau objected primarily to political sins committed as a result of cognitive error. This detail is crucial: the restive personality whose life, as Robert D. Richardson, Jr., points out, *was* the mind, objected fundamentally to intellectual mistakes. His correctives in "Slavery in Massachusetts," then, were based on antique logic and current events, and throughout, on an insistence on the possibilities of redemption through nature. This position was, like religious faith itself in the nineteenth century, susceptible to failure of nerve—especially if nature, like God, were not read correctly.

DESIGN WAS A crucial line of reasoning to nineteenth-century nature writers, who saw in it the ideal admixture of the scientific and the spiritual temperaments. It is a skeptic's argument with a proviso for piety, one that combines cool empirical observation with a faithful conclusion: nature, red in tooth and claw, was at least able to furnish the principal evidences of religion.

In the wake of design's dismissal by the theological majority, and by the 1840s its absorption into politics, Thoreau wrote his major works on nature. Design was popularized in the nineteenth century, even as its hold on theology waned, by the Jacksonian Democrats. The logical premise of design, that from observing phenomena we can infer divine purpose and order, was appropriated by writers ranging from James K. Polk to John O'Sullivan to Walt Whitman. It was not a hard sell: manifest destiny dovetailed neatly into the national effort at western expansion. Indeed, the teleological proof strikes us now as so thoroughly suited to nineteenth-century politics that the invention of the phrase *manifest destiny,* by O'Sullivan in 1845, seems belated. Like the Frederick Jackson Turner frontier thesis of 1893, manifest destiny was stated formally long *after* it was embraced in American culture.

That currency was based in part on the deployment of a version of the design argument, itself current, familiar, and, for its advocates, apparently orthodox. Thoreau promptly became engaged in political resistance to the form that design, by the 1840s, had assumed in America. Like many theories, design sometimes determined the outcome of an argument more than Thoreau did. Thoreau was impressed by the intellectual rigor of design (and he was something of an antiquarian): design was deductive, apparently scientific, and also carefully idealistic. But Thoreau had only limited success in reclaiming it from the most offensive politics of his day. It was difficult to deploy the pleasurable logic of the argument without then mimicking its latter-day political conclusions.

Design for Thoreau was generally in evidence when he wrote of the "text" of nature, as a set of specimens and vistas that confirmed cosmic planning and intent. The mode of writing he made his specialty was this: the walk through nature that could be both delightful and instructive, owing to the beauties and morals to be found right in one's path. Rarely content to observe without drawing moral conclusions, Thoreau was an inveterate "reader" of nature. William Paley's famous example of crossing a heath and comparing a rough stone in his path to a delicate watch, and from the incident inferring the order and balance of the universe, is a model for nature writing such as Thoreau's, whose first works also recount such crossings—though, to be sure, never the crossings of specifically English "heaths."

A Walk to Wachusett, as an example, displays certain standard effects in a Thoreau walking tour: the lure of the horizon, the heavy allusions to classical and oriental authors, the discovery of exotic difference only a few miles from home, the praise of humble botanical specimens as noble and thrilling, and the well-placed "chance" encounters with rustics such as mowers or carpenters or woodchoppers. And throughout it, Thoreau reiterates an Emersonian sentiment of nearly secular design, stated this way: "[in nature] we see laws which never fail."[2] (These laws seem to Thoreau less fallible than laws of human invention, such as the Fugitive Slave Law.) Similarly, in *Natural History of Massachusetts,* Thoreau praises the "law one and invariable" in nature.[3] His use of the term *law* illustrates, here as later, his engagement with the various shapes design had begun to assume.

Tentative about the specifically divine attributes of "divine life" in *A Walk* (it is interchangeable with morality, and elsewhere to oracular insight, but unattributed to God), Thoreau began to notice America, a theme that was to become a favorite. *A Walk* cherishes those aspects of the natural world that promise national discovery and success, particularly those places that "may afford a theme for future poets" (137). Thoreau notes (the year is 1843) that "one could write an epic to be called the leaf," an uncanny prediction of Whitman's American leaf-epic ten years later. Although Thoreau's setting was always interpolated with far-flung locales such as Parnassus, Arabia, Helvellyn, or Polynesia, he recurs to American coordinates with American perspectives: "the sun's rays fell on us two alone, of all New England men" (145).

Through all this mileage, though, Thoreau avoided the conclusion that design offered—the existence of the creator—and in its place offered a variety of substitutes. Looking at nature to educe models of order for human affairs is a basic premise of design, and essential to Thoreau's nature writing. But if his rejection of Christian proofs suggests to some critics his "liberal" credentials,[4] his engagement with corresponding proofs of national virtue is politically more complicated. His nationalism was not automatic, nor entirely comprehensible under the aegis of "nature's nation"; he did not replace God with America. Thoreau protested the excesses of his times (the Mexican War, the Fugitive Slave Law) and was an abolitionist. And yet his enthusiasms are briskly patriotic.

Writing about the text of a specifically American nature was hardly Thoreau's invention, for, as the inexhaustible genre criticism of *Walden* demonstrates, Thoreau had a dizzying number of literary influences.[5] Lawrence Buell has reviewed some of the background texts to *Walden:* almanacs such as William Howitt's *Book of the Seasons;* works of "homiletic naturism" such as Edward Hitchcock's *Religious Lectures on Peculiar Phenomena in the Four Seasons;* regional nature writing such as Susan Fenimore Cooper's *Rural Hours;* picturesque sketches in the best-selling *Home Book of the Picturesque;* and natural histories such as Lyell's *Geology* and Audubon's *Birds.* Of these five genres, Buell notes their common construction of nature "in the image of American cultural nationalism," an effort that also describes Thoreau's construction of nature. While these background texts may not strike us as the heart of the national literature, Buell reminds us how commonly American literary history "presents the spectacle of having identified representation of the natural environment as a major theme while marginalizing the literature devoted most specifically to it." And as Perry Miller notes of the study of nature in America, "To adore and to understand were first of all an escape from provinciality, and not a patriotic assertion. And yet it was patriots who made the assertion."[6]

Thoreau's own patriotism has been pointed out elsewhere, too, in the comparisons of his work to that of the Hudson River painters, such as Thomas Cole and J. F. Cropsey.[7] Barbara Novak has claimed for the Hudson River School that "nineteenth-century nature worship was more strongly nationalistic in America than elsewhere." Thoreau never mentions a landscape painter by name in his journals, but he expresses their sentiments. His proposed epic on the leaf may have come from an extravagant apostrophe of Thomas Cole's: "O for a single blade of grass! if it were only one inch in length, it would cheer my drooping spirits." Cole proclaimed in his 1835 aesthetic manifesto, "Essay on American Scenery," that American nature possessed a "distinctive wildness," superior to that of Europe because "in civilized Europe the primitive features of scenery have long since been destroyed or modified."[8] Thoreau, also fed up with civilization, grumbles that lovers of European painting care "but little about trees but much more about Corinthian columns." In his view, even John Ruskin's *Modern Painters* failed to describe "nature as Nature."[9]

A 1993 retrospective of Thomas Cole's works in the National Museum of American Art in Washington, D.C., made clear the arc of the average landscape painter's career, which, like the epic poet's, runs from pastoral to national: in Cole's case, from small landscapes to his ambitious American allegory, *The Course of Empire.* (Even Audubon's *Birds* has been exalted from mere ornithology to become an example of the organic proofs behind national history.)[10]

The easy drift from local to national matters, then, was the habit of mind

Thoreau readily absorbed. It is a drift given intellectual endorsement by the design argument, with its small examples proving large premises. For Thoreau, as with most of his contemporaries, the effort of describing American nature was at once opaque and explicit, so that he sometimes struggled with and against manifest destiny without acknowledging his rhetorical complicity in it. Whether engaged in natural sciences or Luminist aesthetics, Thoreau was embroiled—not without dissent—in the campaign of these disparate nineteenth-century cultural endeavors: seeing the design of nature's nation.

"WALKING" HAS COMMONLY been read as Thoreau's wilderness manifesto, not a song of praise to the nation. His biographer notes that, after all, Thoreau didn't think about America nearly as much as he did about nature. The essay is also the outcome of Thoreau's efforts in the 1850s to codify his somewhat contradictory views on politics and nature. If *Walden* is his major work, acknowledges the biographer, "Walking" is his major essay.[11]

It is also his most exasperating. Originally two lectures, "Walking" and "Wildness," they were combined into a single essay by Thoreau, not entirely to the satisfaction of many readers, who pronounce it unorganized and the ending "a highly miscellaneous conglomeration of barely related paragraphs."[12] Many critics also complain of Thoreau's affective fallacy in action—that an essay about wildness must be, itself, characterized by wildness. Such disorganization is also blamed on Thoreau's status as a Romantic, so that emotional outbursts and turbulent streams of thought cannot be expected to assume a conventional form.[13] (This argument is a regrettable misreading of both Romanticism and Thoreau.) While not dismissing the charges of haphazard construction, I will focus on Thoreau's strongly made case for design in the essay, which we can locate in his structural irregularities.

Thoreau praises wildness; America excels at wildness; thus Thoreau praises America. This straightforward logical structure is in evidence throughout the essay, seen in inoffensive puffs of national pride and as part of a nineteenth-century commonplace of the national literature, such as Cole's "Essay on American Scenery." And yet Thoreau's fondness for wildness, like Cole's, relies on an observer who is distinctly nonwild. Wildness, on the whole, was a category with little possibility of being correct: it was always a comparative statement, never an absolute one, and one entirely susceptible to that worst of observer states for Thoreau, the noninnocent eye.

It is difficult to imagine Thoreau agreeing to a concept, wildness, that he could easily wave away philosophically, like a fly. Retaining wildness, then— given its flaws—suggests that Thoreau was as interested in the eye that *saw* wildness and (as in the virtues of the lily in "Slavery in Massachusetts") could perceive and love it. Only a mind well trained in patterns of design, Thoreau claims, can perceive and love wildness. Which advances the question: can all—can *any*—Americans manage such insights?

The good mind (we might call it, in modern terms, the "cognitive elite") was Thoreau's political observer. This observer's vexed politics follow a familiar Thoreauvian model: to assert an inoffensive axiom of democracy; to refute it indirectly, paradoxically, and whimsically; and to conclude the opposite of the opening position, owing to the perceptual advantages possessed by this refuting good mind. Thoreau's sympathy in democratic directions seldom holds up to the end of his writings. This routine of contradiction conveys his continuing struggle with "democracy" as the Jacksonian Democrats conducted it.

Frequently Thoreau's opening positions are oriented toward democratic assumptions, such as his endorsement of an egalitarian wildness, which explicitly rejects the requirements of privilege—class, money, tradition, property, social status—in favor of the simple rewards of nature. This theme is familiar enough from *Walden* and also, certainly, from the tone of Andrew Jackson's own presidential campaigns, which capitalized on voters' fears of aristocratic decadence and instead offered more trustworthy (if cruder) symbols of self-reliance and frontier life. (Jackson startled the Washington elite, but not his voters, when he served cider at his inaugural parties.) But just as frequently, Thoreau objects to features of democratic politics, such as nativism, wars of aggression, and the raw drive to make money, and he posits a set of sympathies quite at odds with Jackson's party. "Walking" displays both kinds of advocacy—both broadly pro-democracy, and anti-Jacksonian Democrat—as well as Thoreau's difficulty in reconciling them into one unified design.

Thoreau's interest in a subject that interested many in the Democratic party, the exploration and conquest of the West, is a case in point. Thoreau seems to have been the best read of the Transcendentalists in New World exploration literature, and he knew a range of such texts, from Hakluyt's *Diverse Voyages* and William Bartram's *Travels* to Emory's *Report,* Pike's *Journals,* and Lewis and Clark's *Journals.*[14] His reading was broad and frequent. His later works *Cape Cod* and *The Maine Woods* both contain long, detailed catalog-style passages of explorers' names and achievements. Like Emerson, Thoreau regarded exploration as an example of human excellence; but his restless perusals of its literature seem to suggest that no single instance of exploration was quite perfect.

"Walking," for example, presents a number of encouragements on the westward sweep of the course of empire. "Westward I go free," declares Thoreau. "Eastward I go only by force."[15] The West, he confirms, is where the future lies: "the earth seems more unexhausted and richer on that side." Finally, his manifesto: "I must walk toward Oregon, and not toward Europe." Even this expansive mood, though, is retrenched when we see what Thoreau thought of explorers themselves. In 1784, Thomas Jefferson wrote *Notes on the State of Virginia* in order to refute the findings of Georges Buffon that American species were less hardy, American climates less healthful, and American scenery less beautiful than in Europe. In "Walking," Thoreau, too, targets this European claim, and quotes Sir Francis Head's extravagant catalog of American virtues, a list as gushing as Buffon is skeptical: "The heavens of America appear infinitely higher, the sky is bluer, the air is fresher, the cold is intenser, the moon looks larger, the stars are brighter, the thunder is louder, the lightning is vivider, the wind is stronger, the rain is heavier, the mountains are higher, the rivers longer, the forests bigger, the plains broader." Thoreau concludes, in a Jeffersonian economy of words, that "this statement will do at least to set against Buffon's account" (221–222).

But in the case of another of Jefferson's enterprises, the Lewis and Clark expedition, Thoreau is less sanguine. He assails the institution that sponsored the expedition, the American Philosophical Society (APS), also commonly known in the eighteenth and nineteenth centuries as the Society for the Diffusion of Useful Knowledge.[16] APS was organized by Benjamin Franklin in Philadelphia on the model of the French Academy and the Royal Society, in order to provide lecture venues and intellectual encouragement for philosophers, writers, and scientists, and generally to establish a national headquarters for intellectual inquiry.

Jefferson was president of APS while he was president of the United States. When Congress funded the exploration of the Louisiana Purchase, Jefferson asked the scientist members of the Society to train Meriwether Lewis for twelve months in botany, anthropology, geology, navigation, chemistry, astronomy, and all the other field sciences Lewis and Clark might require. The Society took (and still takes) a proprietary interest in the expedition and Lewis's preparations. It holds today all the archival materials from the expedition, including the journals, the specimens, and a longboat.

Thoreau is cynical about the notion of "useful knowledge" in "Walking," calling instead for a Society for the Diffusion of Useful Ignorance. A little learning, he finds, stands in the way of real education: "what is our boasted so-called knowledge but a conceit that we know something, which robs us of the advantage of our actual ignorance?" (239). Echoing Emerson's "American Scholar," Thoreau's position is one of measured skepticism toward scholarliness without originality, or endless study without native wit. One historian has observed that the cultural backwardness of nineteenth-century America was explained away when cultural achievements were traded for exploits in taming nature: "stumps and cultivated fields," he suggests of Jacksonians, "represented American substitutes for learned societies."[17] Targeting the very learned society known for its sponsorship of Lewis and Clark, Thoreau objects, in this strikingly Jacksonian manner, to exploration when it is not tempered with enough "ignorance"—a sense of wonder or a willingness to be surprised. Ignorance of this type characterizes Thoreau's good mind, and it happens to resemble quite vividly the Jacksonian preferments of sylvan simplicity over urban sophistication. Evidently the Lewis and Clark expedition, for all its intrepid movement west, was too "learned."

So while the patriotic refutation of Buffon suited Thoreau's notions of American virtue, the Lewis and Clark expedition—in some sense, the historical outcome of Jefferson's anti-Buffon position—did not. The reason for Thoreau's distinction is not entirely clear—we wonder whether there can really be much qualitative difference—but it is symptomatic of his view of America generally. It was good to theorize and dispute about national promise while America remained poised at the moment *before* full exploration; but it was far from good to insist on its being explored, even—perhaps *especially*—for the purpose of useful knowledge.

Christopher Columbus posed a similar problem for Thoreau. At age sixteen, in rhetoric class, Thoreau displayed an Emersonian interest in Columbus, selecting him over Herschel and Newton for an essay topic.[18] In "Walking," Columbus appears again, afflicted with the worst case in history of what Thoreau calls "the westward tendency." Columbus "felt it more strongly than any before" (219–220). One gathers that the westward tendency, like any compulsion, can be a burden as well as a gift, like prophesying. It is useful to remind ourselves that Thoreau, a nature writer, traveled very little, and the ten miles around Concord was his preferred *terra incognita*. Columbus, in this light, seems a victim of the West as much as a hero of exploration, just as a persuasive reply to Buffon seems to lead tragically to the excesses of the Lewis and Clark expedition.

For all the optimism and promise of American landscapes, and their expansive and egalitarian properties, then, there is a countercurrent in "Walking" of antidemocratic (and, it seems, provincial) views. Columbus, for yet another Transcendentalist, was by no means an Everyman: he was more a Representative Man, like Napoleon, whom Thoreau also introduces into the essay as an eccentric, not as an ideal. And Jefferson's politics were amenable insofar as they remained in Virginia and replied back to Europe, but were inappropriate when they launched the conquest of the continent from a learned society in Philadelphia. Thoreau found his own project of walking a practice of "a chivalric and heroic spirit" for a "select class." In a somewhat parodic description of aristocratic principles of heredity, Thoreau insists with seriousness that "you must be born into the family of the Walkers." The straightforward egalitarianism of "Walking"—where "no man owns the landscape"—is difficult to sustain in the face of this bracing insistence on social distinctions (207).

The endpoint of this back-and-forth motion seemed to rest (as we have seen before) where Thoreau usually found it: in the examination of the good mind. He introduced this examination by posing a "naive" question—namely, Why was America discovered?

As with other naive questions in Thoreau, the influence was most likely Emerson's *Nature,* with its simple query "To what end is nature?" But Thoreau's adoption of this particular rhetorical strategy does not seem entirely friendly to Emerson, an attitude in evidence later in the essay as well. Thoreau mentions, for example, that the shrubs outside his window, including the rhodora, were "all standing in the quaking sphagnum," one of his standard hierarchies of botany, wherein the humbler species, sphagnum moss, is preferred to the flowers (227). (Recall the lily in "Slavery in Massachusetts.") He may well have had in mind Emerson's poem "The Rhodora," which, as I discuss in chapter 4, presents an early analysis of the design argument by Emerson characterized by only mild skepticism. Just as Thoreau found that useful knowledge was no knowledge at all, the rhodora detail indicates that the design argument was erected on shaky (that is, "quaking") ground. His disapproval of Emerson for writing about nature as he did suggests that Thoreau found Emerson too uncritical of providential logic, or soft on design. Providence asserts that, from all appearances, God wanted Americans to sweep westward; Thoreau's "Walking" objects to this regrettable reliance on appearances.

As with naive questions generally, Thoreau's tone when he inquires, "Why was America discovered?" is shifty. While it may sound like it opens the American discovery to praise, Thoreau's question also conveys some despair at the Columbian arrival, as if the promise of that event had been reneged upon. The stringently nondemocratic features of "Walking" speak to just such a broken promise, or fallen state: one can hear the voice of the embittered conservative. Thoreau notes, early in the essay, that he walks because he had "committed some sin to be atoned for" (208). The scale of "Walking" is always toward the national horizon, so that we may infer how widespread the "sin" is. This despair reflects Thoreau's selective rejection of Jacksonian democracy, asking *why was America discovered* when doing so would only demand atonement.

This odd alloy is on display throughout the essay: recall that although the West was a "richer" area for Thoreau, it was also in the unusually phrased "more unexhausted" direction, an indirection in grammatical and rhetorical terms. Such laments are in force throughout the essay, particularly when Thoreau describes America in a range of aesthetic terms, displaying just how many fallen worldviews, or designs, can be leveled at it. Wildness is only one. This paragraph is overloaded with others:

> The landscape-painter uses the figures of men to mark a road. He would not make that use of my figure. I walk out into a Nature such as the old prophets and poets, Menu, Moses, Homer, Chaucer, walked in. You may name it America, but it is not America; neither Americus Vespucius, nor Columbus, nor the

rest were discoverers of it. There is a truer account of it in mythology than in any history of America, so called, that I have seen (214).

It is not America: and Thoreau offers several ways of not-looking at not-America. He lists landscape painting (in the pastoral tradition, it seems); classical, pre-Christian, epic, or medieval poetry; and the traditional New World of early exploration. Each possibility seems equal to the others, all are "truer than history," and Thoreau's lament is that none of these possibilities can dominate history. All we know is that America is not America.

The elevation of America from Jackson's banal present tense to transcendent and mythic time is accomplished by walking in nature and contemplating mythologies, an effort to redeem what is obviously fallen by recurring to vast landscapes with vast metaphysics. Comparatively, politics is described in "Walking" as "but a narrow field" (213). Thoreau posits a design of America that is inclusive—one might almost say, democratic—so long as it does not traffic in democracy itself.

EMERSONIAN CRITICS SOMETIMES claim that "The American Scholar" is about America or about scholarship, but not about both. Some Thoreauvians have divided, in their readings of "Slavery in Massachusetts," along similar lines, either finding Thoreau's powerful political jeremiad the engine of the piece, disregarding the vivid pastoral ending, or conversely that the lily image is the centerpiece and the politics simply a performance, heated enough to show what outrage sounds like, but finally giving way to "literary" matters. The essay has challenged critics to fix a cause-effect relationship—indeed, *any* relationship—to the political complaint and the pastoral inset in the text.[19]

During the incident that provoked Thoreau to write (and deliver as a speech) "Slavery in Massachusetts"—the enforcement in 1854 of the Fugitive Slave Law in Massachusetts to return Anthony Burns to his owners in the South—the luminaries of New England were mixed in their responses. Emerson was writing *English Traits;* Nathaniel Hawthorne was occupied in Liverpool; Bronson Alcott made antislavery speeches; and Theodore Parker stormed Burns's prison to liberate him. Thoreau, like Parker, seized the moment, and the attack on the Fugitive Slave Law in "Slavery in Massachusetts" is direct and furious. This fury resembles that of Thoreau's earlier work, *Resistance to Civil Government.* But even in this mood, Thoreau worked with a few sobering intellectual tasks in mind: as in the case of *Resistance to Civil Government,* which replies in part to William Paley's political writings, "Slavery in Massachusetts" contains a deliberate attack on not just bad law or bad politics, but a bad worldview. If Emerson was generally confused by cases of trenchant error,[20] Thoreau responded with exasperation.

In order to provide context for this reading of "Slavery in Massachusetts," I would like first to review a similar method on display in *Walden* in order to suggest the background for Thoreau's construction of "Slavery." *Walden*, like Emerson's *Nature*, is a "naturalist's conversion story," in which Thoreau attempts to account for his redeemed view of the landscape. But his appeal to Emersonian self-reliance also displays "the cultural function of radicalism," or the somewhat overdetermined features of his dissent.[21] Thoreau's indebtedness to his own times in this regard—a writer who sneered at all debt as "inherited Irish poverty"—also means that *Walden* displays mixed politics. The protest Thoreau sets up in opposition to Jacksonian market economics offers (as Bercovitch points out) a counter model actually quite amenable to Jacksonians: a simple man who lives in purifying poverty; a natural man who lives by seasons and not by government controls; a rugged individualist. This lone and hidebound male figure was a commonplace in the Democrats' political writing (Andrew Jackson, for example, was elected in 1828 in part by the popular campaign to associate "Old Hickory" with Daniel Boone), and one that exploited its associations with radicalism: Richard Slotkin points out, for instance, the strong associations between Jacksonians and Jacobins.[22]

But as Buell notes, the pastoral ideal in *Walden* "ought to be looked at as *conservative* . . . rather than as a form as dissent," offering a nostalgic fantasy rather than a model for reform.[23] Thus, although Thoreau wanted *Walden* to perform rites of separation and dissent, he was indebted to his own contemporary political culture for the very persona of the work. He also countermanded the radicalism of his own rugged individual by focusing heavily on the redemptive, and surely retrograde, sanctuary offered in nature.

With such a mixed set of political impulses in play, the more complex forms of dissent that *Walden* contains—namely, the deployment of design —require a reckoning with their intended targets of attack. Using the design argument to attack both radicals *and* conservatives imparts some of the complexity, for instance, that distinguishes Thoreau from the gallery of assenters identified by Bercovitch—who finds *Walden* "not a summons to dissent," but a buttress of institutional stability.[24] This position is in need of reappraisal.

The "Sounds" chapter in *Walden* takes a cue from the preceding "Reading" chapter—the call to keep Homer's *Iliad* at hand and open on the desk, even if you are busy with your beans. "Sounds" poses the question of nature's capacity also to be read like a book; it depends, similarly, on our capacity to keep it nearby and open. Thoreau was quite interested in hermeneutical strategies and the uses to which the text of nature could be put.

Thoreau's remark on the pernicious influence of clocks that heads this chapter appears in "Sounds": the detail suggests a familiarity and a fluency with the imagery and terms of the design argument. Thoreau had read Paley's political writings (*Resistance to Civil Government* is in part a reply to them), and of course, Paley's *Natural Theology* was a standard text in most college curriculums. "Sounds" contains additional rejoinders to the commonplaces of natural theology, attempting to replace its logical conclusions with more incantatory insights.

Thoreau's view of the railroad, for example, with its jarring sense details (the "scream" of the whistle), has largely been assessed as the literature of the invaded pastoral. Thoreau's was far from the first such portrait of a technological monster: he knew Carlyle's *Sartor Resartus,* in which a steam engine threatens to grind the hero to death; Hawthorne's description of the railway's invasion of Sleepy Hollow; Daniel Webster's speech on the Northern Railroad; and of course Emerson's "Young American." (Leo Marx calls each of these "incursion" texts.) [25] Thoreau's sense of the railroad blames it, ironically, for our subservience to its convenience: "Have not men improved somewhat," he notes, "in punctuality since the railroad was invented? Do they not talk and think faster in the depot than they did in the stage-office?" [26]

But the railroad in "Sounds," if extraordinarily disruptive and polluting, inspires more than just his most wicked irony. Rather than a complaint about the rigid timetable and noise and terror, staged against the catalog of bird sounds Thoreau prefers, the railroad is described in details that mark it as a symbol of Deism, as the clock complaint had strongly hinted. As such, it is the engine—overmechanized, terrible, fascinating—of design. Thoreau suggests in "Sounds" that if design implies that the cosmos runs like a railroad, then design is a deeply flawed explanation of the universe. Thoreau, as I noted, admired the rigor of thought behind such an intellectual system: here he calls it, ambivalently (and perhaps with Carlyle in mind), the "heroism" of railroad passengers in commerce, who "go to sleep only . . . when the sinews of their iron steed are frozen" (119). (*Walden,* of all Thoreau's works, makes clear that heroic stature is always mock heroic: "The Battle of the Ants" suggests as much.)

Terry Eagleton reminds us of such scenes of the railroad: "If I pore over the railway timetable not to discover a train connection but to stimulate in myself general reflections on the speed and complexity of modern existence, then I might be said to be reading it as literature." [27] (Henry Adams, half a century after Thoreau, observed the railroad's mechanization of genius in America: "From the moment that railways were introduced, life took on extravagance.") [28] Thoreau, in his portrait of the railroad, is performing a reading. His fable of the invaded pastoral becomes an allegory, in fact, of *bad* reading. While the conceit of the railroad chiefly concerns its mythic properties (it is a "traveling demigod"), Thoreau also emphasizes its cosmic features, which are "like a comet," cars "moving off with planetary motion," with nearly immeasurable "velocity and . . . direction" (116). The Newtonian astronomical emphasis is hard to miss: Thoreau satirizes the grandiosity behind the railroad, which visits "our system" from time to time; and conversely, he satirizes the manner in which Deism, a rationalist monster, has reduced the cosmos to a railway timetable. The contrast in "Sounds" between railroad and nature is an exercise in bad versus good "readings": while design can prompt an appreciation of cosmic order, it can also overdetermine our own heat and motion, just as with the faster talkers in the railway depot.

The catalog in Emerson's lecture "The Uses of Natural History" is a lengthy series of animal nomenclature, which culminates in a powerful metaphysical insight:

> You are impressed with the inexhaustible gigantic riches of nature. The limits of the possible are enlarged, and the real is stranger than the imaginary. The universe is a more amazing puzzle than ever, as you look along this bewildering series of animated forms, the hazy butterflies, the carved shells, the birds, beasts, insects, snakes, fish, and the upheaving principle of life everywhere incipient, in the very rock aping organized forms. Whilst I stand there I am impressed with a singular conviction that not a form so grotesque, so savage, or so beautiful, but is an expression of something in man the observer. We feel that there is an occult relation between the very worm, the crawling scorpions, and man. *I am moved by strange sympathies. I say I will listen to this invitation. I will be a naturalist.*[29]

Thoreau's first catalog concludes with a similar crescendo, but it is targeted at commerce:

> Commerce is unexpectedly confident and serene, alert, adventurous, and unwearied. It is *very natural in its methods* withal, far more so than many fantastic enterprises and sentimental experiments, and hence its singular success. *I am refreshed and expanded* when the freight train rattles past me, and I smell the stores which go dispensing their odors all the way from Long Wharf to Lake Champlain, reminding me of foreign parts, of coral reefs, and Indian oceans, and tropical climes, and the extent of the globe. *I feel more like a citizen of the world at the sight* of the palm-leaf which will cover so many flaxen New England heads the next summer, the Manilla hemp and cocoa-nut husks, the old junk, gunny bags, scrap iron, and rusty nails (119; emphasis added).

The nobility of the rusty nails and scrap iron seems a parody of "the very worm, the crawling scorpions," and Thoreau's sense of refreshment and expansion at seeing a freight train an inversion of Emerson's "strange sympathies." And should we miss this joke, Thoreau puns with this paragraph on Emerson's 1841 lecture title "The Method of Nature," here claiming that commerce, too, "is very natural in its methods." It was in part Emerson who encouraged in Thoreau the notion of the "text" of nature, and this passage from "Sounds" continues this way: "This car-load of torn sails is more legible and interesting now than if they should be wrought into paper and printed books. Who can write so graphically the history of the storms they have weathered as these rents have done? They are proof-sheets which need no correction" (119). The pun on "proof-sheets"—not only printer's pages for corrections, but also sheets that offer *proof* with no correction or rebuttal—reminds us that Thoreau was performing a reading in "Sounds" in order to enact, as design does, a proof of a first cause or ordering principle. But who would agree to such a principle—torn sails? In "Sounds" Thoreau yokes the railroad to nature and the conjunction is, as it were, unnatural: it is what the world looks like when viewed through the lens of bad design. It is no wonder that the railroad image has been read so frequently as destructive and monstrous.

But nature is still a text and can still be read, as "Sounds" concludes. The hermeneutics advocated in the chapter are incomplete and focused chiefly on rejecting one model, and not yet posing another. The chapter notes that Emerson's claims can be parodied, and more significantly that Paley's theological confidence has left out, in its rage for order, whether or not a universe organized according to the design argument is a good one.

There are some clues in "Sounds" to the suggested model of design Thoreau was developing in the 1850s. He notes, for example, that the parodic heroism of businessmen is more impressive than the men "who stood up for half an hour in the front line at Buena Vista" (118). Buena Vista was a celebrated 1847 battle in the Mexican War, and an obvious synecdoche for the war Thoreau despised. The battle was rendered into romantic terms instantly following the news of it: because it had been waged in rough terrain (as at Roncesvalles), against impossible odds (as at Agincourt), with infantry against better-equipped cavalry (as at Thermopylae), American journalists and writers made it the most celebrated victory of the Mexican War. The event registered throughout the national literature, including a poem, *The Siege of Monterey,* by one William C. Falkner, the great-grandfather of the novelist.[30] Buena Vista, depending on one's point of view in the nineteenth century, became either a confirmation of American territorial promise (in the *Literary World,* American poets were excused from the rigors of writing the epic because the whole country was now "engaged in acting an Epic")[31] or a disaster of foreign policy and the crisis over slavery. Thoreau's antipathy, of course, is well known. The Mexican War itself was associated entirely, for Thoreau, with the worst excesses of manifest destiny. Quite apart from his night in jail in 1846, his residence at Walden Pond commenced on July 4, 1845, and was, among other things, a protest against the annexation of Texas occurring the same day.

His comparison, then, of commercial "heroes" on the railroad whose mettle surpasses that of the soldiers at Buena Vista takes a further step in his rejection of providential rhetoric. The civilized world in *Walden* is full of symbols of its own misunderstanding and intellectual errors. If the railroad effectively illustrates the overly mechanistic theology of design, and its heroes strike Thoreau as heroic to the extent of their absorption into the mechanism, then the analogy of Buena Vista marks out the machinery of manifest destiny, too, as similarly alienating. The Mexican War, like design, was the product of a fallen worldview. Thoreau's association of the two—the design-railroad and the Buena Vista front line—indicates that he perceived the similar logic behind the two endeavors. Design claimed, in error, that heat and motion could be described not only intelligibly, but to the greater glory of the heater and the mover. Buena Vista, analogously linked by Thoreau to this "heroic" effort, was a comparable (though not as impressive) heroism, to the greater glory of the United States—a claim also in error. Thoreau's interest was in describing a similar flaw of reasoning in theology and in politics, and we then discover his recurrent sense that American design was worth resuscitating from those two fallen discourses.

IF *WALDEN* IS Thoreau's recognition of the flaws of a worldview based on design or on manifest destiny, then "Slavery in Massachusetts" entertains similar objections, and the relationship between the two parts of the essay is comprehensible if it is read, as in *Walden,* as instruction on good and bad design. Thoreau's notion of design in the essay is broadened to include the sense of how eccentrically we Americans look at the world, a logic that follows easily from design itself. Indeed, Thoreau's interest in a specific design argument became, during the 1850s, the dominant term for not simply *one* way of looking, but for the *best* way.

Like "Sounds" in *Walden,* "Slavery in Massachusetts" presents a plainly overdetermined pastoral artistic convention: in the former case, the invading railroad; in the latter, the lily. In both cases, the image is intended to announce our arrival in a pastoral setting, as a type of stage cue for Thoreau's drama about landscapes. Suppose, he suggests, you began to look at nature: what would you see first? For most American observers in the 1850s, the pastoral would be the primary response, including specific botanical displays and the rustic calm of an environment outside the city. The pastoral, like any visual convention, circulated this "restricted number of spatial signs."[32]

Thoreau would have known the ideological limits of the pastoral as well as its visual limits, identified by Buell as "simultaneously . . . counterinstitutional and institutionally sponsored" (50). In other words, in the first place, the pastoral offers retreat from (and implied critique of) its opposites, namely corruption, commerce, heat, noise, dirt, and death. But this retreat is always in danger of encouraging safe pieties about nature as a means of neutralizing that dissent and rendering the entire gesture essentially conservative. In the case of Rachel Carson's *Silent Spring,* for instance, her pastoral opening can be read as a nostalgic fantasy, not a call to arms—which is, Buell notes, *precisely* the way the corporate defenders of the pesticide DDT hoped it would be read. D. H. Lawrence's cynicism about this risk was clear: "Absolutely the safest thing to get your emotional reactions over is NATURE."[33]

Thoreau's "Slavery in Massachusetts," then, had to assess this problem, and override it. When I describe this strategy as a lesson in good and bad readings, I am not invoking Stanley Cavell's *Senses of Walden,* which relies primarily on Thoreau's chapter "Reading." Cavell's argument, that *Walden* is about the philosophical edification of writing (and reading) a book like *Walden,* posits a hermetic seal around Thoreau's own sense of the circulation of ideas between writer and audience; it does not admit of much real experience, whether in nature or in politics or in bad ideas. A writer who commenced with a chapter called "Economy" (as opposed to, say, "Reading") would have had to acknowledge that his book was not only about his book. And if *Walden* seems to contain less of the outright political content that "Slavery in Massachusetts" does (Cavell asserts mysteriously that Thoreau's residence at Walden Pond began on the Fourth of July only "by accident"), it is still preoccupied with—indeed, marked by—its political times, as the main body of *Walden* criticism has acknowledged.[34] This assessment of Cavell is by way of repeating that for Thoreau, reading was at least equally a political act as it was a philosophical one.

"Slavery in Massachusetts" stages a pastoral moment in its ending as a cue to reading the previous pages of politics and to keeping those politics radical—the lily as "murder to the state." Thoreau intended to expose the pastoral as a faulty worldview, as he had done in *Walden,* which, in that text, had accomplished a political critique.

Thoreau's rhetorical question, which commences the lily passage, suggests as much: "What signifies the beauty of nature when men are base?"[35] As in the balance between the Fugitive Slave Law and the lily in the essay overall, "base men" and the "beauty of nature" are set up as opposing terms. And the question is undeniably a hostile one. But toward what is Thoreau most hostile? On the one hand, his question quiets the comparative drone of his politics, seems to change the subject, and makes the previous performance sound rhetorically like mere prologue. Base men are no match, rhetorically or spiritually, for the beauty of nature: lesser matters fade from view before higher truths. Thoreau notes that "Nature has been partner to no Missouri Compromise. I scent no compromise in the fragrance of the water-lily" (108). The pastoral effect of providing refuge from the impurities of politics is in full force in the passage, implicating the political crisis of Anthony Burns's return to slavery in what seems, in Thoreau's view, the final censure: the logic of the Fugitive Slave Law is not even susceptible to the laws of nature.

The pastoral reading, though easily shown, is somewhat unsatisfactory and evasive. The ending to "Slavery in Massachusetts" is, after all, without thunder. Buell paraphrases it thus: "Righteous indignation dissolves into a sulk."[36] The question is: how did Thoreau get so naive?

The solution is in the exposure of pastoral ideology implied in Thoreau's use of it. If we adjust the emphasis of his question about the beauty of nature, we hear a different reproach: that beauty, before base men, does not even "signify"; nature does not triumph after all. And ultimately, Thoreau's sense of hope at the conclusion of "Slavery in Massachusetts" derives not from pastoral refuge or political expediency—not, in other words, deciding between nature and base men—but from a recognition of an alternative worldview.

In order to show this recognition in "Slavery in Massachusetts," it is helpful to know one case of Thoreau's ideas about a "worldview," which for him was simultaneously a cognitive and a metaphysical question. His chief biographer, Robert D. Richardson, Jr., notes the time Thoreau invested in reading about John Ruskin's aesthetics during the 1850s.[37] An enthusiast from the first appearance of *Modern Painters* in 1843, Thoreau's favorite work by Ruskin was *Elements of Drawing*. A guidebook for fledgling artists, Ruskin's text insists throughout on the removal of "memory knowledge" and the elevated experience of "visual appearances only." (Richardson notes helpfully that Georges Seurat and Claude Monet both found *Elements of Drawing* prophetic, making possible the development of modern painting.) Thoreau read carefully through the suggested exercises, which emphasize seeing over drawing. Here is one of Ruskin's practice sessions:

> [Sit] about three yards from a bookcase (not your own, so that you may *know* none of the titles of the books), to try to draw the books accurately, with the title of the backs and the patterns on the bindings as you see them. You are not to stir from your place to seek what they are, but to draw them simply as they appear, giving the perfect look of neat lettering, which nevertheless, must be (as you will find it on most of the books) absolutely illegible.

This technique, it seems, draws on Romantic notions of "defamiliarization." It demands that the viewer-painter forget how to "read" the scene before him, whether the reading is of book titles or landscapes, and instead of seeing the world he knows, he observes a world he doesn't. The method causes the observer to notice how his "observations" have often been planned in advance. Ruskin concludes that "the whole experience of painting depends on the recovery of what may be called the innocence of the eye . . . without consciousness of what [colors and shapes] *signify*."[38] Ruskin's technique, then, rejects any overdetermined or traditional visual systems—such as those in, say, the pastoral—and instead attempts to view landscapes more deliberately. (Thoreau offers a similar rationale in *Walden* about *living* deliberately.) Ruskin's aesthetics, according to Richardson, are present throughout Thoreau's journals in the 1850s and strongly influenced a later essay, "Autumnal Tints." Ruskin taught Thoreau to account for, if not to discard entirely, the ways in which his visual apprehension of nature was likely not to be innocent.

Ruskin's innocent eye works toward immunity from what nature might "signify"—the same verb as in Thoreau's query in "Slavery in Massachusetts." Thoreau's sense of how to look at the lily in "Slavery in Massachusetts" would have been implicated in the question of how it "signified," or how its innocence was lost. That is why the pastoral reading of the ending of "Slavery in Massachusetts," with its tendency to implicate Thoreau as an escapist, is inaccurate. Thoreau would not have resuscitated the overdetermined symbol of the lily *merely* in the service of the pastoral. The pastoral was not innocent enough. But still to select an entirely overloaded floral image for his conclusion represents Thoreau's attempt to reclaim an innocent eye (*not* a pastoral eye, I emphasize) where it was clearly most needed—in the midst of the political crisis of Anthony Burns.[39]

The essay bears out Thoreau's impatience with the pastoral and his preference for a better visual—and political—system, even before it is fully present in the ending. The primary example is in Thoreau's assertion that "there are . . . two parties, . . . the party of the city, and the party of the country"; and "it is much more important to know what the country thinks [of a political issue] than what the city thinks." Thoreau sounds here like a standard champion of rural merits over urban demerits, or an advocate of the pastoral. But, he continues, the problem with the country is that we never get to its real views, because "she has few, if any organs, though which to express herself. The editorials which she reads, like the news, come from the seaboard" (99). Thoreau puns here on *organs* (he means sense organs, like eyes and ears, or perhaps an internal organ, like a brain), so that Boxboro, Massachusetts, Thoreau's specimen country scene, has no brain: it is inhabited by subhumans. Country people, Thoreau insists, must "cultivate self-respect," another pun, on the current produce of those who *cultivate*, or farm, for a living.

How, then, does Thoreau propose to help us see? The argument of "Slavery in Massachusetts" rests primarily on Thoreau's analysis of the law, and his conclusions that "the law will never make men free; it is men who have got to make the law free." He claims finally that the lily "suggests what kind of laws have prevailed longest and widest, and still prevail" (108). In both the political complaint and the appeal to nature, each part is characterized by the presence of the law. Unspecified appeals to law were frequent in the period, as it happens: Senator William Seward spoke bitterly of the slavery crisis in 1850 and appealed to "the higher law than the Constitution which regulates our authority."[40] (He even became known popularly as "Higher-Law Seward," a fact Emerson recorded in his journal in 1850.)[41] Indeed, Thoreau had devoted a chapter of *Walden* to the topic ("Higher Laws"), in which he determined, through his increasing "natural" dislike of a meat diet, the reverence due to the human body according to laws of nature. The law, then, represented the object of a transcendent appeal, away from one's culture. In Thoreau's view, such transcendence was the only relevant practice of Christianity left the modern believer: his religious faith is on display in his essays not as specifically Christian worship but as a nonspecific affection for the divine, such as the "gods" present in *A Walk to Wachusett.*

The law in both the political jeremiad and the pastoral inset of "Slavery in Massachusetts" offers a key to the relationship between the two parts. Law provides the organizing principles in both sections. Thoreau's arrangement of these principles is analogous and meant to balance each section of the essay in light of the other. In the first part of the essay, law represents, variously, the Constitution, the Fugitive Slave Law, and the individual moral sense. The inadequacy of the first two terms—indeed, their sad corruptibility—leads by necessity to appeals to the third. Similarly, in the lily section, the law represents the cycle of nature, the visual system of the pastoral, and a third term that approximates the moral sense outlined in the political section of the essay: Thoreau calls it "a moral quality." And similarly, the third term arises from the inadequacy of the first two.

This arrangement of appeals to law indicates Thoreau's engagement with an essential method of design argument, the analogy. Design rests, as I have described previously, on a chain of analogical association: the universe is like a machine; a machine has a mechanic; thus, the universe has a divine mechanic. Thoreau's habit of mind as an observer of nature had been oriented this way for some years, and a journal entry from 1850 offers an example: "These expansions of the river skim over before the river itself takes on its icy fetters. What is the analogy?"[42] Thoreau's nature writing frequently uses a "random" specimen of natural beauty to elicit a moral or philosophical truth, as Paley had done with the analogy of the watch and the stone.

Thoreau had also absorbed the logic of the design argument that leaps to immediate moral facts from observable laws of nature. Natural laws, which may sound like the strictly scientific phrase "laws of nature," would have provided an easy drift to "intuited, self-evident ethico-moral or political laws."[43] In other words, nature was perpetually in the process of proving some truth or other about human affairs, and this proving was a particular and emphatic method of the design argument.

Thoreau's skepticism toward the law, in the political sense, prompted his analogous skepticism toward law in the sense of its ordering our perceptions of nature. The shiftiness of perceptions, where we may imagine Ruskin's innocent eye suddenly finding focus on a scene, suggests that the "moral quality" apparently at the endpoint of Thoreau's analogies in the essay depends on how you look at things. The essay correspondingly recurs to visual metaphors and details. Thoreau notes that the governor of Massachusetts is no governor to him personally because "I never saw him of whom I speak," and therefore "so far am I from being governed by him" (94). Indeed, the governor's visibility seems to Thoreau in inverse proportion to the ability to govern well: "When freedom is most endangered, he dwells in the deepest obscurity" (92). Thoreau develops a view of the fallen moral state of Massachusetts, and how he has come to perceive it: "I cannot persuade myself that I do not dwell wholly within hell" (106). The recognition, he notes, has been a fall from paradise, perceptible visually:

> Suppose you have a small library, with pictures to adorn the walls,—a garden laid out around,—and contemplate scientific and literary pursuits, and discover all at once that your villa, with all its contents, is located in hell, and that the justice of the peace has a cloven foot and a forked tail,—do not these suddenly lose their value *in your eyes?* (107; emphasis added)

This library scene is not unlike Ruskin's practice session for training the innocent eye—though of course Thoreau would not read *Elements of Drawing* until it appeared in 1857. In any event, Thoreau's example of the sudden clarity of the scene, wherein, as the scales fall from the eyes, the observer glimpses the true value of a life lived under immoral laws, suggests that his "moral quality" rests on the fitness of the perceptions. The essay reveals its reliance on the jeremiad genre—the exhortation to improve a lapsed state of affairs, addressed explicitly to those who don't see this lapse. You know the repugnance of the Fugitive Slave Law, claims Thoreau, or the inadequacy of any other system of "laws," only when you are perceiving correctly. And when you perceive correctly, you also perceive the blindness of your fellow citizens. His lily metaphor, then—"so pure and fair to the *eye* . . . as if to *show* us what purity and sweetness reside within" (108; emphasis added) —carries the weight of this lone seer's gift. As in a jeremiad, too, Thoreau enjoys the solitude of his insights, which he entertains while alone with the lily, not with the crowds in town. The lily is a sign of hope, in the end, only to the man who "is fitted to perceive and love it" (108).

Thoreau's rejection of the inaction of his fellow citizens toward Anthony Burns corresponds to his rejection of the pastoral as another realm of "inaction," so that, in all, the essay attacks complacency while offering a specific psychological program for stirring up protest. It is a vast politics, by any standard: Thoreau will settle for nothing less than complete cognitive overhaul. It is also an eccentric politics, ignoring what seems to be at the heart of the matter—changing the bad law that follows fugitive slaves into free states and repeals their free status—and instead emphasizing the ways in which this bad law is to the intellectual discredit of Americans. Thoreau's oversimplified summation of the Anthony Burns affair—"trying a MAN, to find out if he is not really a SLAVE" (92)—becomes more intriguing when we note that the purpose of the essay is to explain just how such an error is made. It is also, in this sense, a sentimental politics, calling for a restoration of an innocent worldview, a restoration that all Americans are capable of, rather than assessing realistically—in the words of one modern realist— what is to be done. In this way, Thoreau's dilemma is the "liberal" dilemma in the nineteenth century: how to reclaim the mass of the people without resorting to the vulgarities and compromises of populism; and how to maintain any kind of faith in his fellow citizens without becoming trapped by idealism.

And perhaps uniquely in the nineteenth century, Thoreau insists that nature, while proof of a great number of things, does not prove self-evident truths. The process of finding in nature the confirmation of design, after all, is a backward or inductive proof; in the case of manifest destiny, it is mere expediency. In design, Thoreau found intellectual satisfactions from the sheer number of examples that challenged and invigorated the design argument, and in the variety of specimens and processes in nature that he investigated firsthand. (His profession was recorded in the Concord census as "surveyor.") There were none of the same satisfactions in surveying the Democratic party. Nature worked, and often like a ticking watch; politics didn't. And more important, the worldview that permitted the good mind access to nature's workings also showed vividly why the models from nature were in political terms ineffectual, and more often malign. Thoreau grasped that in nature, we must, by necessity, translate our observations into human terms (the pastoral, the poetic, the botanical, the geological), and therefore "use" nature to account for the limits of human knowledge: thus he replied to Emerson's naive question in *Nature*—"To what end is nature?"—and explained precisely to what end nature is. And that, for Thoreau, was design. But a comparable approach to politics, to justify any of the usual range of political options regarding, say, the Fugitive Slave Law (none of which Thoreau could accept), was not only a bad politics, but a bad idea—worth dissent by design.

Epilogue

The Case against the Hamptons

Who hath heard such a thing? who hath seen such things? Shall the earth be made to bring forth in one day? or shall a nation be born at once? for as soon as Zion travailed, she brought forth her children.
Isaiah 66:8

Where does design go after 1861, after Fort Sumter, First Bull Run, and the admission of a free Kansas? Probably Nevada: the setting for *Roughing It.* Mark Twain's "young and ignorant" narrator arrives in Nevada Territory and meets Governor Nye and his fourteen Irish henchmen biding their time, collecting "little territorial crumbs" of federal allocation. To secure his flunkies gainful employment, Governor Nye has a scheme: a railroad survey, "from Carson City westward to a certain point!" When the governor is reminded of the obstacle posed by the Sierra Nevada mountains, he does not miss a beat: "Well, then, survey it eastward to a certain point!" The pork-barrel scheme for the Irishmen induces geographical delirium and gets the best of what Thoreau saw mistakenly as the inevitable westward tendency. Just to keep funds rolling in, Governor Nye calls for the "certain point" to extend eastward indefinitely—"To the Atlantic Ocean, blast you!—and then bridge it and go on!"

It strikes me that the American West may have invited the furious providential thinking described in this book simply by being so improbable: *who*, asks the prophet, *hath heard such a thing?* In the end, many Americans noticed that the course of empire could have advanced any old way.

Such contingent views of continental expansion seem to me, on the whole, kept quiet in the national canon, which allegedly broadcasts from literary headquarters in New England to provincial outposts farther and farther west. (The South, in this model, may be of equal vintage to New England, but the Mason-Dixon line marked its exile and banishment; it is still imagined to be on the receiving end of Culture.) On this Plymouth Rock I will build a culture: the theory of the advance of American literature follows, unwittingly, the Frederick Jackson Turner thesis of westward expansion; it is no wonder that Turner called the frontier a "palimpsest," in which erasures and edits are part of the landscape. It is a place where Westerners do their Eastern literary drills, like penmanship exercises.

But as I have suggested, Westerners have never seen cultural transmission in quite this way. The explorers who brought their narratives back East for annexation into, say, classic texts of Transcendentalism were no longer merely under Eastern tutelage, at least not when they could acknowledge that Eastern metaphors had failed them. Such admissions in exploration writing occur chiefly in forms of aesthetic dementia, such as the picturesque, the designed, the destined.

I suppose I cherish exploration narratives exactly for this repetitive melodrama of statements of absolute knowledge, followed by their eventual collapse in the field. My own image of exploration is not of a westward, triumphant errand of right and empire, but rather of a series of accidents, so unprovidential that explorers cannot keep their luggage dry—luggage that included, of course, only the essentials: theodolytes, sketch pads, laxative pills, presidential medals, quill pens, and volumes of light verse. Jean Nicolet, exploring the Great Lakes and intending to sail to Asia, even planned ahead and brought in his luggage a "Chinese" silk robe, which he donned in order to blend in with the startled Winnebagoes on the shores of Lake Superior. In *Roughing It,* Twain's young narrator insists they bring the weighty English dictionary on the stagecoach to Nevada; for most of the bumpy journey it vaults through the air and, like Eve's progeny with the serpent, bruises his head.

I might have offered evidence for this proposition about the West—of its being not inevitably Western and thus the beneficiary of an elaborate tradition of arguments about inevitability—with a different set of readings, such as Native American writings or frontier women's diaries, or the newly rediscovered accounts by African American cowboys, or the writings of Asian Americans and Mexican Americans in California. These fields of study seem to me well launched and frankly secure in their collective effort to change our views of American literary history. The old joke about the Native American's first words to Christopher Columbus ("So, are you over here on a Fulbright?") ought to remind us who, in that scenario, was giving out the grants. No one I have read in this field thinks that canon is an entirely useless concept; the adjustments and the debate usually have to do with who is in it. Likewise, the four points of the compass are probably overdue for their overhaul as a "social construct," but no one is mad enough to build a bridge from Carson City across the Atlantic and call it Western. (It is true, though, that London Bridge now spans Arizona, in a town renamed, in 1968, English Village.) If we take seriously the view of a canon as no less handy a legend than westward expansion is (which is what literary archaeology is for, after all) then exploration narratives belong in the canon for the same reasons that other alleged "artifact" texts do. The texts I chose might have been by different authors, but the argument, how the canon decenters itself, is at their heart.

TWAIN WAS RIGHT about the temporary and contingent quality of Western places, and the ways in which the West existed primarily in the mind. *Roughing It* is preoccupied with the "flush times" that result from speculation in silver: not value produced from mining itself, but the imaginary values that rumor and fantasy can bestow on a mine that produces nothing. *Roughing It* may even offer its most astringent comment on the fugitive nature of the West, by ending west of the West, in Hawaii. Meanwhile, though, in Nevada, there is a famous lawsuit, *Hyde vs. Morgan*. Hyde's ranch is on the valley floor, just beneath Morgan's. When a landslide causes Morgan's ranch to slide down the hillside on top of Hyde's, Morgan quite sensibly claims ownership—he now owns, as he always did, his same land: "the cabin was standing on the same dirt and same ranch it always had stood on." Morgan is puzzled why Hyde, if he had a genuine claim, didn't "stay and hold possession" as thirty-eight feet of landslide descended on him. The judge, ex-governor Roop, ignores Morgan's logic and decides the case in favor of God's designs for Nevada:

> Gentlemen, [he said,] it ill becomes us, worms as we are, to meddle with the decrees of Heaven. It is plain to me that Heaven, in its inscrutable wisdom, has seen fit to move this defendant's ranch for a purpose. . . . No—Heaven created the ranches, and it is Heaven's prerogative to rearrange them, to experiment with them, to shift them around at its pleasure.[1]

Twain tells the story of the lawsuit as a hilarious send-up of Jacksonian design reasoning in the West, inasmuch as divine purposes can be read not only in landslides but also in lawsuits, or the kind of land-based litigiousness that continental expansion generated in the new territories. Morgan's spurious claims to Hyde's land as, simply and self-evidently, Morgan's "same dirt" rearranged by Providence are surely parodic of Western land thefts and displacements generally, whether against Native Americans, Mexicans, or Anglo ranchers too weak to stare down a Yankee landslide and "hold possession." Hyde wins the lawsuit, as it happens, but effectively loses. Judge Roop exonerates Morgan: "Hyde has been deprived of his ranch by the visitation of God! And from this decision," he concludes, "there is no appeal."

Like losers in lawsuits, many explorers with no appeal achieved their obscurity by arriving in the American West from the wrong direction. Lewis and Clark were hardly the first to take on the territory of Louisiana: Jefferson's forays into the West included John Ledyard's quixotic scheme to arrive at Philadelphia by way of St. Petersburg, Siberia, Nootka Sound, and the Rocky Mountains; and a series of nameless Pacific entries to the inner regions by British mariners that made Jefferson deeply anxious about the

American trade monopoly. Explorers perhaps have never had the luxury of poetic reverie about their geographical lot, as in Walt Whitman's poem, "Facing West from California's Shores" (written at the same time as Twain's adventures in Nevada), in which Whitman declares the advance of the westward latitude line to be utterly transparent, certainly tragic, possibly banal. The poem is a gazetteer of the places that human memory and history have encompassed, which "the circle [has] almost circled": "Hindustan and Kashmere," Asia, the Spice Islands, thence to the western edge of the New World. "But where," demands Whitman's speaker in the poem's coda, in the same tone as Isaiah, "is what I started for so long ago? / And why is it yet unfound?"

Such questions seem to me the undertone of exploration narratives, busy with their theodolites and medals and laxatives: the grief and exasperation of unmet promises, the dry fact that *there is no there there.* The point is that American exploration tended in the nineteenth century more and more heavily toward the devices of fiction, or of fictionalizing. We can indict, for this development, the aesthetic dementia I mentioned, or explorers' decreasing demands on empiricism, or their weakened attempts to "balance" competing landscape theories, or simply (as the sections squared off against each other) their loss of ambivalence.

And American literature in the nineteenth century tended to the same extremes. Nathaniel Hawthorne declared that his own genre, romance, was "a certain latitude," a nice encapsulation of geographical metaphor into one splendid kind of American fiction: it is a line of "latitude," or license, that extends, the further it travels, into fancy. The royal charters granted Virginia, Maryland, and other early colonies the territory between certain latitudes, or sometimes heading off at diagonals, infinitely, without western boundary, so that in an old-fashioned historical atlas of America you find a frenzied fantasy map of the continent, dyed preemptively in stripes and angles of jarring Yankee tones. Likewise, we map our literature the way that John Donne mapped his beloved's body: "O my America! O my newfound land!" he cries ecstatically, making that primal error again, the one that assures us we can entirely embrace our imagination, or indeed imagine the thing we embrace.

And surely Jay Gatsby, that Westerner, had seen a geographical prophecy in his youthful reading of *Hopalong Cassidy,* and found out that the excesses of latitude moved in a complete circle around the globe, or in Gatsby's case, the egg.[2] It is, after all, Tom and Daisy Buchanan, the Chicagoans, who are the most screwed up. They take geographical liberties when they go to the place that we must call "*back* East," a place of apparent return that Whitman can rebut in a half-stanza. But "they smashed things up," bellyaches Nick Carraway, himself a Minnesotan. Fitzgerald has Nick Carraway admit that Gatsby's is a "story of the West, after all"—this Eastern novel, the one that pines most for the Hamptons, the transatlantic bridge, the English Village, and the wonder of the Old World. This mysterious jaunt eastward is the secret theme in American literature, as secret as Gatsby's beginnings in North Dakota. Yes, the novel ends on designing Dutch sailors ogling what is west of them, but the real gaze of the novel is Gatsby's, from West Egg eastward to East Egg. And even more ardent than this geographical gaze is Gatsby's attempt, finally, to win over the Eastern natives in the manner of Nicolet: with grand silks. "It makes me sad," sobs Daisy, speaking like a Winnebago, "because I've never seen such—such beautiful shirts before."

NOTES

INTRODUCTION

1. Vladimir Nabokov, *Lolita, or the Confessions of a White Widowed Male* (New York: G. P. Putnam's Sons, 1955), 88.

2. See the range of opinions in some general works on the design argument: John Donnelly, ed., *Logical Analysis and Contemporary Theism* (New York: Fordham University Press, 1972); Peter Addinall, *Philosophy and Biblical Interpretation: A Study in Nineteenth-Century Conflict* (Cambridge: Cambridge University Press, 1991); Robert H. Hurlbutt, *Hume, Newton, and the Design Argument* (Lincoln: University of Nebraska Press, 1965); Philip P. Wiener, ed., *Dictionary of the History of Ideas,* 5 vols. (New York: Scribners, 1973–74); and Frederick Copleston, S.J., *A History of Philosophy,* vol. 7 (New York: Doubleday, 1994).

3. Aristotle, *The Metaphysics,* 2 vols., trans. Hugh Tredennick (Cambridge: Harvard University Press, 1989–90); Thomas Aquinas, *The Five Ways: St. Thomas Aquinas' Proofs of God's Existence,* ed. Anthony John Patrick Kenny (New York: Schocken Books, 1969); Edward Herbert, Lord Cherbury, *De Veritate prout distinguitur a revelatione, a verisimili, a possibili, et a falso* (1624; reprint, Bristol: J. W. Arrowsmith Ltd., 1937); and John Toland, *Christianity Not Mysterious* (1696; reprint, New York: Garland, 1978).

   On this topic generally, see John Tulloch, *Rational Theology and Christian Philosophy in England in the Seventeenth Century,* 2 vols. (Edinburgh and London: Blackwood and Sons, 1872). Tulloch's table of contents lists these names as the major players in this intellectual and theological development: Lord Falkland, John Hales, William Chillingworth, Jeremy Taylor, Edward Stillingfleet, Benjamin Whichcote, John Smith, Ralph Cudworth, Henry More, and in general the Cambridge Platonists or Latitudinarians.

4. Joseph Addison, "An Ode," in *The Works of the English Poets, from Chaucer to Cowper,* vol. 9, ed. Alexander Chambers, 21 vols. (London: J. Johnson et al., 1810), 571; William Derham, *Physico-theology: or, A demonstration of the being and attributes of God, from His works of creation: Being the substance of sixteen sermons preached in St. Mary-*

le-Bow-Church, London, at the Honourable Mr. Boyle's lectures in the years 1711 and 1712 (London: Printed for W. Innys, 1742); William Paley, *Natural Theology; or, Evidences of the Existence and Attributes of the Deity, collected from the appearances of Nature* (London: R. Faulder, 1804).

5. Norman Hampson, *The Enlightenment* (New York: Penguin, 1968), 12: "The abbé Pluche was such a virtuoso in this [theological] genre that it is only fair to point out that he did not claim, as Voltaire and subsequent writers have misquoted him as doing, that tides were created to enable ships to enter ports. He merely pointed out that this was one of their advantages."

   See Noël Antoine Pluche's *Spectacle de la Nature: or, Nature display'd. Being discourses on such particulars of natural history as were thought most proper to excite the curiosity, and form the minds of youth, translated from the original French,* 7 vols. (London: J. Pemberton, R. Francklin, and C. Davis, 1735–48).

6. Perry Miller, *The Life of the Mind in America from the Revolution to the Civil War* (New York: Harcourt Brace Jovanovich, 1965), 276.

7. John O'Sullivan, "An Introductory Statement of the Democratic Principle," in *Social Theories of Jacksonian Democracy: Representative Writings of the Period 1825–1850,* ed. Joseph L. Blau (New York: The Liberal Arts Press, 1954).

8. Henry David Thoreau, "Walking," in *Excursions and Poems,* ed. Bradford Torrey and Francis H. Allen (Boston: Houghton Mifflin, 1906).

9. Andrew Jackson, "A Political Testament," from *Farewell Address of Andrew Jackson to the People of the United States: and the Inaugural Address of Martin Van Buren, President of the United States* (Washington, 1837), in Blau, *Social Theories,* 2, 20.

10. Myra Jehlen, *American Incarnation: The Individual, the Nation, and the Continent* (Cambridge: Harvard University Press, 1986), 2; Wayne Franklin, *Discoverers, Explorers, Settlers: The Diligent Writers of Early America* (Chicago: University of Chicago Press, 1979), 1; F. O. Matthiessen, *American Renaissance: Art and Expression in the Age of Emerson and Whitman* (New York: Oxford University Press, 1941), ix.

11. Walt Whitman, "The Workings of Democracy," *Brooklyn Daily Eagle,* April 20, 1847, in Blau, *Social Theories,* 129.

12. Henry David Thoreau, "Walking" (New York: The Riverside Press, 1914), 31.

13. In 1832–33 the Society for the Diffusion of Useful Knowledge produced an inexpensive general-interest periodical (these details confirm its aims at a broad readership rather than an elite one) called *The Penny Magazine.* From the preface to its first issue:

There have been no excitements for the lovers of the marvellous—no tattle or abuse for the gratification of a diseased taste for personality—and, above all, *no party politics.* The subjects which have uniformly been treated have been of the broadest and simplest character. Striking points of Natural History—Accounts of the great Works of Art in Sculpture and Painting—Descriptions of such Antiquities as possess historical interest—Personal Narratives of Travellers—Biographies of Men who have had a permanent influence on the condition of the world—Elementary Principles of Language and Numbers—established facts in Statistics and Political Economy—these have supplied the materials for exciting the curiosity of a million of readers. This consideration furnishes the most convincing answer to the few (if any there now remain) who assert that General Education is an evil. The people will not abuse the power they have acquired to read, and therefore to think.

This journal is available online at http://english.cla.umn.edu/lkd/pm/Penny Mag.html. The society also produced the Library of Entertaining Knowledge, suggesting again its mainly nonspecialist readership. Thoreau's acquaintance with this periodical is unknown.

14. Whitman, "Workings," in Blau, *Social Theories,* 129.
15. Thomas R. Hietala, *Manifest Design: Anxious Aggrandizement in Late Jacksonian America* (Ithaca, N.Y.: Cornell University Press, 1985), 8–9.
16. Marvin Meyers, *The Jacksonian Persuasion: Politics and Belief* (Stanford: Stanford University Press, 1957).
17. W. E. Channing's petition is in W. H. Channing, *The Life of William Ellery Channing* (Boston: n.p., 1880), 504. The Kneeland story is told in Anne C. Rose, *Transcendentalism as a Social Movement, 1830–1850* (New Haven: Yale University Press, 1981), 26–27; it is picked up by Barbara Packer in "The Transcendentalists," in *The Cambridge History of American Literature,* vol. 2, *Prose Writing 1820–1865,* ed. Sacvan Bercovitch (Cambridge: Cambridge University Press, 1995), 404–6. Brownson's remark appears in Rose, *Transcendentalism,* 27; the source is Orestes Brownson, *A Discourse of the Wants of the Times* (Boston: James Munroe, 1836), 10.
18. He did deliver several speeches, considered elsewhere in this book. There is a film version of Jackson's life: *The Gorgeous Hussy* (1936), in which Joan Crawford plays Mrs. Andrew Jackson. The phrase *manifest destiny* is not in the script.
19. Tzvetan Todorov, *The Conquest of America: The Question of the Other* (New York: Harper and Row, 1984), 190, 156.
20. Sacvan Bercovitch, *The Rites of Assent: Transformations in the Symbolic Construction of America* (New York: Routledge, 1993), 35.
21. Hietala, *Manifest Design,* 132, 156. His original source for both quotations is Representative Samuel Gordon of New York in *Congressional Globe,* 29th Cong., 2d sess., 391 (February 11, 1847).
22. Annette Kolodny, "Letting Go Our Grand Obsessions: Notes toward a New Literary History of the American Frontiers," *American Literature* 64 (March 1992): 1–18.
23. Frank Bergon, "Wilderness Aesthetics," *American Literary History* 9 (Spring 1997): 128–61; Myra Jehlen, "Exploration and Empire," in *The Cambridge History of American Literature,* vol. 1, *1590–1820,* ed. Sacvan Bercovitch (Cambridge: Cambridge University Press, 1995), 149–61.
24. William Gilpin, "On Picturesque Travel," in *Three Essays* (London: n.p., 1794), 47.
25. Edward Halsey Foster, *The Civilized Wilderness: Backgrounds to American Romantic Literature, 1817–1860* (New York: Free Press, 1975), 14, 64.
26. Henry Adams, *The Education of Henry Adams* (1918; reprint, New York: Penguin, 1995), 232.
27. John O'Sullivan, "An Introductory Statement," in Blau, *Social Theories,* 28.
28. Nabokov, 212.
29. Ralph Waldo Emerson, *The Journals and Miscellaneous Notebooks of Ralph Waldo*

Emerson, ed. William H. Gilman, Ralph H. Orth, et al., 16 vols. (Cambridge: Harvard University Press, Belknap Press, 1960–1982), 5:218.

30. Albert J. von Frank, *The Sacred Game: Provincialism and Frontier Consciousness in American Literature, 1630–1860* (Cambridge: Cambridge University Press, 1985), 107.

31. Anders Stephanson, *Manifest Destiny: American Expansion and the Empire of Right* (New York: Hill and Wang, 1996), 51. Stephanson does not list a source for Channing's quotation.

32. George Bancroft, "The Office of the People in Art, Government, and Religion," in Blau, *Social Theories,* 266.

33. Stephanson, *Manifest Destiny,* 54.

34. Barbara Packer, "Emerson and the Shadow of Race," lecture at Claremont Graduate School, March 22, 1994.

35. Letter to the editor, *New York Times,* December 1860, in Kenneth M. Stampp, ed., *The Causes of the Civil War* (New York: Simon and Schuster, 1991), 76. Editorial, Charleston *Mercury,* February 28, 1860, in Stampp, *Causes,* 148.

36. Edgar Allan Poe, "To Helen," in *The Fall of the House of Usher and Other Writings,* ed. David Galloway (New York: Penguin, 1987), 68.

37. The quotation is from February 1855. Joel Porte, ed., *Emerson in His Journals* (Cambridge: Harvard University Press, Belknap Press, 1982), 458.

38. Robert D. Richardson, Jr., *Henry Thoreau: A Life of the Mind* (Berkeley: University of California Press, 1986), 24.

CHAPTER 1. NATURAL CAUSES

1. The facts of this little-known story, and the quotations from Lewis's and McKeehan's letters, appeared first in Donald Jackson, "The Race to Publish Lewis and Clark," *Pennsylvania Magazine of History and Biography* 85, no. 2 (1985), 163–77, and are retold by Gary E. Moulton in the introduction to *The Journal of Patrick Gass, May 14, 1804–September 23, 1806,* vol. 10 of *The Journals of the Lewis and Clark Expedition,* 12 vols., ed. Gary E. Moulton (Lincoln: University of Nebraska Press, 1983–99). Patrick Gass's book was originally published as *Journal of the voyages and travels of a corps of discovery, under the command of Capt. Lewis and Capt. Clarke of the Army of the United States, from the mouth of the River Missouri through the interior parts of North America to the Pacific Ocean, during the years 1804, 1805 and 1806. Containing an authentic relation of the most interesting transactions during the expedition; a description of the country; and an account of its inhabitants, soil, climate, curiosities and vegetable and animal productions* (Philadelphia: Printed for M. Carey, 1811).

2. Patrick Gass, *Voyage des capitaines Lewis et Clarke, depuis l'emboulure du Missouri, jusqu'à l'entrée de la Colombia dans l'océan Pacifique; fait dans les années 1804, 1805, et 1806, par ordre du gouvernement des États-Unis: contenant le journal authentique des événements les plus remarquables du voyage, ainsi que la description des habitants, du sol, du climat, et des productions animales et végétales des pays situés à l'ouest de l'Amérique Septentrionale. Rédigé en anglais par Patrice Gass, employé dans l'expédition; et traduit en française par A. J. N. Lallemant . . . Avec des notes, deux lettres du capitaine Clarke, et une carte gravée par J. B. Tardieu* (Paris: Arthus-Bertrand, 1810); Patrick Gass,

Tagebuch einer Entdeckungs-Reise durch Nord-America, von der Mündung des Missouri an bis zum Einfluss der Columbia in den Stillen Ocean, gemacht in den Jahren 1804, 1805 und 1806, auf Befehl der Regierung der Vereinigten Staaten, von den beiden Capitäns Lewis und Clarke. Uebers. von Ph. Ch. Weyland (Weimar: H.S. privil. Landes-Industrie-Comptoirs, 1814).

3. Of course, vol. 12 of the Nebraska edition of the Lewis and Clark *Journals* includes all the field drawings.

4. Elliott Coues, *History of the Expedition . . . of Lewis and Clark* (New York: F. P. Harper, 1893), 1:189 n. 12. Without evidence, Coues attributes the plates to Gass. Art historian Kenneth Haltman remarks on that in the introduction to his doctoral dissertation (see note 11). Haltman also mentions that Gass was the expedition's official carpenter, and in the plate entitled *Capt. Clark and His Men Build a Line of Huts,* the architecture of the shelters is so complex that it is possible to theorize that Gass, with his carpenter's eye, was the artist.

5. I am referring chiefly to Ken Burns, whose documentary *Lewis and Clark* was a paean to national pride and Western landscapes.

6. William H. Goetzmann, *New Lands, New Men: America and the Second Great Age of Discovery* (New York: Viking, 1986), 3, 11, and 115; Clyde A. Milner II, et al., eds., *The Oxford History of the American West* (New York: Oxford University Press, 1994), 157; Myra Jehlen, "Exploration and Empire," in *The Cambridge History of American Literature,* vol. 1, *1590–1820,* ed. Sacvan Bercovitch (Cambridge: Cambridge University Press, 1995), 149–61.

7. Blake Allmendinger, in the contentious introduction to his recent *Ten Most Wanted: The New Western Literature* (New York: Routledge, 1998), reviews the embarrassment of scholars who study subliterary works such as Westerns. Jane Tompkins, in what Allmendinger finds a typical move, starts her book about Westerns with the daring assertion, "I make no secret of the fact: I love Westerns." See *West of Everything: The Inner Life of Westerns* (New York: Oxford University Press, 1992), 3.

8. Annette Kolodny, "Letting Go Our Grand Obsessions: Notes toward a New Literary History of the American Frontiers," *American Literature* 64 (March 1992): 14.

9. John Ledyard, *Journey through Russia and Siberia, 1787–1788: The Journal and Selected Letters,* ed. with an introduction by Stephen D. Watrous (Madison: University of Wisconsin Press, 1966).

10. See Marshall Sahlins, "The Apotheosis of Captain Cook," in *Between Belief and Transgression: Structuralist Essays in Religion, History, and Myth,* ed. Michel Izard and Pierre Smith, trans. John Leavitt (Chicago: University of Chicago Press, 1982), 73–102. Note also the conclusion of the chief biographer of Cook in the twentieth century: he is "our Hero." See John Beaglehole, *The Life of Captain James Cook* (Stanford: Stanford University Press, 1974).

11. Kenneth Haltman, "Figures in a Western Landscape: Reading the Art of Titian Ramsay Peale from the Long Expedition to the Rocky Mountains, 1819–1820" (Ph.D. diss., Yale University, 1992). *Christian and Pliable in the Slough of Despond* (1781), anonymous, line etching, 14 by 25.7 centimeters, Print Collection, Winterthur Library, Winterthur, Delaware.

12. Bear attacks were, it seems, always a large part of Western storytelling. Gass's picture of the bear treeing "an American" is probably part of a new genre. Elliott

West in *The Oxford History of the American West,* 138–40, collects two examples of bear-attack artwork from *Davy Crockett's Almanack* and an unknown Assiniboin artist's painting in the *Bureau of American Ethnology Forty-Sixth Annual Report.* In both cases the bear is, West says, the "worthy antagonist" of human interlopers.

13. John Bunyan, *The Pilgrim's Progress, Part 1* (Menston, England: Scolar Press, 1970, facsimile reprint of 2d ed., 1678), 12–13.

14. Jackson reprints McKeehan's long diatribe in his article "The Race to Publish Lewis and Clark." It originally appeared in the *Pittsburgh Gazette,* April 14, 1807. Jackson says: "It occupied the whole of page 2 . . . and seems to have been overlooked by the biographers of Lewis and Clark and the subsequent editors of their journals." It appears, of course, in Moulton, *Journals of Lewis and Clark,* vol. 10, xvi–xvii.

15. See, on this topic, Allmendinger, *Ten Most Wanted;* Lee Clark Mitchell, *Westerns: Making the Man in Fiction and Film* (Chicago: University of Chicago Press, 1996); Elizabeth Cook-Lynn, "Why I Can't Read Wallace Stegner," in *Why I Can't Read Wallace Stegner and Other Essays: A Tribal Voice* (Madison: University of Wisconsin Press, 1996); and Kolodny, "Letting Go."

16. John Seelye, "Beyond the Shining Mountains: The Lewis and Clark Expedition as Enlightenment Epic," *Virginia Quarterly Review* 63 (Winter 1987): 36–53.

17. Seelye, "Shining Mountain," 41, is the main source of this "buddy movie" dichotomy. It also appears in Jehlen, "Exploration and Empire"; Bernard DeVoto's introduction to *The Journals of Lewis and Clark* (New York: Houghton-Mifflin, 1952); and Stephen Ambrose, *Undaunted Courage: Meriwether Lewis, Thomas Jefferson, and the Opening of the American West* (New York: Simon and Schuster, 1996); and is finally well reappraised in Frank Bergon, "Wilderness Aesthetics," *American Literary History* 9 (Spring 1997): 128–61.

18. Peter Gay terms it the "shadow" in *The Enlightenment: An Interpretation,* 2 vols. (New York: Knopf, 1966–69); "pathos" appears in John P. Diggins, "Slavery, Race, and Equality: Jefferson and the Pathos of the Enlightenment," *American Quarterly* 28 (2 Summer 1976): 206–28; "heightened uncertainty" is the term in Robert A. Ferguson, *The American Enlightenment, 1750–1820* (Cambridge: Harvard University Press, 1997), 36 ff.

19. See a few examples: Alan Heimert, *Religion and the American Mind: From the Great Awakening to the Revolution* (Cambridge: Harvard University Press, 1969); Daniel Walker Howe, *Making the American Self: Jonathan Edwards to Abraham Lincoln* (Cambridge: Harvard University Press, 1997); Kenneth Silverman, "From Cotton Mather to Benjamin Franklin," in *The Columbia Literary History of the United States,* ed. Emory Elliott (New York: Columbia University Press, 1988), 101–12; and Kevin Van Anglen, "Reading Transcendentalist Texts Religiously: Emerson, Thoreau, and the Myth of Secularization," in *Seeing into the Life of Things: Essays on Literature and Religious Experience,* ed. John L. Mahoney (New York: Fordham University Press, 1998), 152–70.

20. Michael J. Colacurcio, "A Better Mode of Evidence: The Transcendental Problem of Faith and Spirit," *Emerson Society Quarterly* 54 (1st Quarter 1969): 12–22.

21. Heimert, *Religion,* 3–4.

22. Colacurcio, "Better Mode," 12.

23. Jehlen, "Exploration and Empire," 131.

24. On William Bartram, see Christopher Looby, "The Constitution of Nature: Taxonomy as Politics in Jefferson, Peale, and Bartram," *Early American Literature* 22 (1987): 252–73; Douglas Anderson, "Bartram's Travels and the Politics of Nature," *Early American Literature* 25 (1990): 3–17; Pamela Regis, *Describing Early America: Bartram, Jefferson, Crevecoeur, and the Rhetoric of Natural History* (De Kalb: Northern Illinois University Press, 1992); and Michael Branch, "Indexing American Possibilities: The Natural History Writing of Bartram, Wilson, and Audubon," in *The Ecocriticism Reader: Landmarks in Literary Ecology,* ed. Cheryll Glotfelty and Harold Fromm (Athens: University of Georgia Press, 1996).

On Captain John Smith, see Everett Emerson, "History and Chronicle," in Elliott, *Columbia Literary History;* Philip F. Gura, "John Who? Captain John Smith and Early American Literature," *Early American Literature* 21 (1986–87): 260–67; Myra Jehlen, "History Before the Fact; or, Captain John Smith's Unfinished Symphony," *Critical Inquiry* 19, no. 4 (Summer 1993): 677–92; and Leo J. Lemay, "Captain John Smith," in *The History of Southern Literature,* ed. Louis D. Rubin, Jr., et al. (Baton Rouge: Louisiana State University Press, 1985).

25. Ian Watt, *The Rise of the Novel* (Berkeley: University of California Press, 1957), 63; Lennard J. Davis, "The Fact of Events and the Event of Facts: New World Explorers and the Early Novel," *The Eighteenth Century* 32, no. 3 (Autumn 1991): 240; Michael McKeon, *The Origins of the English Novel, 1600–1740* (Baltimore: Johns Hopkins University Press, 1987), 315.

26. McKeon, *Origins,* 113.

27. Edward Said, *Culture and Imperialism* (New York: Knopf, 1993).

28. Robert A. Ferguson, "'We Hold These Truths': Strategies of Control in the Literature of the Founders," in *Reconstructing American Literary History,* ed. Sacvan Bercovitch (Cambridge: Harvard University Press, 1986), 5.

29. Ambrose, *Undaunted Courage,* 461–65.

30. Moulton, *Journals,* 6:309. Subsequent parenthetical citations in the text refer to the Moulton edition of the *Journals.*

31. Stephen Greenblatt, *Marvelous Possessions: The Wonder of the New World* (Chicago: University of Chicago Press, 1991), 16.

32. Professor Starr Jenkins (emeritus, California State University, San Luis Obispo) suggests in his essay "The Rugged Return of Lewis and Clark," *Nugget* (March 1971), 5–6, that Jefferson had counted on the explorers' picking up a merchant ship along the coast to take them back. I am grateful to Professor Jenkins for sending this essay to me in manuscript form.

33. Greenblatt, *Marvelous Possessions,* 125; Thomas Jefferson, *Notes on the State of Virginia,* ed. William Peden (New York: Norton, 1972).

34. Larzer Ziff, *Writing a New Nation: Prose, Print, and Politics in the Early United States* (New Haven: Yale University Press, 1991), 150–58.

35. See Eric Cheyfitz, *The Poetics of Imperialism: Translation and Colonization from* The Tempest *to* Tarzan (New York: Oxford University Press, 1991), 110–11, and in general chapter 6, "The Empire of Poetics."

36. Thomas Jefferson to Meriwether Lewis, quoted in DeVoto, *Journals,* 482.

37. Ibid., 485.

38. Susan J. Rosowski, "The Western Hero as Logos; or, Unmaking Meaning," *Western American Literature* 32, no. 3 (November 1997): 289.

39. Seelye, "Shining Mountains," 46.
40. In the two leading studies of early American exploration narratives, for example (Stephen Greenblatt, *Marvelous Possessions,* and Tzvetan Todorov, *The Conquest of America* [New York: Harper and Row, 1984]), Christopher Columbus is described in detail during his *encounter* with the people of the West Indies; reencounter is omitted.
41. Leo Marx, *The Machine in the Garden: Technology and the Pastoral Ideal in America* (New York: Oxford University Press, 1964).
42. William Boelhower, *Through a Glass Darkly: Ethnic Semiosis in American Literature* (New York: Oxford University Press, 1987), 48; Jehlen, "Exploration and Empire," 155.
43. Boelhower, *Through a Glass,* 44.

CHAPTER 2. ZEBULON PIKE,
FEDERALIST GLOOM, AND WESTERN LANDS

1. On the influence of Lewis and Clark on Poe, see Robert Lawson-Peebles, *Landscape and Written Expression in Revolutionary America* (Cambridge: Cambridge University Press, 1988), 263–77, and Edwin Fussell, *Frontier: American Literature and the American West* (Princeton: Princeton University Press, 1965).
2. John Conron, ed., *American Picturesque* (University Park: Penn State University Press, 2000), 291.
3. See Daniel Walker Howe, *The Political Culture of the American Whigs* (Chicago: University of Chicago Press, 1979), 90, and Michael F. Holt, *The Rise and Fall of the American Whig Party* (New York: Oxford University Press, 1999), 2.
4. See Hubert Howe Bancroft, *History of the Northwest Coast,* vols. 27–28 of *The Works of Hubert Howe Bancroft* (San Francisco: The History Company, 1886), and also Vernon L. Parrington, *Main Currents in American Thought,* vol. 2, *The Romantic Revolution in America, 1800–1860* (New York: Harcourt Brace, 1927), for details on Irving's financial dependence on Astor. The insight about Irving's achievement of being an aristocratic kept writer, and similarly about Astor's acquisition of an object of patronage, comes from Peter Antelyes, *Tales of Adventurous Enterprise: Washington Irving and the Poetics of Western Expansion* (New York: Columbia University Press, 1990).
5. Edith Wharton, *The Age of Innocence* (1920; reprint, London: Virago Press, 1988), 100.
6. Daniel Walker Howe, *The Unitarian Conscience: Harvard Moral Philosophy, 1805–1861* (Cambridge: Harvard University Press, 1970), 9.
7. Marvin Meyers, *The Jacksonian Persuasion: Politics and Belief* (Stanford: Stanford University Press, 1957), 186, discusses the "imported nightmares" of French radicalism.
8. Parrington, *Main Currents,* 195, reviews the drift from anti-Jacobinism to Jacksonian sentiments. The "compromise" quotation is from a letter of Irving's quoted in Parrington, *Main Currents,* 201; the original citation is from Pierre M. Irving, ed., *The Life and Letters of Washington Irving* (London: n.p, 1864), 2: 312–13.
9. Holt, *Rise and Fall,* 249, quoting William E. Robinson in the *New York Tribune,*

June 2, 1846; Ralph Waldo Emerson, *The Journals and Miscellaneous Notebooks of Ralph Waldo Emerson,* ed. William H. Gilman, Ralph H. Orth, et al. (Cambridge: Harvard University Press, Belknap Press, 1960–82), 8:87, quoted in Howe, *Political Culture,* 37.

10. Robert A. Ferguson, *The American Enlightenment, 1750–1820* (Cambridge: Harvard University Press, 1994), 6.

11. David Hackett Fischer uses Ames's line as an epigraph to his *Revolution of American Conservatism: The Federalist Party in the Era of Jeffersonian Democracy* (New York: Harper and Row, 1965), xi; there is no attribution. See also Shaw Livermore, Jr., *The Twilight of Federalism: The Disintegration of the Federalist Party, 1815–1830* (Princeton: Princeton University Press, 1962), 8.

12. Under the alias "Launcelot Langstaff, esq.," Irving refers to the breeches as "Mr. Jefferson's red *what-d'ye call-'ems.*" Washington Irving, *Salmagundi* No. II (Wed. Feb. 4, 1807), from *Works,* vol. 18, Knickerbocker edition (New York: Putnam, 1869).

13. Edward Stafford, a Republican newspaper editor, in Holt, *Rise and Fall,* 951.

14. Meyers, *Jacksonian Persuasion,* 117. The quotation is from Martin Van Buren's 1839 state of the union address.

15. Tom Stoppard, *Arcadia* (London: Faber and Faber, 1993).

16. Stephen Copley and Peter Garside, eds., *The Politics of the Picturesque: Literature, Landscape, and Aesthetics since 1770* (Cambridge: Cambridge University Press, 1994), 1.

17. Kenneth Haltman, "Figures in a Western Landscape: Reading the Art of Titian Ramsay Peale from the Long Expedition to the Rocky Mountains, 1819–1820" (Ph.D. diss., Yale University, 1992), 46.

18. "The Drowziad, by a Dozer" (Charleston, 1829). Cited in Bruce Robertson, "The Picturesque Traveler in America," in *Views and Visions: American Landscape before 1830,* ed. Edward J. Nygren and Bruce Robertson (Washington, D.C.: Corcoran Gallery, 1986), 189–211.

19. S. T. Coleridge, "The Delinquent Travellers," in *Poetical Works,* ed. Ernest Hartley (New York: Oxford University Press, 1969), 445–47.

20. On Paulding, see Beth L. Lueck, "James Kirke Paulding and the Picturesque Tour: 'Banqueting on the Picturesque' in the 1820s and '30s," *University of Mississippi Studies in English* 9 (1991): 167–88.

21. Haltman, "Western Landscape," 46; Barbara Maria Stafford, *Voyage into Substance: Art, Science, Nature, and the Illustrated Travel Account, 1760–1840* (Cambridge: MIT Press, 1984), 7; Meriwether Lewis, June 13, 1805, in Gary E. Moulton, ed., *The Journals of the Lewis and Clark Expedition,* 12 vols. (Lincoln: University of Nebraska Press, 1983–99), 4:285.

22. Barbara Novak, *Nature and Culture: American Landscape and Painting, 1825–1875* (New York: Oxford University Press, 1980), 228; Haltman, "Western Landscape," 164. A *repoussoir* is a figure or object in the extreme foreground, used with the intention of creating spatial depth and of drawing the spectator into the picture. "Planar recession" means simply a series of pictorial planes that move "back" into the far horizon. A prospect is a vanishing point, where a landscape's horizon loses focus but conveys distance. A *coulisse* (Fr. "wing") is an object on the side of a landscape scene that draws the eye toward the view in the

distance; it aids the sense of perspective. See Sir David Piper, ed., *The Random House Dictionary of Art and Artists* (New York: Random House, 1988).

23. Copley, *Politics of the Picturesque*, 6.
24. Stoppard, *Arcadia*, 25; Stafford, *Voyage*, 322–24 and 322; she quotes from James Hakewell's *Picturesque Tour of Jamaica* (1825).
25. Stafford, *Voyage*, 353.
26. Copley, *Politics of the Picturesque*, 7.
27. Conron, *American Picturesque*, 6, 9.
28. Studies of the Picturesque have focused more on the English Picturesque than the American. The main study in the English tradition is Christopher Hussey, *The Picturesque: Studies in a Point of View* (Hamden, Conn.: Archon Books, 1967). Also quite fine are John Barrell, ed., *Paintings and the Politics of Culture: New Essays on British Art, 1700–1850* (New York: Oxford University Press, 1992), and Anne Janowitz, *England's Ruins: Poetic Purpose and the National Landscape* (London: Basil Blackwell, 1990). A collection that seeks to broaden somewhat the English focus of Picturesque studies is Copley, *Politics of the Picturesque*, especially the essay by John Whale, "Romantics, Explorers, and Picturesque Travellers." Finally, as this book was being prepared for publication, John Conron published his *American Picturesque*.

   Irving and the picturesque tradition are reviewed in David R. Anderson, "A Quaint, Picturesque Little Pile: Architecture and the Past in Washington Irving," in *The Old and New World Romanticism in Washington Irving*, ed. Stanley Brodwin (Westport, Conn.: Greenwood Press, 1986), 139–49; Brigitte Bailey, "Irving's Italian Landscapes: Skepticism and the Picturesque Aesthetic," *Emerson Society Quarterly* 32 (1st Quarter 1986): 1–22; and Bruno Montfort, "Washington Irving et le pittoresque post-romantique," *Revue française d'études americaines* 14, no. 42 (November 1989): 439–53. Among other nineteenth-century writers, Charles Brockden Brown's interest in the picturesque is surveyed in Beth L. Lueck, "Charles Brockden Brown's *Edgar Huntly:* The Picturesque Traveler as Sleepwalker," *Studies in American Fiction* 15, no. 1 (Spring 1987): 25–42, and in Dennis Berthold, "Charles Brockden Brown, *Edgar Huntly,* and the Origins of the American Picturesque," *William and Mary Quarterly* 41, no. 1 (January 1984): 62–84. Nathaniel Hawthorne's picturesque is examined in Beth L. Lueck, "Hawthorne's Ironic Traveler and the Picturesque Tour," in *Hawthorne's American Travel Sketches*, ed. Beth L. Lueck and Dennis Berthold (Hanover, N.H.: University Press of New England, 1989).
29. Richard Chase, *The American Novel and Its Tradition* (Baltimore: Johns Hopkins University Press, 1957), 1–12; Michael T. Gilmore, *American Romanticism and the Marketplace* (Chicago: University of Chicago Press, 1985), 12.
30. The *Oxford English Dictionary* (2d ed., 1989) states the etymology this way: "Picturesque: . . . of language, narrative, etc.; strikingly graphic or vivid; sometimes implying disregard of fact in the effort for effect." Examples: "1868. 'Picturesque history is seldom to be trusted.' 1874. 'the highly picturesque language of the Aryan people.' 1907. Mark Twain: 'Repetition of pet poetic picturesqueness.'"
31. Stafford, *Voyage*, 3.
32. Zebulon Montgomery Pike, *The Journals of Zebulon Montgomery Pike, with Letters*

and Related Documents, ed. Donald Dean Jackson (Norman: University of Oklahoma Press, 1966). Further citations appear parenthetically in the text.

33. The latter three in this list are cited by Stafford.
34. For this quick survey, I used the OCLC or WorldCat FirstSearch database and searched for the title phrases "Picturesque Tour" or "Voyage pittoresque." The best years were 1820–1840. Here is the breakdown in that database of the number of books by decade:

1760–69: 7

1770–79: 6

1780–89: 16

1790–99: 11

1800–09: 26

1810–19: 19

1820–29: 36

1830–39: 34

1840–49: 21

1850–59: 21

1860–69: 18

1870–79: 11

1880–89: 6

35. On this topic, see Michael Davitt Bell, "Beginnings of Professionalism," in *Cambridge History of American Literature,* vol. 2, *Prose Writing, 1820–1865,* ed. Sacvan Bercovitch (Cambridge: Cambridge University Press, 1995), 39. See also William Charvatt's essential *Profession of Authorship in America, 1800–1870* (Miami: Ohio State University Press, 1968).
36. Copley, *Politics of the Picturesque,* 5.
37. New England *Palladium,* August 13, 1805.
38. John Barrell, "Geometry and the Garden," in *Paintings and the Politics of Culture,* 44; Christopher Hussey, *The Picturesque.*
    See four studies of Thoreau's attention to contemporary aesthetics: Richard N. Masteller and Jean Carwile Masteller, "Rural Architecture in Andrew Jackson Downing and Henry David Thoreau: Pattern Book Parody in *Walden,*" *New England Quarterly* 57, no. 4 (1984): 483–510; Steven Fink, "Building America: Henry Thoreau and the American Home," *Prospects* 11 (1988): 327–66; Richard J. Schneider, "Thoreau and Nineteenth-Century American Landscape Painting," *Emerson Society Quarterly* 31 (2nd Quarter 1985): 67–88; and Gordon V. Boudreau, "H. D. Thoreau, William Gilpin, and the Metaphysical Ground of the Picturesque," *American Literature* 45 (1973): 357–69.
39. Quoted in Whale, "Romantics," p. 177 in Copley, *Politics and the Picturesque;* the original source is William Gilpin, "On Picturesque Travel," in *Three Essays* (London, 1794), 41.

40. Eve Kosofsky Sedgwick, *Between Men: English Literature and Male Homosocial Desire* (New York: Columbia University Press, 1985), 13–14; emphasis added.
41. See W. Eugene Hollon, "Zebulon Montgomery Pike and the Wilkinson-Burr Conspiracy," *Proceedings of the American Philosophical Society* 91, no. 5 (December 1947): 447–56, 453 n. 30. Hollon's review of the evidence has provided me with the facts of this historical episode, and I cite his article here, once, as the source of my information on the Burr Conspiracy in this chapter.
42. *The National Intelligencer,* December 24, 1806.
43. This epithet appears in the *Natchez Weekly Chronicle* of July 27, 1809, and is quoted by Hollon, "Zebulon Montgomery Pike," 455.
44. Fischer, *Revolution of American Conservatism,* 423, 461, 473.
45. D. H. Lawrence, *Studies in Classic American Literature* (New York: Viking, 1961), 47.
46. Mary Louise Pratt, *Imperial Eyes: Travel Writing and Transculturation* (New York: Routledge, 1992), 78.
47. *Black's Law Dictionary,* 6th ed. (St. Paul, Minn.: West Publishing Co., 1990), defines *sedition* as communication or agreement which has as its objective the stirring up of treason or certain lesser commotions, or the defamation of the government; *mutiny* as rising against lawful or constituted authority, particularly in military service; and *treason* as a breach of allegiance to one's government, usually committed through levying war or by giving aid or comfort to the enemy. Thus, Pike distinguishes carefully. I gratefully acknowledge the assistance of Professor Peter Appel, University of Georgia School of Law, for an illuminating explication of this point of law.
48. John Seelye, in "Beyond the Shining Mountains: The Lewis and Clark Expedition as an Enlightenment Epic," *Virginia Quarterly Review* 63 (Winter 1987): 36–53, makes this claim for the circumstances of Lewis's death by a gunshot wound. The narrative biography of Lewis, Stephen Ambrose's *Undaunted Courage: Meriwether Lewis, Thomas Jefferson, and the Opening of the American West* (New York: Simon and Schuster, 1996), also tells this story.
49. Harlin M. Fuller and LeRoy R. Hafen, eds., *The Journal of Captain John R. Bell, Official Journalist for the Stephen H. Long Expedition to the Rocky Mountains, 1820* (Glendale, Calif.: The Arthur H. Clarke Co., 1957), 186.
50. Three contemporary works on the Burr Conspiracy that review these facts are: Thomas Perkins Abernethy, *The Burr Conspiracy* (New York: Oxford University Press, 1954); Donald Barr Chidsey, *The Great Conspiracy: Aaron Burr and His Strange Doings in the West* (New York: Crown, 1967); and Manly Wade Wellman, *Napoleon of the West: A Story of the Aaron Burr Conspiracy* (New York: I. Washburn, 1970).
51. Hollon, "Zebulon Montgomery Pike," 447 n. 1. Hollon notes that "trappers and traders . . . insisted upon calling it Pike's Peak." The political allegiances of these frontiersmen are unclear: in light of Pike's disrepute, was their nomenclature satiric or loyal? Or simply alliterative?

CHAPTER 3. THE LAND WITHOUT QUALITIES

1. On Thoreau's attention to the picturesque, see Richard N. Masteller and Jean Carwile Masteller, "Rural Architecture in Andrew Jackson Downing and Henry

David Thoreau: Pattern Book Parody in *Walden,*" *New England Quarterly* 57, no. 4 (1984): 483–510; Steven Fink, "Building America: Henry Thoreau and the American Home," *Prospects* 11 (1988): 327–66; Richard J. Schneider, "Thoreau and Nineteenth-Century American Landscape Painting," *Emerson Society Quarterly* 31 (2nd Quarter 1985): 67–88; and Gordon V. Boudreau, "H. D. Thoreau, William Gilpin, and the Metaphysical Ground of the Picturesque," *American Literature* 45 (1973): 357–69.

2. Howard Lamar, ed., *Account of an Expedition from Pittsburgh to the Rocky Mountains, under the Command of Major Stephen H. Long* (Barre, Mass.: Imprint Society, 1972), xxxv. This edition will be cited parenthetically by page number in the text.

3. Long's fame is for the exploration itself, and not for the journal of the expedition; when we discuss the published *Account* at all, we must note that Edwin James, Long's second in command, kept the daily log. The literary collaboration between the two has not been investigated by historians, and the manuscript, kept in James's hand, seems uncorrected by Long and unchanged for publication, except for the usual corrections to spelling and punctuation. Surely, though, Long read it before it was published. Although James is the writer of the narrative under discussion in this part of the chapter, I refer to it as Long's, simply because it was his troupe, his leadership, and his determinations about the landscape that dominate the account. (It's also the way the text is usually referred to by readers.) Long is in no sense "narrated" by James, since the two explorers had none of the differences of personality that Lewis did with Clark.

4. Carlo Rotella, "Travels in a Subjective West: The Letters of Edwin James and Major Stephen Long's Scientific Expedition of 1819–1820," *Montana* 41, no. 4 (Autumn 1991): 23.

5. Richard H. Dillon, "Stephen Long's Great American Desert," *Proceedings of the American Philosophical Society* 111, no. 2 (April 1967): 93.

6. Ruben Gold Thwaites, ed., *James' Account of S. H. Long's Expedition, Part III* (Cleveland: A. H. Clark, 1905), 174 n, cited in Dillon, "Great American Desert," 93.

7. Barbara Maria Stafford, *Voyage into Substance: Art, Science, Nature, and the Illustrated Travel Account, 1760–1840* (Cambridge: MIT Press, 1984), 154.

8. Dillon, "Great American Desert," 95.

9. Bruce Greenfield, *Tales of Adventurous Enterprise: Washington Irving and the Poetics of Western Expansion* (New York: Columbia University Press, 1990), 14.

10. See, for instance, the references to Spanish exploration in E. O. Beaman's journal of the Grand Canyon.

11. Rotella, "Travels," 22, citing Edwin James to John James, October 26, 1820, in James Letters, Western Americana, Beinecke Library, Yale University, New Haven. These letters of Edwin James were made available for scholarly study only in 1983.

12. Rotella, "Travels," 21, citing from ibid. in the Edwin James Letters.

13. "Selkirk, Thomas Douglas" in *The Columbia Encyclopedia*, 5th ed., ed. Barbara A. Chernow and George A. Vallasi (New York: Columbia University Press, 1989), 741.

14. Harlin M. Fuller and LeRoy R. Hafen, eds., *The Journal of Captain John R. Bell, Official Journalist for the Stephen H. Long Expedition to the Rocky Mountains, 1820* (Glendale, Calif.: The Arthur H. Clarke Co., 1957), 311.

15. "Major Long's Second Expedition," *North American Review* XII (June 1825): 178; emphasis original.

16. Fuller and Haven, *Journal of Captain John R. Bell,* 336.

17. Francis Parkman, *The Oregon Trail,* ed. E. N. Feltskog (Madison: University of Wisconsin Press, 1969).

18. William H. Goetzmann, *Exploration and Empire: The Explorer and the Scientist in the Winning of the American West* (New York: Norton, 1966), 231 ff.

19. This quotation is from Thomas R. Hietala, *Manifest Design: Anxious Aggrandizement in Late Jacksonian America* (Ithaca, N.Y.: Cornell University Press, 1985), 265 n. 9. Hietala's original source is Congressman Joshua Bell (Kentucky), *Congressional Globe,* 29th Cong., 2d sess., App. 249 (January 19, 1847).

20. Robert D. Richardson, Jr., *Emerson: The Mind on Fire* (Berkeley: University of California Press, 1995), 508.

21. Gloria Anzaldúa, *Borderlands/La Frontera: The New Mestiza* (San Francisco: Aunt Lute Books, 1987), 25.

22. See, in the field of cartography in European exploration writing, J. B. Hartley and David Woodward, eds., *The History of Cartography* (Chicago: University of Chicago Press, 1987); David Woodward, ed., *Art and Cartography: Six Historical Essays* (Chicago: University of Chicago Press, 1987); Stephen Greenblatt, *Marvelous Possessions: The Wonder of the New World* (Chicago: University of Chicago Press, 1991); Margarita Zamora, *Reading Columbus* (Berkeley: University of California Press, 1993), esp. 102–17; Mary B. Campbell, *The Witness and the Other World: Exotic European Travel Writing, 400–1600* (Ithaca, N.Y.: Cornell University Press, 1988); and Tom Conley, "Montaigne and the Indies: Cartographies of the New World in the Essais, 1580–1588," in *1492–1992: Re/Discovering Colonial Writing,* ed. Rene Jara and Nicholas Spadaccini (Minneapolis: Prisma Institute, 1989).

23. On the famous jail episode of Thoreau's life, see Walter Harding and Carl Bode, eds., *The Days of Henry Thoreau* (New York: New York University Press, 1958), 199–208.

24. The Mexican War ended in 1848 with the Treaty of Guadalupe-Hidalgo; the Gadsden Purchase of 1853 was arranged by President Franklin Pierce, to purchase another thirty thousand square miles, which were then thought to contain the most practicable route for the southern railroad routes to the Pacific.

25. Norman J. W. Thrower, "William H. Emory and the Mapping of the American Southwest Borderlands," *Terrae Incognitae* 22 (1990): 41 ff.

26. William H. Emory, *Report on the United States and Mexican Boundary Survey* (Washington, D.C.: Cornelius Wendall, 1857), 1:xvi. Further references to the *Report* will appear parenthetically as page numbers in the text.

27. The facts in this paragraph and the next about opposition to the Mexican War are taken directly from Glyndon G. Van Deusen, *The Jacksonian Era, 1828–1848* (New York: Harper and Row, 1963), 241–42.

28. Goetzmann, *Exploration and Empire,* 254; Thrower, "William H. Emory," 80.

29. John R. Bartlett, *Personal Narrative of Exploration and Incidents* (New York: D. Appleton and Co., 1854).

30. Alexander von Humboldt, *Ansichten der Natur* (Views of Nature), trans. E. C. Otte and Henry G. Bohn (London: Henry G. Bohn, 1850).

31. Mary Louise Pratt is the source for this idea of Gerbi's, in her book *Imperial Eyes:*

Travel Writing and Transculturation (New York: Routledge, 1992), 120, in an illuminating chapter on von Humboldt's "invention" of America as nature, which I cite further herein.

32. Dorothy Zuersher, "Benjamin Franklin, Jonathan Williams, and the United States Marine Corps" (Ph.D. diss., University of North Carolina, Greensboro, 1974).

33. Bache's letters are held in the American Philosophical Society in Philadelphia.

34. See Christopher Mulvey, Anglo-American Landscapes: A Study of Nineteenth-Century Anglo-American Travel Literature (Cambridge: Cambridge University Press, 1983), esp. 255 ff., on the topic of American novelty as a visual liability.

35. See, for example, William H. Goetzmann, Army Exploration in the American West, 1803–1863 (New Haven: Yale University Press, 1959); Robert Hine, Bartlett's West: Drawing the Mexican Boundary (New Haven: Yale University Press, 1968); and Joseph Richard Werne, "Major Emory and Captain Jimenez: Running the Gadsden Line," Journal of the Southwest 29, no. 2 (1987): 203–21.

36. Bruce Robertson, "Venit, Vidit, Depinxit: The Military Artist in America," in Views and Visions: American Landscape Before 1830, ed. Edward J. Nygren and Bruce Robertson (Washington, D.C.: Corcoran Gallery, 1986), 83–103.

CHAPTER 4. EMERSON'S 1830s

1. Wilde remarks on dish painting while on tour in San Jose, California. The San Jose Mercury carried this story, omitting Wilde's cautions against the perils of the decorative arts. The anecdote is reprinted in Lloyd Lewis and Henry Justin Smith, Oscar Wilde Discovers America (New York: Harcourt Brace, 1936), and in Wilde, The Writings of Oscar Wilde, vol. 11, pt. 2 (New York: Gabriel Wells, 1925), 73–4.

2. Ralph Waldo Emerson, The Journals and Miscellaneous Notebooks of Ralph Waldo Emerson, ed. William H. Gilman, Ralph H. Orth, et al. (Cambridge: Harvard University Press, Belknap Press, 1960–82), 2:153. Hereafter cited in the text and notes as JMN.

3. Jonathan Bishop, Emerson on the Soul (Cambridge: Harvard University Press, 1964), 53.

4. Walt Whitman, Reflections on Democracy, selected from editorials in the Brooklyn Daily Eagle published in C. Rodgers and J. Black, eds., The Gathering of the Forces (New York, 1920) and reprinted in Joseph L. Blau, ed., Social Theories of Jacksonian Democracy: Representative Writings of the Period 1825–1850 (New York: The Liberal Arts Press, 1954), 130.

5. Carolyn Porter, Seeing and Being: The Plight of the Participant Observer in Emerson, James, Adams, and Faulkner (Middletown, Conn.: Wesleyan University Press, 1981), 61.

6. Daniel Walker Howe, The Political Culture of the American Whigs (Chicago: University of Chicago Press, 1979), 89, quoting a journal entry by Ralph Waldo Emerson, June [?] 1840, JMN 7:376.

7. Stephen Whicher, Freedom and Fate: An Inner Life of Ralph Waldo Emerson (Philadelphia: University of Pennsylvania Press, 1953); Robert D. Richardson, Jr., "Emerson and Nature," in The Cambridge Companion to Ralph Waldo Emerson, ed. Joel Porte and Saundra Morris (Cambridge: Cambridge University Press, 1999),

97–15. See also, of course, Richardson's excellent biography, *Emerson: The Mind on Fire* (Berkeley: University of California Press, 1995).

8. Lee Rust Brown, *The Emerson Museum: Practical Romanticism and the Pursuit of the Whole* (Cambridge: Harvard University Press, 1997).

9. See Julie Ellison, *Emerson's Romantic Style* (Princeton: Princeton University Press, 1984), 85, and Richard Poirier, *The Renewal of Literature: Emersonian Reflections* (New Haven: Yale University Press, 1987), 13.

10. Robert Weisbuch, "Post-Colonial Emerson and the Erasure of Europe," in Porte and Morris, *Cambridge Companion.*

11. Kevin Van Anglen, "Reading Transcendentalist Texts Religiously: Emerson, Thoreau, and the Myth of Secularization," in *Seeing into the Life of Things: Essays on Literature and Religious Experience,* ed. John L. Mahoney (New York: Fordham University Press, 1998), 152–70.

12. Miller also notes the ecumenical variety of this naturalist Christianity: "In one fashion or other, various religious interests, aroused against the Enlightenment, allied themselves with forces we lump together as 'romantic.'" Perry Miller, *Errand into the Wilderness* (Cambridge: Harvard University Press, Belknap Press, 1956), 208, 210.

13. Maurice Gonnaud, *An Uneasy Solitude: Individual and Society in the Work of Ralph Waldo Emerson* (Princeton: Princeton University Press, 1987), 105–6; Len Gougeon, *Virtue's Hero: Emerson, Antislavery, and Reform* (Athens: University of Georgia Press, 1990), 20; John Carlos Rowe, *At Emerson's Tomb: The Politics of Classic American Literature* (New York: Columbia University Press, 1997), chapter 2, esp. 19–21; Robert Milder, "The Radical Emerson?" in Porte and Morris, *Cambridge Companion,* 50.

14. My objection to the term *liberal* is chiefly historical. The word *liberal* means, in social, political, or cultural contexts, generous or free of restraint. The ideological connotation is later and secondary. Our early-twenty-first-century conception of liberal versus conservative does not apply to the nineteenth century. Thus we may find the strict usage of the term in a magazine of 1860: "The old Whig party . . . [has] a liberal spirit." *DeBow's Review* 29, issue 1 (July 1860): 38.

Likewise, Alexander Hamilton praised "a liberal construction of the powers of the national government." See his "Letter to Edward Carrington," in Hamilton, *The Works of Alexander Hamilton,* ed. Henry Cabot Lodge (New York: G. P. Putnam's Sons, 1904), VIII: 264. He simply meant he was not a strict constructionist: he proposed to read the Constitution in a free, nonliteral fashion. And when Gibbon spoke of Theodosius's "liberal opinions concerning the duties of kings," he simply meant that Theodosius's views were not bigoted. See Edward Gibbon, *The History of the Decline and Fall of the Roman Empire* (London: Methuen, 1913), xxx, 142.

By applying this sense to theology, *liberal* began to mean, early in the nineteenth century, Christians not chauvinistically attached to details of dogma; hence Oliver Wendell Holmes's lines "Thine eyes behold / A cheerful Christian of the liberal fold" (O. W. Holmes, "A Rhymed Lesson," in *The Complete Poetical Works* [Boston: Houghton, Mifflin and Company, 1895]) mean that we are looking at an unbigoted Christian—probably a Universalist. The predominant sense of the word *liberal* in controversial terms, throughout the nineteenth century, was simply this: Christians disinclined to dogmatism. In America the word specifically meant Unitarians and Universalists, who explicitly denied traditional doctrines of Christianity on the nature of God (Trinitarian), of Christ (divine in substance), and of mankind (innately sinful): "It may be inferred that Transcendentalism was a movement within the limits of 'liberal' Christianity or Unitarianism, as it was called." See O. B. Frothingham, *Transcendentalism in New England, A History* (New York: G. P. Putnam's Sons, 1886), 128. Thus Daniel Walker Howe clearly explains the word *liberal* in this way: "[Unitarians] applied [the term] to themselves . . . in the sense of 'broad-minded' or 'unsectarian.' By this designation they expressed their unwillingness to accept adherence to a strictly defined Calvinist creed as a test for church membership" (Daniel Walker Howe, *The Unitarian Conscience: Harvard Moral Philosophy, 1805–1861* [Cambridge: Harvard University Press, 1970], 4–5).

But also, at the end of the eighteenth century, *liberal* became a (friendly) term for those who wanted, by constitutional reform, to increase the political, social, and economic freedom of the individual. Oddly, the word *libéralisme* has in European discourse consistently and clearly meant political arrangements that actually decrease the social and political control of the individual: even now, the policy of Ronald Reagan and Margaret Thatcher and their admirers is called "neoliberalism" in European politics. At the November 1999 summit in Florence, Italy, of center-left Western leaders, Bill Clinton spoke of a liberal renaissance, while Lionel Jospin spoke of stemming neoliberalism; they meant the same thing.

In literary criticism, Vernon L. Parrington applies the term accurately and narrowly, as the contrary of Calvinism. See his book *Main Currents in American Thought*, vol. 2, *The Romantic Revolution in America, 1800–1860* (New York: Harcourt Brace, 1927), 309 ff., where he details the "social conscience" that arose from liberal Christian (that is, Unitarian) thought. But Sacvan Bercovitch's excellent study *The Rites of Assent: Transformations in the Symbolic Construction of America* (New York: Routledge, 1993), has discussed thoroughly the etiology of what he calls nineteenth-century liberalism without first justifying the use of the term to mean "politically left" or "tending to vaunt the rights of man" or something like it. We seem to be meant to take it on faith.

In America, where the Bill of Rights guaranteed the classical liberal constitutional program, there would scarcely be liberals or antiliberals in the European sense. Andrew Jackson himself never used the word to describe a political orientation; he once wrote only that his Indian policy "is not only liberal, but generous." See Thomas R. Hietala, *Manifest Design: Anxious Aggrandizement in Late Jacksonian America* (Ithaca, N.Y.: Cornell University Press, 1985), 137 n. 8; the original source is James D. Richardson, ed., *Messages and Papers of the Presidents*, 10 vols. (New York, 1897), vol. 3 (Dec. 6, 1830): 1084–85.

I have searched in a database of some fifty American periodicals from the period 1820 to 1870 for the term *liberal*, in the misunderstood political sense of "progressive" or "antislavery" or "pro-suffrage" or simply "in favor of granting extended personal liberties to everyone." The word simply does not appear in such a context. Instead, it is used to describe a man's generosity or breadth of thought: "Edward Bates of Missouri was regarded with so much favor, at one time, on account of his liberal advocacy of public improvements at the West." See "Presidential Candidates and Aspirants," *DeBow's Review* 29, issue 1 (July 1860): 93.

Thus, in America, the L-word has gone begging. Indeed, it often became a term of abuse. When the *New York Tribune* on April 22, 1854 (p. 5/col. 5), sneered, "The 'Liberals' of Maine have called a 'State Democratic Mass Convention' at Portland," it was the nativist Know-Nothings that the paper had in mind. Almost a century later, the *New York Times* sighed that since the Russian Revolution, "Liberal has been a word of confusion. Everybody who was not a Conservative became a Liberal or Radical or Red, whichever came first to the mind" (January 23, 1940, p. 20/col. 4). Inasmuch as *liberal* has had any use in America, it has been misapplied since the 1930s, by themselves and others, to what would be called Social Democrats or Socialists in Europe.

Liberal, then, is a vague theological term in Europe, with a specific meaning in America (Unitarian); a vague political term in America with a specific meaning in Europe (one in favor of constitutional libertarianism); and also a term misused in American politics as a euphemism for "socialist." It is improvident to call Emerson and the other highbrow New Englanders "liberals" because they began to adopt progressive views on abolition, the role of women, and such issues in the 1840s or 1850s. They were driven to these positions, typically, by their theological liberalism, to be sure; but no American of that epoch, not even a Calhounite southerner, would have consented to being described as antiliberal. The members of the antebellum New England avant garde were simply more loyal to the spirit of the age, which blew through causes such as dress reform, phrenology, mesmerism, and teetotalism as much as it did through abolitionism. They were not the nineteenth-century Left.

15. David Van Leer, *Emerson's Epistemology: The Argument of the Essays* (Cambridge: Cambridge University Press, 1986), 26–28.

16. The phrase is from William Bradford, *Of Plymouth Plantation, 1620–1647* (New York: Modern Library, 1981), 35.

17. See the introduction for a fuller description of design. See also the range of opinions in some general works on the design argument: John Donnelly, ed., *Logical Analysis and Contemporary Theism* (New York: Fordham University Press, 1972); Peter Addinall, *Philosophy and Biblical Interpretation: A Study in Nineteenth-Century Conflict* (Cambridge: Cambridge University Press, 1991); Robert H. Hurlbutt, *Hume, Newton, and the Design Argument* (Lincoln: University of Nebraska Press, 1965); Philip P. Wiener, ed., *Dictionary of the History of Ideas*, 5 vols. (New York: Scribners, 1973–74); and Frederick Copleston, S.J., *A History of Philosophy*, vol. 7 (New York: Doubleday, 1994).

18. On the relation of Puritans to providential history, see Perry Miller's two standard texts, *Nature's Nation* (Cambridge: Harvard University Press, Belknap Press, 1967), and *Errand into the Wilderness,* and Sacvan Bercovitch, *The Puritan Origins of the American Self* (New Haven: Yale University Press, 1975). See also the comprehensive study by Antonello Gerbi, *The Dispute of the New World: The History of a Polemic, 1750–1900,* trans. Jeremy Moyle (Pittsburgh: University of Pittsburgh Press, 1973).

19. Philip S. Foner, ed., *The Complete Writings of Thomas Paine* (New York: The Citadel Press, 1945), 1:21.

20. Harry Hayden Clark, "Emerson and Science," *Philological Quarterly* 10, no. 3 (1931): 225–60, 230 n. 28.

21. Perry Miller, "God's Controversy with New England," in *The New England Mind: The Seventeenth Century* (Cambridge: Harvard University Press, 1939), 463. Emphasis added.

22. Bercovitch, *Puritan Origins*, 160 and 153.

23. The best general accounts of Puritan typology include Karen Rowe, *Saint and Singer: Edward Taylor's Typology and the Poetics of Meditation* (Cambridge: Cambridge University Press, 1986), 1–17, and the annotated bibliography in Sacvan Bercovitch, ed., *Typology and Early American Literature* (Amherst: University of Massachusetts Press, 1972), 245–337.

24. William Paley, *Natural Theology; or, Evidences of the Existence and Attributes of the Deity, Collected from the Appearances of Nature* (London: R. Faulder, 1804), chapter 6, esp. 32–33.

25. Miller, *New England Mind*, 226–29.

26. Volume and page numbers cited parenthetically in the text for *Nature* (1836), "Nature" (1841), "The Method of Nature," "The Poet," "Swedenborg, or the Mystic," and "The Rhodora" refer to Emerson, *The Collected Works of Ralph Waldo Emerson*, ed. Alfred R. Ferguson, Joseph Slater, et al., 4 vols. to date (Cambridge: Harvard University Press, Belknap Press, 1971–). I abbreviate this title as *CW*.

    For "The Uses of Natural History," "On the Relation of Man to the Globe," and "The Naturalist," I cite Emerson, *The Early Lectures of Ralph Waldo Emerson 1833–1842*, ed. Stephen E. Whicher and Robert E. Spiller, 3 vols. (Cambridge: Harvard University Press, Belknap Press, 1959–72). I abbreviate this title as *EL*.

27. The "starvation diet" metaphor is from Barbara Packer, *Emerson's Fall: A New Interpretation of the Major Essays* (New York: Continuum, 1982), 39. Howe, *Unitarian Conscience*, 29.

28. Hurlbutt, whose book *Hume, Newton, and the Design Argument* is a standard text on this subject, says late in his study that "the design argument is still very commonly seen in popular discussion . . . so commonly that my assertion need not, I think, be supported by citations" (p. 170). He continues, describing the impact of Hume's *Dialogues,* by characterizing Paley and William Whewell as "resurrect[ing] the design argument in its logically weakest but psychologically most compelling form, as if Hume's *Dialogues* had never been written." Finally, Hurlbutt concludes, "the design argument fared well at the hands of most nineteenth-century believers, despite Hume's criticism" (p. 177).

29. William Ellery Channing, "The Evidences of Revealed Religion," in *Unitarian Christianity and Other Essays,* ed. Irving H. Bartlett (New York: Liberal Arts Press, 1957), 64.

30. Howe, *Unitarian Conscience*, 80–82.

31. This quotation is from Howe, *Unitarian Conscience*, 72. The original source is James Walker, "Religion and Physical Science," in *Sermons Preached in the Chapel of Harvard College* (Boston, 1861), 129.

32. Miller, *New England Mind*, 213. Emphasis added.

33. Richardson, in *Mind on Fire,* clarifies this means of transmission with some care.

Not only did Reed instruct Emerson in Swedenborg, but Fredric Hedge taught him Kant and Coleridge. Moreover, Mary Moody Emerson taught him Plato, Edwards, Plotinus, Locke, the Romantics, Spinoza, Boehme, and Madame de Staël, among others. See pp. 198, 164–69, and 23–28.

34. Whicher, *Freedom and Fate,* 87.

35. Richardson, in *Mind on Fire,* dates the composition of "The Rhodora" to early May 1834, which places it nearest to "The Naturalist" in time.

36. Anne Janowitz, *England's Ruins: Poetic Purpose and the National Landscape* (London: Basil Blackwell, 1990), 92.

37. *CW* vol. 9, "Poems," 37–38.

38. Richardson, *Mind on Fire,* 177.

39. Cited in John Dixon Hunt, *Gardens and the Picturesque* (Cambridge: MIT Press, 1992), 106.

40. See Kenneth Walter Cameron, *A Commentary on Emerson's Early Lectures* (Hartford, Conn.: Transcendental Books, 1961), 37, 39, 55, 75, 76, 82.

41. Kenneth Walter Cameron, *Ralph Waldo Emerson's Reading* (Hartford, Conn.: Transcendental Books, 1962).

42. Walter Harding, *Emerson's Library* (Charlottesville: University Press of Virginia, 1967).

43. Kenneth Walter Cameron, *Emerson and Thoreau as Readers* (Hartford, Conn.: Transcendental Books, 1958 and new ed. 1972). This volume is the source of the three items cited.

44. *JMN* 4:76, *JMN* 4:108–9, *JMN* 5:149–50.

45. Andrew Jackson, "A Political Testament," in *Farewell Address of Andrew Jackson to the People of the United States: And the Inaugural Address of Martin Van Buren, President of the United States* (Washington, D.C., 1837); reprinted in Blau, *Social Theories,* 2.

46. Richardson, *Mind on Fire,* 125.

47. Paley, *Natural Theology,* 4.

48. William Ellery Channing, "A Letter to the Hon. Henry Clay, on the Annexation of Texas to the United States," August 1, 1837, in *The Works of William E. Channing* (New York: Burt Franklin, 1882), 775.

49. See, for example, Kenneth Walter Cameron, *Emerson's Prose Poem: The Structure and Meaning of* Nature (Hartford, Conn.: Transcendental Books, 1988), and Merton M. Sealts, ed., *Emerson's* Nature: *Origin, Growth, Meaning* (New York: Dodd, Mead, 1969).

50. See Richardson, *Mind on Fire,* 418–22.

51. John Michael, *Emerson and Skepticism: The Cipher of the World* (Baltimore: Johns Hopkins University Press, 1988), 4.

52. Kenneth Burke, "I, Eye, Ay—Emerson's Early Essay 'Nature': Thoughts on the Machinery of Transcendence," in *Transcendentalism and Its Legacy,* ed. Myron Simon and Thornton H. Parsons (Ann Arbor: University of Michigan Press, 1966), 3–24.

53. See Andrew Delbanco, *William Ellery Channing: An Essay on the Liberal Spirit in America* (Cambridge: Harvard University Press, 1981), on the topic of nature and its precarious position in Unitarian theology.

CHAPTER 5. EMERSON'S *NATURE*

1. The gospel of John, however, does end with the image of a burning lump of coal: "As soon then as they were come to land, they saw a fire of coals there, and fish laid thereon, and bread."

2. Barbara Packer, *Emerson's Fall: A New Interpretation of the Major Essays* (New York: Continuum, 1982), 24.

3. See, for example, Kenneth Walter Cameron, *Emerson's Prose Poem: The Structure and Meaning of* Nature (Hartford, Conn.: Transcendental Books, 1988); Merton M. Sealts, ed., *Emerson's* Nature: *Origin, Growth, Meaning* (New York: Dodd, Mead, 1969); and Kenneth Burke, "I, Eye, Ay—Emerson's Early Essay 'Nature': Thoughts on the Machinery of Transcendence" in *Transcendentalism and Its Legacy*, ed. Myron Simon and Thornton H. Parsons (Ann Arbor: University of Michigan Press, 1966), 3-24.

4. The text of *Nature* is cited from vol. 1 of Ralph Waldo Emerson, *The Collected Works of Ralph Waldo Emerson*, ed. Alfred R. Ferguson, Joseph Slater, et al., 4 vols. to date (Cambridge: Harvard University Press, Belknap Press, 1971-). Hereafter I cite it in the text parenthetically as *CW*.

5. Sacvan Bercovitch, *The American Jeremiad* (Madison: University of Wisconsin Press, 1978), chapter 6, esp. 202.

6. Richard Poirier, *A World Elsewhere: The Place of Style in American Literature* (London: Chatto and Windus, 1967), 69.

7. Ralph Waldo Emerson, *The Journals and Miscellaneous Notebooks of Ralph Waldo Emerson*, ed. William H. Gilman and Ralph H. Orth et al. (Cambridge: Harvard University Press, Belknap Press, 1960-82), 7:80 and 12:404. Hereafter referred to as *JMN*.

8. May 14, 1834. Joseph Slater, ed., *The Correspondence of Emerson and Carlyle* (New York: Columbia University Press, 1964).

9. See Arthur M. Schlesinger, *The Age of Jackson* (New York: Little, Brown, 1945), for a somewhat indignant view of this state of mind, esp. 384-86: "[Emerson] lingered indecisively, accepting without enthusiasm certain relations to government but never confronting directly the implications of acceptance. . . . Yet here he failed himself, and ignored the responsibilities of his own moral position."

10. Packer, *Emerson's Fall*, 28.

11. "On the Relation of Man to the Globe," *The Early Lectures of Ralph Waldo Emerson 1833-1842*, ed. Stephen E. Whicher and Robert E. Spiller, 3 vols. (Cambridge: Harvard University Press, Belknap Press, 1959-72), 49.

12. See the first epigraph to chapter 4.

13. Quoted in Bertrand Russell, *The History of Western Philosophy* (London: Routledge, 1991), 623-33.

14. Perry Miller, *Errand into the Wilderness* (Cambridge:Harvard University Press, Belknap Press, 1956), 211.

15. Schlesinger, *Age of Jackson*, 146.

16. Schlesinger, for instance, organizes his chapters on the age this way: "Jacksonian Democracy as an Intellectual Movement," "Jacksonian Democracy and the Law," "Jacksonian Democracy and Industrialism," "Jacksonian Democracy

and Religion," "Jacksonian Democracy and Utopia," "Jacksonian Democracy and Literature."

17. This interesting passage came to my attention in Wai-Chee Dimock's *Empire for Liberty: Melville and the Poetics of Individualism* (Princeton: Princeton University Press, 1989), 4. Dimock's source is *Young Hickory Banner* 15 (October 1846), quoted in Albert Weinberg, *Manifest Destiny: A Study of Nationalist Expansionism in American History* (Baltimore: Johns Hopkins University Press, 1935), 119.

18. "Letter from General Jackson," *Niles National Register* (August 31, 1844): 449.

19. All quotations from "Ode" in this chapter refer to *The Complete Works of Ralph Waldo Emerson, with a Biographical Introduction by Edward Waldo Emerson* (New York: The Riverside Press Cambridge Edition, Houghton-Mifflin Company, 1904), 9:76–79.

20. Barbara Packer, "Emerson and the Shadow of Race," lecture at Claremont Graduate School, March 22, 1994, 12.

21. *Overland Monthly and Out West Magazine* 3, no. 2 (August 1869), 191.

CHAPTER 6. THOREAU AND THE DESIGN OF DISSENT

1. For the former, formalist, view of *Walden*, see Charles Anderson, *The Magic Circle of Walden* (New York: Holt, 1968), and, to a lesser extent, Sherman Paul, *The Shores of America: Thoreau's Inward Exploration* (Urbana: University of Illinois Press, 1958), and Ethel Seybold, *Thoreau: The Quest and the Classics* (New Haven: Yale University Press, 1951). For the latter, political, view, see, among others, Myra Jehlen, *American Incarnation: The Individual, the Nation, and the Continent* (Cambridge: Harvard University Press, 1986); Annette Kolodny, *The Lay of the Land: Metaphor as Experience and History in American Life and Letters* (Chapel Hill: University of North Carolina Press, 1975); and Kolodny, *The Land Before Her: Fantasy and Experience of the American Frontiers, 1630–1860* (Chapel Hill: University of North Carolina Press, 1984).

2. Henry David Thoreau, "A Walk to Waschusett," in *Excursions, and Poems,* vol. 5 of *The Writings of Henry David Thoreau,* ed. Carl F. Hovde, William Howarth, and Elizabeth Hall Witherell (Princeton: Princeton University Press, 1980), 146. Further citations will appear parenthetically in the text.

3. Henry David Thoreau, "Natural History of Massachusetts," in *Excursions, and Poems,* 127.

4. Sacvan Bercovitch, for instance has propounded this view, especially in chapter 9 of *The Rites of Assent: Transformations in the Symbolic Construction of America* (New York: Routledge, 1993).

5. See Linck C. Johnson, "Revolution and Renewal: The Genres of *Walden,*" in *Critical Essays on Henry David Thoreau's* Walden, ed. Joel Myerson (Boston: G. K. Hall, 1988), 215–35.

6. Lawrence Buell, *The Environmental Imagination: Thoreau, Nature Writing, and the Formation of American Culture* (Cambridge: Harvard University Press, Belknap Press, 1995), 6, 9 (see also the appendix, 397–423: *Walden* is part novel, autobiography, travel narrative, sermon, treatise, almanac, regional fiction, picturesque sketch, natural history, and poem); Perry Miller, *The Life of the Mind in*

America from the Revolution to the Civil War (New York: Harcourt Brace Jovanovich, 1965), 277.

7. See Barbara Novak, *Nature and Culture: American Landscape Painting, 1825–1875* (New York: Oxford University Press, 1980), 16–17; Levi St. Armand, "Luminism in the Work of Henry David Thoreau: The Dark and the Light," *Canadian Review of American Studies* 11 (1980): 13–30; John Conron, "Bright American Rivers: The Luminist Landscapes of Thoreau's 'A Week on the Concord and Merrimack Rivers,'" *American Quarterly* 32 (1980): 143–66; Richard J. Schneider, "Thoreau and Nineteenth-Century American Landscape Painting," *Emerson Society Quarterly* 31, no. 2 (1985): 67–88; and Kevin Radaker's three articles: "'A Separate Intention of the Eye': Luminist Eternity in Thoreau's *A Week on the Concord and Merrimack Rivers*," *Canadian Review of American Studies* 18, no. 1 (1987): 41–60; "'To Witness Our Limits Transgressed': The Scientific and Nationalistic Perspectives of Henry Thoreau and Frederic Church in Describing the Maine Wilderness," *Yearbook of Interdisciplinary Studies in the Fine Arts* 2 (1990): 447–71; and "Henry Thoreau and Frederic Church: Confronting the Monumental Sublimity of the Maine Wilderness," *Yearbook of Interdisciplinary Studies in the Fine Arts* 1 (1989): 267–88.

8. The "blade of grass" quote of Cole's is mentioned by Novak, *Nature and Culture*, 111, who cites Louis L. Noble, *The Course of Empire, Voyage of Life, and Other Pictures of Thomas Cole*, ed. Elliot S. Vessell (1853; reprint, Cambridge: Harvard University Press, 1964), 292–93. The connection to Thoreau is mine. See Thomas Cole, "Essay on American Scenery," in *The American Landscape: A Critical Anthology of Prose and Poetry*, ed. John Conron (New York: Oxford University Press, 1974), 571.

9. Henry David Thoreau, *The Writings of Henry D. Thoreau: Journal*, ed. John C. Broderick and John Sattelmeyer, 8 vols. (Princeton: Princeton University Press, 1981–), October 6, 1857.

10. On the Luminist show at the National Gallery, see William H. Truettner and Alan Wallach, eds., *Thomas Cole: Landscape into History* (New Haven: Yale University Press; Washington, D.C.: National Museum of American Art, Smithsonian Institution, 1994). On Audubon, see C. Irmscher, "Violence and Artistic Representation in John James Audubon," *Raritan* 15, no. 2 (1995): 34, and Peter Roop and Connie Roop, eds., *Capturing Nature: The Writings and Art of John James Audubon* (New York: Walker, 1993).

11. Robert D. Richardson, Jr., *Henry Thoreau: A Life of the Mind* (Berkeley: University of California Press, 1986), 287.

12. Walter Harding, *A Thoreau Handbook* (New York: New York University Press, 1961), 70.

13. See, for example, Frederick Garber, "Unity and Diversity in *Walking*," *Emerson Society Quarterly* 56 (1969): 35–40.

14. John Aldrich Christie, "A Bibliography of Travel Works Read by Thoreau," in *Thoreau as World Traveler* (New York: Columbia University Press, 1965), 313–33.

15. Henry Thoreau, "Walking," in *Excursions and Poems*, ed. Bradford Torrey and Francis H. Allen (Boston: Houghton Mifflin, 1906), 210 ff.

16. See the introduction to this book, note 12, for other possibilities of "useful knowledge" societies intended by Thoreau.

17. Thomas R. Hietala, *Manifest Design: Anxious Aggrandizement in Late Jacksonian America* (Ithaca, N.Y.: Cornell University Press, 1985), 137.

18. Christie, *Thoreau as World Traveler,* 46.

19. To assess "Slavery in Massachusetts," there are a number of basic studies that offer a range of views on the concept of the pastoral. See, first, Leo Marx, *The Machine in the Garden: Technology and the Pastoral Ideal in America* (New York: Oxford University Press, 1964), on the presence of pastoral nostalgia in the nineteenth century; also Roderick Nash, *Wilderness and the American Mind* (New Haven: Yale University Press, 1973), and Lee Clark Mitchell, *Witnesses to a Vanishing America: The Nineteenth-Century Response* (Princeton: Princeton University Press, 1981), for adjustments to Marx's basic position. Lawrence Buell has codified the problems of pastoral critique in *Environmental Imagination.*

20. The phrase is from Michael J. Colacurcio, "'The Corn and the Wine': Emerson and the Example of Herbert," *Nineteenth Century Literature* 42 no. 1 (June 1987): 5.

21. Bercovitch, *Rites of Assent,* 190 ff. and 21.

22. Richard Slotkin, *Regeneration through Violence: The Mythology of the American Frontier, 1600–1860* (Hanover, N.H.: University Press of New England, 1973), 395.

23. Buell, *Environmental Imagination,* 2; emphasis in original.

24. Bercovitch, *Rites of Assent,* 5.

25. Leo Marx provides these four examples of railroad portraiture in *Machine in the Garden.*

26. Henry David Thoreau, *Walden,* ed. J. Lyndon Shanley (Princeton: Princeton University Press, 1989), 118. Subsequent citations are given parenthetically in the text.

27. Terry Eagleton, *Literary Theory: An Introduction* (Minneapolis: University of Minnesota Press, 1983), 9.

28. Henry Adams, *The Education of Henry Adams* (1918; reprint, New York: Penguin, 1995), 230.

29. Ralph Waldo Emerson, *The Early Lectures of Ralph Waldo Emerson 1833–1842,* ed. Stephen E. Whicher and Robert E. Spiller, 3 vols. (Cambridge: Harvard University Press, Belknap Press, 1959–72), 10; emphasis in original.

30. Robert W. Johansen, *To the Halls of the Montezumas: The Mexican War in the American Imagination* (New York: Oxford University Press, 1985), 209.

31. Johansen, *To the Halls,* 207.

32. Barbara Maria Stafford, *Voyage into Substance: Art, Science, Nature, and the Illustrated Travel Account, 1760–1840* (Cambridge: MIT Press, 1984), 353.

33. Buell, *Environmental Imagination,* 50 and 44; D. H. Lawrence, *Studies in Classic American Literature* (Garden City, N.Y.: Doubleday, 1951), 33.

34. Stanley Cavell, *The Senses of Walden* (New York: Viking Press, 1974), 43–44. For *Walden* criticism, see some of these works on the potentially long list: recently Buell, *Environmental Imagination,* 323 n. 529; Richardson, *Henry Thoreau,* 33 ff.; Leo Stoller, "Thoreau's Doctrine of Simplicity," *New England Quarterly* 29 (1956): 443–61, and *After Walden* (Stanford: Stanford University Press, 1957); John C. Broderick, "Thoreau, Alcott, and the Poll Tax," *Studies in Philology* 53 (1956): 612–26.

35. Henry David Thoreau, "Slavery in Massachusetts," in *Reform Papers,* ed. Wendell

Glick (Princeton: Princeton University Press, 1973), 108. Further citations of this essay will appear parenthetically in the text.

36. Buell, *Environmental Imagination,* 38.

37. Richardson, *Henry Thoreau,* 357–62.

38. Ibid., 359, citing John Ruskin, *Elements of Drawing* (1857; reprint, New York: Dover, 1971), 27; emphasis in original.

39. On the Burns episode, see Albert J. von Frank, *The Trial of Anthony Burns: Freedom and Slavery in Emerson's Boston* (Cambridge: Harvard University Press, 1998).

40. William H. Seward, cited in Samuel Eliot Morison, *The Oxford History of the American People* (New York: Penguin, 1972), 2:337. I note also the discussion of American hostility, during the 1820s and 1830s, to the tradition of the English Common Law. See Miller, *Life of the Mind,* 99–116. Thus the entire discussion of "higher laws," with its rhetorical flourishes designed to obstruct Southern demands about the constitutionality of slavery, had its first hearing before the crises of the 1840s and 1850s, when national pride focused the debate on the real use and content of the law in America. Thoreau came of age during this debate, and though he eventually refused to engage in legalistic discussions of slavery, he knew its range.

41. Joel Porte, ed., *Emerson in His Journals* (Cambridge: Harvard University Press, Belknap Press, 1982), 412.

42. Thoreau, *Journal,* Nov. 25, 1850.

43. Robert H. Hurlbutt, *Hume, Newton, and the Design Argument* (Lincoln: University of Nebraska Press, 1965), 88.

EPILOGUE

1. Mark Twain, *Roughing It,* illustrated by True Williams, Edward F. Mullen, et al.; ed. Harriet Elinor Smith and Edgar Marquess Branch (Berkeley: University of California Press, 1993).

2. On this topic, see two essays by Richard Lehan: "The Romantic Self and the Use of Place in the Stories of F. Scott Fitzgerald," in *The Short Stories of F. Scott Fitzgerald: New Approaches in Criticism,* ed. Jackon R. Bryer (Madison: University of Wisconsin Press, 1982), and "The Grotesque End Product of the American Dream," in *Readings on* The Great Gatsby, ed. Katie deKoster (San Diego: Greenhaven, 1998).

BIBLIOGRAPHY

Abernethy, Thomas Perkins. *The Burr Conspiracy*. New York: Oxford University Press, 1954.

Adams, Henry. *The Education of Henry Adams*. 1918; reprint, New York: Penguin, 1995.

Addinall, Peter. *Philosophy and Biblical Interpretation: A Study in Nineteenth-Century Conflict*. Cambridge: Cambridge University Press, 1991.

Addison, Joseph. "An Ode." In *The Works of the English Poets, from Chaucer to Cowper*, vol. 9. Ed. Alexander Chambers. 21 vols. London: J. Johnson et al., 1810.

Allmendinger, Blake. *Ten Most Wanted: The New Western Literature*. New York: Routledge, 1998.

Ambrose, Stephen. *Undaunted Courage: Meriwether Lewis, Thomas Jefferson, and the Opening of the American West*. New York: Simon and Schuster, 1996.

Anderson, Charles. *The Magic Circle of Walden*. New York: Holt, 1968.

Anderson, David R. "A Quaint, Picturesque Little Pile: Architecture and the Past in Washington Irving." In *The Old and New World Romanticism in Washington Irving*. Ed. Stanley Brodwin. Westport, Conn.: Greenwood Press, 1986.

Anderson, Douglas. "Bartram's Travels and the Politics of Nature." *Early American Literature* 25 (1990): 3–17.

Antelyes, Peter. *Tales of Adventurous Enterprise: Washington Irving and the Poetics of Western Expansion*. New York: Columbia University Press, 1990.

Anzaldúa, Gloria. *Borderlands/La Frontera: The New Mestiza*. San Francisco: Aunt Lute Books, 1987.

Aquinas, Thomas. *The Five Ways: St. Thomas Aquinas' Proofs of God's Existence*. Ed. Anthony John Patrick Kenny. New York: Schocken Books, 1969.

Aristotle. *The Metaphysics*. 2 vols. Trans. Hugh Tredennick. Cambridge: Harvard University Press, 1989–90.

Bailey, Brigitte. "Irving's Italian Landscapes: Skepticism and the Picturesque Aesthetic." *Emerson Society Quarterly* 32 (1st Quarter 1986): 1–22.

Bancroft, Hubert Howe. *History of the Northwest Coast*. Vols. 27–28 of *The Works of Hubert Howe Bancroft*. San Francisco: The History Company, 1886.

Barrell, John, ed. *Paintings and the Politics of Culture: New Essays on British Art, 1700–1850.* New York: Oxford University Press, 1992.

Bartlett, John R. *Personal Narrative of Exploration and Incidents.* New York: D. Appleton and Co., 1854.

Beaglehole, John. *The Life of Captain James Cook.* Stanford: Stanford University Press, 1974.

Beaman, E. O. "The Cañon of the Colorado, and the Moquis Pueblos." *Appleton's Journal,* April 18, April 25, May 2, May 9, 1874.

Bell, Michael Davitt. "Beginnings of Professionalism." *Cambridge History of American Literature.* Vol. 2, *Prose Writing, 1820–1865.* Ed. Sacvan Bercovitch. Cambridge: Cambridge University Press, 1995.

Bercovitch, Sacvan. *The American Jeremiad.* Madison: University of Wisconsin Press, 1978.

———. *The Puritan Origins of the American Self.* New Haven: Yale University Press, 1975.

———. *The Rites of Assent: Transformations in the Symbolic Construction of America.* New York: Routledge, 1993.

———, ed. *Typology and Early American Literature.* Amherst: University of Massachusetts Press, 1972.

Bergon, Frank. "Wilderness Aesthetics." *American Literary History* 9 (Spring 1997): 128–61.

Berthold, Dennis. "Charles Brockden Brown, *Edgar Huntly,* and the Origins of the American Picturesque." *William and Mary Quarterly* 41 no. 1 (January 1984): 62–84.

Bishop, Jonathan. *Emerson on the Soul.* Cambridge: Harvard University Press, 1964.

Black's Law Dictionary. 6th ed. St. Paul, Minn.: West Publishing Co., 1990.

Blau, Joseph L., ed. *Social Theories of Jacksonian Democracy: Representative Writings of the Period 1825–1850.* New York: The Liberal Arts Press, 1954.

Boelhower, William. *Through a Glass Darkly: Ethnic Semiosis in American Literature.* New York: Oxford University Press, 1987.

Boudreau, Gordon V. "H. D. Thoreau, William Gilpin, and the Metaphysical Ground of the Picturesque." *American Literature* 45 (1973): 357–69.

Bradford, William. *Of Plymouth Plantation, 1620–1647.* New York: Modern Library, 1981.

Branch, Michael. "Indexing American Possibilities: The Natural History Writing of Bartram, Wilson, and Audubon." In *The Ecocriticism Reader: Landmarks in Literary Ecology.* Ed. Cheryll Glotfelty and Harold Fromm. Athens: University of Georgia Press, 1996.

Broderick, John C. "Thoreau, Alcott, and the Poll Tax." *Studies in Philology* 53 (1956): 612–26.

Brown, Lee Rust. *The Emerson Museum: Practical Romanticism and the Pursuit of the Whole.* Cambridge: Harvard University Press, 1997.

Brownson, Orestes. *A Discourse of the Wants of the Times.* Boston: James Munroe, 1836.

Buell, Lawrence. *The Environmental Imagination: Thoreau, Nature Writing, and the Formation of American Culture.* Cambridge: Harvard University Press, Belknap Press, 1995.

Bunyan, John. *The Pilgrim's Progress, Part 1,* 2d ed. 1678. Reprint, Menston, England: Scolar Press, 1970.

Burke, Kenneth. "I, Eye, Ay—Emerson's Early Essay 'Nature': Thoughts on the Machinery of Transcendence." In *Transcendentalism and Its Legacy*. Ed. Myron Simon and Thornton H. Parsons. Ann Arbor: University of Michigan Press, 1966.

Cameron, Kenneth Walter. *A Commentary on Emerson's Early Lectures*. Hartford, Conn.: Transcendental Books, 1961.

———. *Emerson and Thoreau as Readers*. Hartford, Conn.: Transcendental Books, 1958 and new ed. 1972.

———. *Emerson's Prose Poem: The Structure and Meaning of Nature*. Hartford, Conn.: Transcendental Books, 1988.

———. *Ralph Waldo Emerson's Reading*. Hartford, Conn.: Transcendental Books, 1962.

Campbell, Mary B. *The Witness and the Other World: Exotic European Travel Writing, 400–1600*. Ithaca, N.Y.: Cornell University Press, 1988.

Cavell, Stanley. *The Senses of Walden*. New York: Viking Press, 1974.

Channing, William Ellery. *The Life of William Ellery Channing*. Boston: n.p., 1880.

———. "The Evidences of Revealed Religion." In *Unitarian Christianity and Other Essays*. Ed. Irving H. Bartlett. New York: Liberal Arts Press, 1957.

———. "A Letter to the Hon. Henry Clay, on the Annexation of Texas to the United States." In *The Works of William E. Channing*. New York: Burt Franklin, 1882.

Charvatt, William. *The Profession of Authorship in America, 1800–1870*. Miami: Ohio State University Press, 1968.

Chase, Richard. *The American Novel and Its Tradition*. Baltimore: Johns Hopkins University Press, 1957.

Cheyfitz, Eric. *The Poetics of Imperialism: Translation and Colonization from* The Tempest *to* Tarzan. New York: Oxford University Press, 1991.

Chidsey, Donald Barr. *The Great Conspiracy: Aaron Burr and His Strange Doings in the West*. New York: Crown, 1967.

Christie, John Aldrich. *Thoreau as World Traveler*. New York: Columbia University Press, 1965.

Chuinard, Eldon G. "How Did Meriwether Lewis Die? It Was Murder." *We Proceeded On* 18, nos. 1 and 2 (January and May 1992).

Clark, Harry Hayden. "Emerson and Science." *Philological Quarterly* 10, no. 3 (1931): 225–60.

Colacurcio, Michael J. "A Better Mode of Evidence: The Transcendental Problem of Faith and Spirit." *Emerson Society Quarterly* 54 (1st Quarter 1969): 12–22.

———. "'The Corn and the Wine': Emerson and the Example of Herbert." *Nineteenth Century Literature* 42, no. 1 (June 1987): 1–28.

Cole, Thomas. "Essay on American Scenery." In *The American Landscape: A Critical Anthology of Prose and Poetry*. Ed. John Conron. New York: Oxford University Press, 1974.

Coleridge, S. T. "The Delinquent Travellers." In *Poetical Works*. Ed. Ernest Hartley. New York: Oxford University Press, 1969.

The Columbia Encyclopedia. 5th ed. Ed. Barbara A. Chernow and George A. Vallasi. New York: Columbia University Press, 1989.

Conley, Tom. "Montaigne and the Indies: Cartographies of the New World in the Essais, 1580–1588." In *1492–1992: Re/Discovering Colonial Writing*. Ed. Rene Jara and Nicholas Spadaccini. Minneapolis: Prisma Institute, 1989.

Conron, John, ed. *The American Landscape: A Critical Anthology of Prose and Poetry*. New York: Oxford University Press, 1974.

———. *American Picturesque*. University Park: Penn State University Press, 2000.

———. "Bright American Rivers: The Luminist Landscapes of Thoreau's 'A Week on the Concord and Merrimack Rivers.'" *American Quarterly* 32 (1980): 143–66.

Cook-Lynn, Elizabeth. *Why I Can't Read Wallace Stegner and Other Essays: A Tribal Voice*. Madison: University of Wisconsin Press, 1996.

Copleston, Frederick, S.J. *A History of Philosophy*. Vol. 7. New York: Doubleday, 1994.

Copley, Stephen, and Peter Garside, eds. *The Politics of the Picturesque: Literature, Landscape, and Aesthetics since 1770*. Cambridge: Cambridge University Press, 1994.

Coues, Elliott. *History of the Expedition . . . of Lewis and Clark*. 4 vols. New York: F. P. Harper, 1893.

Davis, Lennard J. "The Fact of Events and the Event of Facts: New World Explorers and the Early Novel." *The Eighteenth Century* 32, no. 3 (Autumn 1991): 240–55.

DeBow's Review. Vol. 29, issue 1 (July 1860).

Delbanco, Andrew. *William Ellery Channing: An Essay on the Liberal Spirit in America*. Cambridge: Harvard University Press, 1981.

Derham, William. *Physico-theology: or, A demonstration of the being and attributes of God, from His works of creation: Being the substance of sixteen sermons preached in St. Mary-le-Bow-Church, London, at the Honourable Mr. Boyle's lectures in the years 1711 and 1712*. London: Printed for W. Innys, 1742.

DeVoto, Bernard, ed. *The Journals of Lewis and Clark*. New York: Houghton-Mifflin, 1952.

Diggins, John P. "Slavery, Race, and Equality: Jefferson and the Pathos of the Enlightenment." *American Quarterly* 28 (2 Summer 1976): 206–28.

Dillon, Richard H. *Meriwether Lewis: A Biography*. New York: Coward-McCann, 1965.

———. "Stephen Long's Great American Desert." *Proceedings of the American Philosophical Society* 111, no. 2 (April 1967): 93–108.

Dimock, Wai-Chee. *Empire for Liberty: Melville and the Poetics of Individualism*. Princeton: Princeton University Press, 1989.

Donnelly, John, ed. *Logical Analysis and Contemporary Theism*. New York: Fordham University Press, 1972.

"The Drowziad, by a Dozer." Charleston, 1829.

Eagleton, Terry. *Literary Theory: An Introduction*. Minneapolis: University of Minnesota Press, 1983.

Elliott, Emory, ed. *The Columbia Literary History of the United States*. New York: Columbia University Press, 1988.

Ellison, Julie. *Emerson's Romantic Style*. Princeton: Princeton University Press, 1984.

Emerson, Everett. "History and Chronicle." In *The Columbia Literary History of the United States*. Ed. Emory Elliott. New York: Columbia University Press, 1987.

Emerson, Ralph Waldo. *The Collected Works of Ralph Waldo Emerson*. Ed. Alfred R. Ferguson, Joseph Slater, et al. 5 vols. Cambridge: Harvard University Press, Belknap Press, 1971–.

———. *The Complete Works of Ralph Waldo Emerson, with a Biographical Introduction by Edward Waldo Emerson*. Vol. 9. New York: The Riverside Press Cambridge Edition, Houghton-Mifflin Company, 1904.

———. *The Early Lectures of Ralph Waldo Emerson 1833–1842*. Ed. Stephen E. Whicher and Robert E. Spiller. 3 vols. Cambridge: Harvard University Press, Belknap Press, 1959–72.

———. *The Journals and Miscellaneous Notebooks of Ralph Waldo Emerson.* 16 vols. Ed. William H. Gilman, Ralph H. Orth, et al. Cambridge: Harvard University Press, Belknap Press, 1960–82.

Emory, William H. *Report on the United States and Mexican Boundary Survey.* Vol. 1. Washington, D.C.: Cornelius Wendall, 1857.

Ferguson, Robert A. *The American Enlightenment, 1750–1820.* Cambridge: Harvard University Press, 1994.

———. "'We Hold These Truths': Strategies of Control in the Literature of the Founders." In *Reconstructing American Literary History.* Ed. Sacvan Bercovitch. Cambridge: Harvard University Press, 1986.

Fink, Steven. "Building America: Henry Thoreau and the American Home." *Prospects* 11 (1988): 327–66.

Fischer, David Hackett. *The Revolution of American Conservatism: The Federalist Party in the Era of Jeffersonian Democracy.* New York: Harper and Row, 1965.

Fisher, Vardes. *Suicide or Murder? The Strange Death of Governor Meriwether Lewis.* Chicago: Swallow Press, 1962.

Foner, Philip S., ed. *The Complete Writings of Thomas Paine.* 2 vols. New York: The Citadel Press, 1945.

Foster, Edward Halsey. *The Civilized Wilderness: Backgrounds to American Romantic Literature, 1817–1860.* New York: Free Press, 1975.

Franklin, Wayne. *Discoverers, Explorers, Settlers: The Diligent Writers of Early America.* Chicago: University of Chicago Press, 1979.

Frothingham, O. B. *Transcendentalism in New England, A History.* New York: G. P. Putnam's Sons, 1886.

Fuller, Harlin M., and LeRoy R. Hafen, eds. *The Journal of Captain John R. Bell, Official Journalist for the Stephen H. Long Expedition to the Rocky Mountains, 1820.* Glendale, Calif.: The Arthur H. Clarke Co., 1957.

Fussell, Edwin. *Frontier: American Literature and the American West.* Princeton: Princeton University Press, 1965.

Garber, Frederick. "Unity and Diversity in *Walking.*" *Emerson Society Quarterly* 56 (1969): 35–40.

Gass, Patrick. *Journal of the voyages and travels of a corps of discovery, under the command of Capt. Lewis and Capt. Clarke of the Army of the United States, from the mouth of the River Missouri through the interior parts of North America to the Pacific Ocean, during the years 1804, 1805 and 1806. Containing an authentic relation of the most interesting transactions during the expedition; a description of the country; and an account of its inhabitants, soil, climate, curiosities and vegetable and animal productions.* Philadelphia: Printed for M. Carey, 1811.

———. *Tagebuch einer Entdeckungs-Reise durch Nord-America, von der Mündung des Missuri an bis zum Einfluss der Columbia in den Stillen Ocean, gemacht in den Jahren 1804, 1805 und 1806, auf Befehl der Regierung der Vereinigten Staaten, von den beiden Capitäns Lewis und Clarke. Uebers. von Ph. Ch. Weyland.* Weimar: H.S. privil. Landes-Industrie-Comptoirs, 1814.

———. *Voyage des capitaines Lewis et Clarke, depuis l'emboulure du Missouri, jusqu'à l'entrée de la Colombia dans l'océan Pacifique; fait dans les années 1804, 1805 et 1806, par ordre du gouvernement des États-Unis: contenant le journal authentique des événements les plus remarquables du voyage, ainsi que la description des habitants, du sol, du climat, et des productions animales et végétales des pays situés à l'ouest de l'Amérique Septentrionale. Rédigé en anglais par Patrice Gass, employé dans l'expédition; et traduit en française par A. J. N. Lallemant . . . Avec des notes, deux lettres du capitaine Clarke, et une carte gravée par J. B. Tardieu.* Paris, Arthus-Bertrand, 1810.

Gay, Peter. *The Enlightenment: An Interpretation.* 2 vols. New York: Knopf, 1966–69.

Gerbi, Antonello. *The Dispute of the New World: The History of a Polemic, 1750–1900.* Trans. Jeremy Moyle. Pittsburgh: University of Pittsburgh Press, 1973.

Gibbon, Edward. *The History of the Decline and Fall of the Roman Empire.* Vol. XXX. London: Methuen, 1913.

Gilmore, Michael T. *American Romanticism and the Marketplace.* Chicago: University of Chicago Press, 1985.

Gilpin, William. "On Picturesque Travel." In *Three Essays.* London: n.p., 1794.

Goetzmann, William H. *Army Exploration in the American West, 1803–1863.* New Haven: Yale University Press, 1959.

———. *Exploration and Empire: The Explorer and the Scientist in the Winning of the American West.* New York: Norton, 1966.

———. *New Lands, New Men: America and the Second Great Age of Discovery.* New York: Viking, 1986.

Gonnaud, Maurice. *An Uneasy Solitude: Individual and Society in the Work of Ralph Waldo Emerson.* Princeton: Princeton University Press, 1987.

Gougeon, Len. *Virtue's Hero: Emerson, Antislavery, and Reform.* Athens: University of Georgia Press, 1990.

Greenblatt, Stephen. *Marvelous Possessions: The Wonder of the New World.* Chicago: University of Chicago Press, 1991.

Greenfield, Bruce. *Tales of Adventurous Enterprise: Washington Irving and the Poetics of Western Expansion.* New York: Columbia University Press, 1990.

Gura, Philip F. "John Who? Captain John Smith and Early American Literature." *Early American Literature* 21 (1986–87): 260–67.

Haltman, Kenneth. "Figures in a Western Landscape: Reading the Art of Titian Ramsay Peale from the Long Expedition to the Rocky Mountains, 1819–1820." Ph.D. diss., Yale University, 1992.

Hamilton, Alexander. "Letter to Edward Carrington." *The Works of Alexander Hamilton.* Vol. VIII. Ed. Henry Cabot Lodge. New York: G. P. Putnam's Sons, 1904.

Hampson, Norman. *The Enlightenment.* New York: Penguin, 1968.

Harding, Walter. *Emerson's Library.* Charlottesville: University Press of Virginia, 1967.

———. *A Thoreau Handbook.* New York: New York University Press, 1961.

Harding, Walter, and Carl Bode, eds. *The Days of Henry Thoreau.* New York: New York University Press, 1958.

Hartley, J. B., and David Woodward, eds. *The History of Cartography.* Chicago: University of Chicago Press, 1987.

Heimert, Alan. *Religion and the American Mind: From the Great Awakening to the Revolution.* Cambridge: Harvard University Press, 1969.

Herbert, Edward, Lord Cherbury. *De Veritate prout distinguitur a revelatione, a verisimili, a possibili, et a falso.* 1624. Reprint, Bristol: J. W. Arrowsmith Ltd., 1937.

Hietala, Thomas R. *Manifest Design: Anxious Aggrandizement in Late Jacksonian America*. Ithaca, N.Y.: Cornell University Press, 1985.

Hine, Robert. *Bartlett's West: Drawing the Mexican Boundary*. New Haven: Yale University Press, 1968.

Hollon, W. Eugene. "Zebulon Montgomery Pike and the Wilkinson-Burr Conspiracy." *Proceedings of the American Philosophical Society* 91, no. 5 (December 1947): 447–56.

Holmberg, James J. "'I wish you to see & know all': The Recently Discovered Letters of William Clark to Jonathan Clark." *We Proceeded On* 18, no. 4 (November 1992).

Holmes, Oliver Wendell. "A Rhymed Lesson." In *The Complete Poetical Works*. Boston: Houghton, Mifflin and Company, 1895.

Holt, Michael F. *The Rise and Fall of the American Whig Party*. New York: Oxford University Press, 1999.

Howe, Daniel Walker. *The American Whigs*. New York: John Wiley and Sons, 1983.

———. *Making the American Self: Jonathan Edwards to Abraham Lincoln*. Cambridge: Harvard University Press, 1997.

———. *The Political Culture of the American Whigs*. Chicago: University of Chicago Press, 1979.

———. *The Unitarian Conscience: Harvard Moral Philosophy, 1805–1861*. Cambridge: Harvard University Press, 1970.

Humboldt, Alexander von. *Ansichten der Natur* (Views of Nature). Trans. E. C. Otte and Henry G. Bohn. London: Henry G. Bohn, 1850.

Hunt, John Dixon. *Gardens and the Picturesque*. Cambridge: MIT Press, 1992.

Hurlbutt, Robert H. *Hume, Newton, and the Design Argument*. Lincoln: University of Nebraska Press, 1965.

Hussey, Christopher. *The Picturesque: Studies in a Point of View*. Hamden, Conn.: Archon Books, 1967.

Irmscher, C. "Violence and Artistic Representation in John James Audubon." *Raritan* 15, no. 2 (1995): 1–34.

Irving, Pierre M., ed. *The Life and Letters of Washington Irving*. 4 vols. London: n.p., 1864.

Irving, Washington. *Salmagundi* No. II (Wed. Feb. 4, 1807). *Works*. Vol. 18. Knickerbocker ed. New York: Putnam, 1869.

Jackson, Donald Dean. "The Race to Publish Lewis and Clark." *Pennsylvania Magazine of History and Biography* 85, no. 2 (1985): 163–77.

———, ed. *The Journals of Zebulon Montgomery Pike, with Letters and Related Documents*. Norman: University of Oklahoma Press, 1966.

James Letters, Western Americana, Beinecke Library, Yale University.

Janowitz, Anne. *England's Ruins: Poetic Purpose and the National Landscape*. London: Basil Blackwell, 1990.

Jefferson, Thomas. *Notes on the State of Virginia*. Ed. William Peden. New York: Norton, 1972.

Jehlen, Myra. *American Incarnation: The Individual, the Nation, and the Continent*. Cambridge: Harvard University Press, 1986.

———. "Exploration and Empire." In *The Cambridge History of American Literature*. Vol. 1, *1590–1820*. Ed. Sacvan Bercovitch. Cambridge: Cambridge University Press, 1995.

————. "History Before the Fact: Or, Captain John Smith's Unfinished Symphony." *Critical Inquiry* 19, no. 4 (Summer 1993): 677–92.

Jenkins, Starr. "The Rugged Return of Lewis and Clark." *Nugget* (March 1971).

Johansen, Robert W. *To the Halls of the Montezumas: The Mexican War in the American Imagination.* New York: Oxford University Press, 1985.

Johnson, Linck C. "Revolution and Renewal: The Genres of *Walden.*" In *Critical Essays on Henry David Thoreau's* Walden. Ed. Joel Myerson. Boston: G. K. Hall, 1988.

Kolodny, Annette. *The Land Before Her: Fantasy and Experience of the American Frontiers, 1630–1860.* Chapel Hill: University of North Carolina Press, 1984.

————. *The Lay of the Land: Metaphor as Experience and History in American Life and Letters.* Chapel Hill: University of North Carolina Press, 1975.

————. "Letting Go Our Grand Obsessions: Notes toward a New Literary History of the American Frontiers." *American Literature* 64 (March 1992): 1–18.

Lamar, Howard, ed. *Account of an Expedition from Pittsburgh to the Rocky Mountains, Under the Command of Major Stephen H. Long.* Barre, Mass.: Imprint Society, 1972.

Lawrence, D. H. *Studies in Classic American Literature.* New York: Viking, 1961.

Lawson-Peebles, Robert. *Landscape and Written Expression in Revolutionary America.* Cambridge: Cambridge University Press, 1988.

Ledyard, John. *Journey through Russia and Siberia, 1787–1788: The Journal and Selected Letters.* Ed. with an introduction by Stephen D. Watrous. Madison: University of Wisconsin Press, 1966.

Lehan, Richard. "The Grotesque End Product of the American Dream." In *Readings on* The Great Gatsby. Ed. Katie deKoster. San Diego: Greenhaven, 1998.

————. "The Romantic Self and the Use of Place in the Stories of F. Scott Fitzgerald." In *The Short Stories of F. Scott Fitzgerald: New Approaches in Criticism.* Ed. Jackson R. Bryer. Madison: University of Wisconsin Press, 1982.

Lemay, Leo J. "Captain John Smith." In *The History of Southern Literature.* Ed. Louis D. Rubin, Jr., et al. Baton Rouge: Louisiana State University Press, 1985.

Lewis, Lloyd, and Henry Justin Smith. *Oscar Wilde Discovers America.* New York: Harcourt Brace, 1936.

Livermore, Shaw, Jr. *The Twilight of Federalism: The Disintegration of the Federalist Party, 1815–1830.* Princeton: Princeton University Press, 1962.

Looby, Christopher. "The Constitution of Nature: Taxonomy as Politics in Jefferson, Peale, and Bartram." *Early American Literature* 22 (1987): 252–73.

Lueck, Beth L. "Charles Brockden Brown's *Edgar Huntly:* The Picturesque Traveler as Sleepwalker." *Studies in American Fiction* 15, no. 1 (1987): 25–42.

————. "Hawthorne's Ironic Traveler and the Picturesque Tour." In *Hawthorne's American Travel Sketches.* Ed. Beth L. Lueck and Dennis Berthold. Hanover, N.H.: University Press of New England, 1989.

————. "James Kirke Paulding and the Picturesque Tour: 'Banqueting on the Picturesque' in the 1820s and '30s." *University of Mississippi Studies in English* 9 (1991): 167–88.

"Major Long's Second Expedition." *North American Review* XII (June 1825).

Marx, Leo. *The Machine in the Garden: Technology and the Pastoral Ideal in America.* New York: Oxford University Press, 1964.

Masteller, Richard N., and Jean Carwile Masteller. "Rural Architecture in Andrew

Jackson Downing and Henry David Thoreau: Pattern Book Parody in *Walden.*" *New England Quarterly* 57, no. 4 (1984): 483–510.

Matthiessen, F. O. *American Renaissance: Art and Expression in the Age of Emerson and Whitman.* New York: Oxford University Press, 1941.

McKeon, Michael. *The Origins of the English Novel, 1600–1740.* Baltimore: Johns Hopkins University Press, 1987.

Meyers, Marvin. *The Jacksonian Persuasion: Politics and Belief.* Stanford: Stanford University Press, 1957.

Michael, John. *Emerson and Skepticism: The Cipher of the World.* Baltimore: Johns Hopkins University Press, 1988.

Milder, Robert. "The Radical Emerson?" In *The Cambridge Companion to Ralph Waldo Emerson.* Ed. Joel Porte and Saundra Morris. Cambridge: Cambridge University Press, 1999.

Miller, Perry. *Errand into the Wilderness.* Cambridge: Harvard University Press, Belknap Press, 1956.

———. *The Life of the Mind in America from the Revolution to the Civil War.* New York: Harcourt Brace Jovanovich, 1965.

———. *Nature's Nation.* Cambridge: Harvard University Press, Belknap Press, 1967.

———. *The New England Mind: The Seventeenth Century.* Cambridge: Harvard University Press, 1939.

Milner, Clyde A. II, et al., eds. *The Oxford History of the American West.* New York: Oxford University Press, 1994.

Mitchell, Lee Clark. *Westerns: Making the Man in Fiction and Film.* Chicago: University of Chicago Press, 1996.

———. *Witnesses to a Vanishing America: The Nineteenth-Century Response.* Princeton: Princeton University Press, 1981.

Montfort, Bruno. "Washington Irving et le pittoresque post-romantique." *Revue française d'études americaines* 14 no. 42 (November 1989): 439–53.

Morison, Samuel Eliot. *The Oxford History of the American People.* Vol. 2. New York: Penguin, 1972.

Moulton, Gary E., ed. *The Journals of the Lewis and Clark Expedition.* 12 vols. Lincoln: University of Nebraska Press, 1983–99.

Mulvey, Christopher. *Anglo-American Landscapes: A Study of Nineteenth-Century Anglo-American Travel Literature.* Cambridge: Cambridge University Press, 1983.

Nabokov, Vladimir. *Lolita, or the Confessions of a White Widowed Male.* New York: G. P. Putnam's Sons, 1955.

Nash, Roderick. *Wilderness and the American Mind.* New Haven: Yale University Press, 1973.

The National Intelligencer. December 24, 1806.

New England *Palladium.* August 13, 1805.

New York Times. January 23, 1940, p. 20/vol. 4.

New York *Tribune.* April 22, 1854, p. 5/vol. 5.

Novak, Barbara. *Nature and Culture: American Landscape and Painting, 1825–1875.* New York: Oxford University Press, 1980.

Overland Monthly and Out West Magazine 3, no. 2 (August 1869).

Packer, Barbara. *Emerson's Fall: A New Interpretation of the Major Essays.* New York: Continuum, 1982.

————. "Emerson and the Shadow of Race." Lecture at Claremont Graduate School, March 22, 1994.

————. "The Transcendentalists." *The Cambridge History of American Literature*. Vol. 2, *Prose Writing 1820–1865*. Ed. Sacvan Bercovitch. Cambridge: Cambridge University Press, 1995.

Paley, William. *Natural Theology; or, Evidences of the Existence and Attributes of the Deity, collected from the appearances of Nature*. London: R. Faulder, 1804.

Parkman, Francis. *The Oregon Trail*. Ed. E. N. Feltskog. Madison: University of Wisconsin Press, 1969.

Parrington, Vernon L. *Main Currents in American Thought*. Vol. 2, *The Romantic Revolution in America, 1800–1860*. New York: Harcourt Brace, 1927.

Paul, Sherman. *The Shores of America: Thoreau's Inward Exploration*. Urbana: University of Illinois Press, 1958.

Phelps, Dawson A. "The Tragic Death of Meriwether Lewis." *William and Mary Quarterly* 13, no. 3 (1956).

Pike, Zebulon Montgomery. *The Journals of Zebulon Montgomery Pike, with Letters and Related Documents*. Ed. Donald Dean Jackson. Norman: University of Oklahoma Press, 1966.

Piper, Sir David, ed. *The Random House Dictionary of Art and Artists*. New York: Random House, 1988.

Pluche, Noël Antoine. *Spectacle de la Nature: or, Nature display'd. Being discourses on such particulars of natural history as were thought most proper to excite the curiosity, and form the minds of youth, translated from the original French*. 7 vols. London: J. Pemberton, R. Francklin, and C. Davis, 1735–48.

Poe, Edgar Allan. "To Helen." In *The Fall of the House of Usher and Other Writings*. Ed. David Galloway. New York: Penguin, 1987.

Poirier, Richard. *The Renewal of Literature: Emersonian Reflections*. New Haven: Yale University Press, 1987.

————. *A World Elsewhere: The Place of Style in American Literature*. London: Chatto and Windus, 1967.

Porte, Joel, ed. *Emerson in His Journals*. Cambridge: Harvard University Press, Belknap Press, 1982.

Porter, Carolyn. *Seeing and Being: The Plight of the Participant Observer in Emerson, James, Adams, and Faulkner*. Middletown, Conn.: Wesleyan University Press, 1981.

Pratt, Mary Louise. *Imperial Eyes: Travel Writing and Transculturation*. New York: Routledge, 1992.

"Presidential Candidates and Aspirants." *DeBow's Review* vol. 29, issue 1 (July 1860).

Quaife, M. M., ed. *The Journals of Captain Meriwether Lewis and Sergeant John Ordway, Kept on the Expedition of Western Exploration, 1803–1806*. Madison: State Historical Society of Wisconsin, 1916.

Radaker, Kevin. "Henry Thoreau and Frederic Church: Confronting the Monumental Sublimity of the Maine Wilderness." *Yearbook of Interdisciplinary Studies in the Fine Arts* 1 (1989): 267–88.

————. "'A Separate Intention of the Eye': Luminist Eternity in Thoreau's *A Week on the Concord and Merrimack Rivers*." *Canadian Review of American Studies* 18 no. 1 (1987): 41–60.

————. "'To Witness Our Limits Transgressed': The Scientific and Nationalistic Perspectives of Henry Thoreau and Frederic Church in Describing the Maine Wilderness." *Yearbook of Interdisciplinary Studies in the Fine Arts* 2 (1990): 447–71.

Regis, Pamela. *Describing Early America: Bartram, Jefferson, Crevecoeur, and the Rhetoric of Natural History.* De Kalb: Northern Illinois University Press, 1992.

Richardson, Robert D., Jr. *Emerson: The Mind on Fire.* Berkeley: University of California Press, 1995.

———. *Henry Thoreau: A Life of the Mind.* Berkeley: University of California Press, 1986.

———. "Emerson and Nature." In *The Cambridge Companion to Ralph Waldo Emerson.* Ed. Joel Porte and Saundra Morris. Cambridge: Cambridge University Press, 1999.

Robertson, Bruce. "The Picturesque Traveler in America." In *Views and Visions: American Landscape before 1830.* Ed. Edward J. Nygren and Bruce Robertson. Washington, D.C.: Corcoran Gallery, 1986.

———. "Venit, Vidit, Depinxit: The Military Artist in America." In *Views and Visions: American Landscape Before 1830.* Ed. Edward J. Nygren and Bruce Robertson Washington, D.C.: Corcoran Gallery, 1986.

Roop, Peter, and Connie Roop, eds. *Capturing Nature: The Writings and Art of John James Audubon.* New York: Walker, 1993.

Rose, Anne C. *Transcendentalism as a Social Movement, 1830–1850.* New Haven: Yale University Press, 1981.

Rosowski, Susan J. "The Western Hero as Logos; or, Unmaking Meaning." *Western American Literature* 32, no. 3 (November 1997): 269–92.

Rotella, Carlo. "Travels in a Subjective West: The Letters of Edwin James and Major Stephen Long's Scientific Expedition of 1819–1820." *Montana* 41, no. 4 (Autumn 1991).

Rowe, John Carlos. *At Emerson's Tomb: The Politics of Classic American Literature.* New York: Columbia University Press, 1997.

Rowe, Karen. *Saint and Singer: Edward Taylor's Typology and the Poetics of Meditation.* Cambridge: Cambridge University Press, 1986.

Ruskin, John. *Elements of Drawing.* 1857. Reprint, New York: Dover, 1971.

Russell, Bertrand. *The History of Western Philosophy.* London: Routledge, 1991.

Sahlins, Marshall. "The Apotheosis of Captain Cook." In *Between Belief and Transgression: Structuralist Essays in Religion, History, and Myth.* Ed. Michel Izard and Pierre Smith. Trans. John Leavitt. Chicago: University of Chicago Press, 1982.

Said, Edward. *Culture and Imperialism.* New York: Knopf, 1993.

St. Armand, Levi. "Luminism in the Work of Henry David Thoreau: The Dark and the Light." *Canadian Review of American Studies* 11 (1980): 13–30.

Schlesinger, Arthur M. *The Age of Jackson.* New York: Little, Brown, 1945.

Schneider, Richard J. "Thoreau and Nineteenth-Century American Landscape Painting." *Emerson Society Quarterly* 31 (2nd Quarter 1985): 67–88.

Sealts, Merton M., ed. *Emerson's Nature: Origin, Growth, Meaning.* New York: Dodd, Mead, 1969.

Sedgwick, Eve Kosofsky. *Between Men: English Literature and Male Homosocial Desire.* New York: Columbia University Press, 1985.

Seelye, John. "Beyond the Shining Mountains: The Lewis and Clark Expedition as Enlightenment Epic." *Virginia Quarterly Review* 63 (Winter 1987): 36–53.

Seybold, Ethel. *Thoreau: The Quest and the Classics.* New Haven: Yale University Press, 1951.

Silverman, Kenneth. "From Cotton Mather to Benjamin Franklin." In *The Columbia Literary History of the United States.* Ed. Emory Elliott. New York: Columbia University Press, 1988.

Slater, Joseph, ed. *The Correspondence of Emerson and Carlyle.* New York: Columbia University Press, 1964.

Slotkin, Richard. *Regeneration through Violence: The Mythology of the American Frontier, 1600–1860.* Hanover, N.H.: University Press of New England, 1973.

Stafford, Barbara Maria. *Voyage into Substance: Art, Science, Nature, and the Illustrated Travel Account, 1760–1840.* Cambridge: MIT Press, 1984.

Stampp, Kenneth M., ed. *The Causes of the Civil War.* New York: Simon and Schuster, 1991.

Stephanson, Anders. *Manifest Destiny: American Expansion and the Empire of Right.* New York: Hill and Wang, 1996.

Stoller, Leo. *After Walden.* Stanford: Stanford University Press, 1957.

———. "Thoreau's Doctrine of Simplicity." *New England Quarterly* 29 (1956): 443–61.

Stoppard, Tom. *Arcadia.* London: Faber and Faber, 1993.

Thoreau, Henry David. *Excursions, and Poems.* Vol. V, *The Writings of Henry David Thoreau.* Ed. Carl F. Hovde, William Howarth, and Elizabeth Hall Witherell. Princeton: Princeton University Press, 1989.

———. *The Journal of Henry Thoreau.* Ed. Bradford Torrey and Francis H. Allen. Boston: Houghton Mifflin, 1906.

———. *Walden.* Ed. J. Lyndon Shanley. Princeton: Princeton University Press, 1989.

———. "Slavery in Massachusetts." In *Reform Papers.* Ed. Wendell Glick. Princeton: Princeton University Press, 1973.

Thrower, Norman J. W. "William H. Emory and the Mapping of the American Southwest Borderlands." *Terrae Incognitae* 22 (1990).

Thwaites, Ruben Gold, ed. *James' Account of S. H. Long's Expedition, Part III.* Cleveland: A. H. Clark, 1905.

Todorov, Tzvetan. *The Conquest of America: The Question of the Other.* New York: Harper and Row, 1984.

Toland, John. *Christianity Not Mysterious.* 1696. Reprint, New York: Garland, 1978.

Tompkins, Jane. *West of Everything: The Inner Life of Westerns.* New York: Oxford University Press, 1992.

Truettner, William H., and Alan Wallach, eds. *Thomas Cole: Landscape into History.* New Haven: Yale University Press; Washington, D.C.: National Museum of American Art, Smithsonian Institution, 1994.

Tulloch, John. *Rational Theology and Christian Philosophy in England in the Seventeenth Century.* 2 vols. Edinburgh and London: Blackwood and Sons, 1872.

Twain, Mark. *Roughing It.* Illustrated by True Williams, Edward F. Mullen, et al. Ed. Harriet Elinor Smith and Edgar Marquess Branch. Berkeley: University of California Press, 1993.

Van Anglen, Kevin. "Reading Transcendentalist Texts Religiously: Emerson, Thoreau, and the Myth of Secularization." In *Seeing into the Life of Things: Essays on Lit-*

erature and Religious Experience. Ed. John L. Mahoney. New York: Fordham University Press, 1998.

Van Deusen, Glyndon G. *The Jacksonian Era, 1828–1848.* New York: Harper and Row, 1963.

Van Leer, David. *Emerson's Epistemology: The Argument of the Essays.* Cambridge: Cambridge University Press, 1986.

von Frank, Albert J. *The Sacred Game: Provincialism and Frontier Consciousness in American Literature, 1630–1860.* Cambridge: Cambridge University Press, 1985.

————. *The Trials of Anthony Burns: Freedom and Slavery in Emerson's Boston.* Cambridge: Harvard University Press, 1998.

Walker, James. "Religion and Physical Science." In *Sermons Preached in the Chapel of Harvard College.* Boston, 1861.

Watt, Ian. *The Rise of the Novel.* Berkeley: University of California Press, 1957.

Weinberg, Albert. *Manifest Destiny: A Study of Nationalist Expansionism in American History.* Baltimore: Johns Hopkins University Press, 1935.

Weisbuch, Robert. "Post-Colonial Emerson and the Erasure of Europe." In *The Cambridge Companion to Ralph Waldo Emerson.* Ed. Joel Porte and Saundra Morris. Cambridge: Cambridge University Press, 1999.

Wellman, Manly Wade. *Napoleon of the West: A Story of the Aaron Burr Conspiracy.* New York: I. Washburn, 1970.

Werne, Joseph Richard. "Major Emory and Captain Jimenez: Running the Gadsden Line." *Journal of the Southwest* 29, no. 2 (1987): 203–21.

Wharton, Edith. *The Age of Innocence.* 1920. Reprint, London: Virago Press, 1988.

Whicher, Stephen. *Freedom and Fate: An Inner Life of Ralph Waldo Emerson.* Philadelphia: University of Pennsylvania Press, 1953.

Wiener, Philip P., ed. *Dictionary of the History of Ideas.* 5 vols. New York: Scribners, 1973–74.

Wilde, Oscar. *The Writings of Oscar Wilde.* 12 vols. New York: Gabriel Wells, 1925.

Woodward, David, ed. *Art and Cartography: Six Historical Essays.* Chicago: University of Chicago Press, 1987.

Young Hickory Banner. October 15, 1846.

Zamora, Margarita. *Reading Columbus.* Berkeley: University of California Press, 1993.

Ziff, Larzer. *Writing a New Nation: Prose, Print, and Politics in the Early United States.* New Haven: Yale University Press, 1991.

Zuersher, Dorothy. "Benjamin Franklin, Jonathan Williams, and the United States Marine Corps." Ph.D. diss., University of North Carolina, Greensboro, 1974.

INDEX

Adams, Henry, 10, 140
Addison, Joseph, 3
African Discoveries, 103
Alcott, Bronson, 7, 138
American Philosophical Society, 6, 135
Ames, Fisher, 49
ancestor worship, 2
Anzaldúa, Gloria, 76
Appel, Peter, 168n47
Aquinas, Thomas, 3
argument from design, 3, 16, 17, 28, 29, 32, 45, 46, 65, 93–94, 97, 128, 130, 151; conservatism of, 4, 128; definition of, 2–4, 92–93; as intellectual trap, 14, 15, 48, 90, 128; and landscapes, 15; logical extreme of, 17; and manifest destiny, 5, 15; and nationalism, 90, 93; and natural theology, 3; and providence, 94–96, 97, 128; and Unitarians, 97–98; and U.S. exploration, 2, 93, 128. *See also individual authors*
Aristotle, 3
Audubon, James, 132
Austen, Jane, 31

Bache, A. D., 79
Bancroft, George, 13
Barlow, Almira, 12
Barthelemy, Jean Jacques, 104
Bartram, William, 30, 31, 104, 134
Beechey, Frederick William, 104
Behn, Aphra, 31

Belknap, Jeremy, 104
Bell, John, 73
Bercovitch, Sacvan, 92, 95, 96, 139, 173n14
Bergon, Frank, 9
Berkeley, George, 112, 117, 126, 127
Biddle, Nicholas, 27
Bishop, Elizabeth, 36
Bishop, Jonathan, 90
Blake, William, 101
Bonaparte, Napoleon, xi, 19, 78
Bossu, Jean Bernard, 105
Bradford, William, 31
Brown, "Capability," 50
Brown, Lee Rust, 91
Buell, Lawrence, 132, 139, 143
Buffon, Georges, 6, 11, 79, 80, 82, 85, 135, 136
Bunyan, John, 22, 23
Burns, Ken, 32
Burr Conspiracy, 9, 13, 44, 45, 54, 56–57, 59, 63, 64, 76, 77
Byrd, William, 31

Cabot, John, 106
Cabot, Sebastian, 106
Calhoun, John C., 66
Cavell, Stanley, 144
Channing, W. E., 92; letter to Henry Clay, 109; petition to defend Abner Kneeland, 7; sermon condemning design argument, 97
Channing, W. H., 13, 122

Text: 10/12 Baskerville
Display: Baskerville
Compositor: G&S Typesetters, Inc.
Printer and Binder: Sheridan Books, Inc.